OUR 50-STATE BORDER CRISIS

ALSO BY HOWARD G. BUFFETT

40 Chances: Finding Hope in a Hungry World

OUR 50-STATE BORDER CRISIS

How the Mexican Border Fuels
the Drug Epidemic Across America

HOWARD G. BUFFETT

NEW YORK   BOSTON

Hachette Books
Hachette Book Group
1290 Avenue of the Americas, New York, NY 10104
hachettebooks.com
twitter.com/hachettebooks

First edition: April 2018

All photos taken by the author unless otherwise indicated.

Hachette Books is a division of Hachette Book Group, Inc. The Hachette Books name and logo are trademarks of Hachette Book Group, Inc.

The publisher is not responsible for websites (or their content) that are not owned by the publisher.

The Hachette Speakers Bureau provides a wide range of authors for speaking events. To find out more, go to www.hachettespeakersbureau.com or call (866) 376-6591.

Library of Congress Cataloging-in-Publication Data has been applied for.

ISBNs: 978-0-316-47661-4 (hardcover), 978-0-316-47658-4 (ebook)

Printed in the United States of America

LSC-C

10 9 8 7 6 5 4 3 2 1

This book is dedicated to my wife, Devon.
Her support, understanding, advice, patience, and
love inspire me to keep trying to make a positive
difference for those who suffer.

And, to Billy Rogers.

CONTENTS

CONTENTS

PART III: WHAT NEEDS TO CHANGE

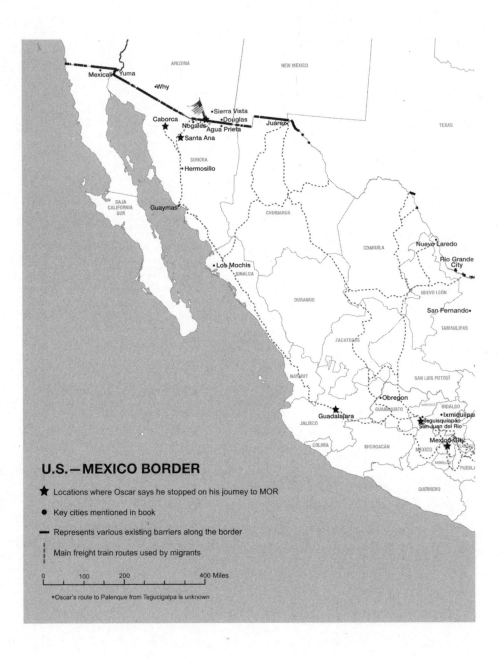

U.S.—MEXICO BORDER

★ Locations where Oscar says he stopped on his journey to MOR

● Key cities mentioned in book

— Represents various existing barriers along the border

▮ Main freight train routes used by migrants

| 0 | 100 | 200 | | 400 Miles |

*Oscar's route to Palenque from Tegucigalpa is unknown

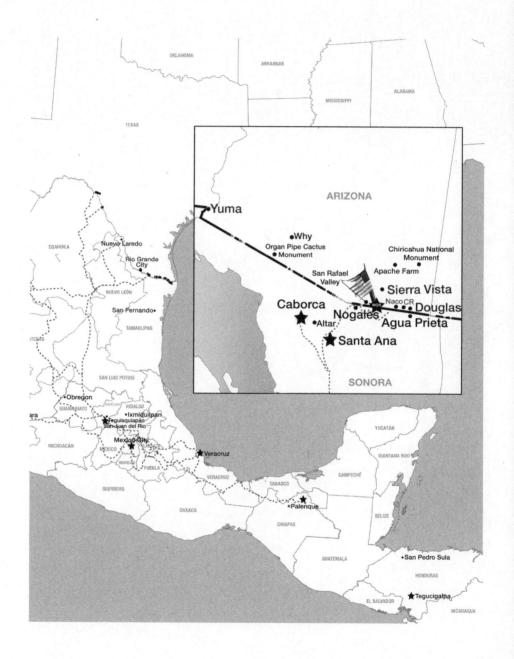

A LIST OF ACRONYMS

ATF: Alcohol, Tobacco, and Firearms
AOR: Border Patrol "Areas of Responsibility"
BP: U.S. Border Patrol
CBP: U.S. Customs and Border Protection
CCSO: Cochise County Sheriff's Office
DACA: Deferred Action for Childhood Arrivals
DEA: Drug Enforcement Administration
DPD: Decatur Police Department
DOD: Department of Defense
DHS: Department of Homeland Security
FBI: Federal Bureau of Investigation
FEMA: Federal Emergency Management Agency
GAO: Government Accountability Office (formerly the General Accounting Office)
GIS: Geographic information system
ICE: Immigration and Customs Enforcement
INL: Bureau of International Narcotics and Law Enforcement Affairs
KIND: Kids in Need of Defense
MCSO: Macon County Sheriff's Office
MS-13: Mara Salvatrucha-13
NBPC: National Border Patrol Council
NGO: Non-governmental organization
NORTHCOM: U.S. Northern Command
NSC: National Security Council

OFAC: U.S. Department of the Treasury's Office of Foreign Assets Control
PAIC: Patrol Agent in Charge
PRI: Partido Revolucionario Institucional
PERF: Police Executive Research Forum
POE: Port of Entry
SOUTHCOM: U.S. Southern Command
TSA: Transportation Security Administration
UDA: Undocumented alien
USCIS: U.S. Citizenship and Immigration Services
USCG: U.S. Coast Guard
WFP: World Food Programme

A NOTE ON NAMES

A number of individuals whose comments and insights appear in this book either live in or have left situations where violence is a constant threat. I use pseudonyms for those at risk, and I have not identified their hometowns or given specific details about where they are living now.

FOREWORD

Howard G. Buffett is one of the most brilliant, outside-the-box thought leaders I've ever met. His ideas often challenge the status quo and force people out of their comfort zones. His foundation specializes in helping vulnerable people in some of the most dangerous and difficult situations on Earth, and he lives by a hard-and-fast rule: You must take risks and not be afraid to fail, because the same stale thinking and ideas will get you nowhere.

As a member of the U.S. Senate Homeland Security Committee and former attorney general of North Dakota, I have considered U.S. border security and the consequences of smuggling illegal narcotics, people, weapons, and other contraband into and out of our country priorities for some time. Unfortunately, this important topic has been burdened with half-truths, false facts, and partisan bickering. In *Our 50-State Border Crisis* Howard courageously takes on an issue that challenges our sense of what it means to be an American. We are at once a nation built on the rule of law, and yet we embrace a longstanding moral obligation to help those in need. We are a nation of immigrants, but to be a nation we must protect our borders from the truly evil cartel forces that cross them every day.

All writers have biases. Howard's bias is for facts. Howard paints a high-definition picture of the border that he has lived as a ranch owner, a law enforcement officer, a humanitarian, and a photographer. The book starts from one very basic set of facts: The U.S. border with Mexico is *not* secure. And yet at the same time we have refugees and economic migrants arriving at our border whose challenges and needs we must address. His stories of his experiences and travels in Mexico and the Northern Triangle countries of Central America, and of his interactions with migrants, violent gang members, ranchers, law enforcement, and leaders struggling to help their countries recover from years of conflict, are vivid and powerful.

I first met Howard several years ago when a friend suggested I talk to him before I traveled to Africa, where our congressional delegation was attending briefings on food security. I was promised a lively and interesting conversation on soil and water conservation. Given the topics, I thought, *Maybe.* Well, within fifteen minutes on the phone I knew Howard was the real deal. He is an expert on the fragility of soils and water issues, and I learned how his foundation was investing in a farm in Arizona to try new soil and water conservation techniques that could be used in Africa.

In the same call, I explained to Howard that I was focusing on the challenges in Central America and Mexico and the resulting border security issues. Through my platform on the Homeland Security Committee, I felt that I had some ability to influence our policy toward those regions. Howard invited me to Arizona to see the soil and water conservation work, but also to see the effort he was making to understand and develop data about border security. The price of my admission to his farm and ranch was that I could not bring any staff, and I had to read his 2013 book *40 Chances: Finding Hope in a Hungry World.*

"You're on," I said. I read *40 Chances*, not because I thought I would find enlightenment, rather because I said I would. Instead, I found I could not put it down. Books about foundations' work so often involve fluffy tales of success, hope, and happiness. In *40 Chances*, I found honest autopsies of failures as Howard has tried to solve hunger crises all over the world: an example about how an intervention may have caused more problems than it solved or how a huge investment had only limited impact. The book showed how money and good intentions don't make complicated situations and issues any less so. The lesson is: You don't abandon the effort, but you must approach solving these problems with honesty.

I was instantly drawn to Howard's brutal honesty, and this book delivers more of it. Howard will always tell you the truth as he sees it. There is no partisan agenda or self-promotion. Howard cares about what works and how to achieve results that don't disrupt delicate relationships. How many philanthropists and investors have you heard or read about who put their failures on display so that others can learn from them? How many will use their own missteps to foster dialogue on how to solve problems? I know of only one.

Howard is the son of a famous investor, and people may be dismissive and think his philanthropy is some kind of an indulgent hobby. That couldn't be further from the truth. This is difficult and sometimes heartbreaking work. Like Howard, I've also traveled on multiple occasions to Mexico and to the Northern Triangle countries. I promise you these problems are real and not easy to solve, and we may never completely solve them. Howard provides the unvarnished, hard truth—that border security is not simply a "border problem." Border insecurity also is driven by choices made by individuals in states across the country who use and abuse illicit narcotics. Addressing border security means tackling the problems in the interior of the United States as well as root causes in neighboring countries whose social fabric is deteriorating from violence and poverty.

Our 50-State Border Crisis is a book for readers who are deeply concerned about the safety and security of the United States and want to understand how we can better achieve it. For best results, check your ideology and preconceptions at the door.

The Honorable Heidi Heitkamp
Senator for North Dakota

PREFACE

Border security is a contentious topic in our nation today. As someone born and raised and living in the border state of Arizona, I can also tell you that it's a subject fraught with myths and misleading stereotypes. The good news is we now have Howard Buffett's book, *Our 50-State Border Crisis*, to help us sort it out.

One of the most important myths Howard explodes in this book is that you are either a humanitarian who cares about immigrants or you are a hard-hearted border security advocate. Howard forges another path: He is a big-hearted realist, and he is a nonpartisan security advocate who believes deeply in the rule of law. Readers of this book will come to understand the complex forces at play on the border. He makes the argument that a strong, secure border both keeps us safe and erodes the ability of the drug cartels to exploit vulnerable people on both sides—and he shows how that is happening today.

Howard is one of the most high-energy, committed philanthropists I know. I've traveled with Howard to some very difficult and dangerous situations from the Democratic Republic of Congo to an El Salvador prison to inner-city Chicago. But the experience I shared with Howard that is most vivid for me was in 2015, when Howard invited me to tour the Arizona border near his foundation's property. I was standing with Howard on a small hill just a stone's throw from the border fence with Mexico. We were watching a group of migrants assembling on the other side. Clearly, they were getting ready to make an illegal entry. As I looked around the U.S. side of the fence, I saw clothing strewn around the base of a tree. There were women's undergarments hanging from its branches.

"What is that over there?" I asked Howard.

"That's a rape tree," Howard said. "The *coyotes* and their contacts will take women and girls they're guiding to the U.S., and part of the 'payment' is they rape them, and then hang their clothing as a trophy." He was so obviously moved by this horrible display and motivated to act to stop it.

Fighting against human trafficking is the area of philanthropy that is closest to my heart. Every single day in this country and around the world vulnerable people, many of them children, are subjected to trafficking for both sex and labor. It has been gratifying to have Howard Buffett's tremendous compassion and support on our side.

As an Arizona native, I know that my state is full of optimistic and hardworking people. Hispanic culture forms the backbone of our communities. It's been painful for me to see politicized rhetoric that disparages Hispanics or pretends they are the cause of the border crisis today. As you will learn in this book, our enemy is not a nation or a race, it is the criminal element—Mexican drug cartels and Central American gangs. The former are pushing massive quantities of lethal, illegal drugs into our country and trafficking huge numbers of terrified people who are running from gang violence in countries including Honduras, Guatemala, and El Salvador. Innocent people are an expendable commodity in this twisted economy. The cartels have come to realize that you sell drugs or guns once, but you can sell a child or a woman for sex over and over and over. We must destroy this criminal business model.

The McCain Institute is committed to advancing leadership based on security, economic opportunity, freedom, and human dignity in the United States and around the world. What I have seen firsthand is that Howard Buffett has a fearless commitment to understanding and battling threats to all these important values. He personally works in law enforcement, riding unglamorous night patrols and supporting first responder programs not only to battle drug dealing in communities but also to help addicts get treatment. He visits respite centers in Mexico so he can understand what is driving people on these incredibly risky journeys north. He talks to the powerful and powerless alike: migrant farmworkers and politicians, drug counselors and generals, Texas and Arizona ranchers and gang members trying to break out of the life, parents who've lost children to drugs and Border Patrol agents who work long shifts alone in dangerous smuggling corridors.

It's tempting to turn away from difficult realities. Howard makes it his business to lean in, understand, and then act. A more secure border will discourage the trafficking that leads to tragic symbols like rape trees. But so will investing in improving livelihoods in the home countries of poor people attempting these dangerous border crossings. Howard's foundation has spent hundreds of millions doing that and is increasing its work in Central America.

I challenge anyone who thinks philanthropy is easy to go on the road with Howard Buffett and see how hard he works and the length he goes to figure out how to help—always with perspective and, even in sticky situations, humor. You'll get a sense of his journeys and his passion in this book, one that can help all of us understand an urgent crisis and work toward solving it.

Cindy McCain
Chair, Human Trafficking Advisory Council
The McCain Institute for International Leadership

INTRODUCTION

When I was growing up in Omaha, my cousin Billy Rogers was one of my favorite people. We'd play basketball together, and he told great jokes and stories. Billy was a jazz guitar prodigy, and he later performed with a well-known group called The Crusaders. But like a lot of the musicians around him in the 1970s, he tried heroin, and he became an addict.

My mother loved Billy. She helped him move to San Francisco where my brother, Peter, also lived, to try to help Billy overcome his addiction. Peter hired Billy to work in his recording studio. One day, Billy asked Peter to borrow twenty dollars to go buy lunch. He never came back to work. Eventually, my mother and Peter found Billy in his apartment. He was dead from an overdose.

Billy was a great person—smart, funny, and kind. And he was a heroin addict. I wish we'd all known more about addiction in those days and had been able to get him the treatment he needed.

Today, the exploding number of overdose deaths from heroin, fentanyl, and other opioids has become an almost daily topic in the news. The increase in addictions is now a nationwide epidemic. It's reaching into every corner of our society, lowering our lifespans, straining our economic resources, and fracturing our social fabric. Overdose calls are bankrupting emergency response budgets. U.S. businesses are finding they can't hire and retain drug-free workers.

Perhaps you have read or heard about America's addiction epidemic, but you feel like it's someone else's problem—someone you may dismiss as weak or in any case very different from you. I have not thought that way for a long time, for two reasons. First, the painful loss, many years ago, of Billy; second, my extensive involvement, over the last five years, in local law enforcement in Illinois and Arizona.

Following Billy's death, I've been committed to trying to help people facing hardships. As a philanthropist, I've spent almost two decades trying to invest in meaningful agricultural and livelihood development projects around the world. But I have come to the conclusion that when the rule of law is absent it is almost impossible to achieve real progress. I have witnessed that even hundreds of millions of aid dollars, provided by my foundation and others, invested in some of the most difficult and violent places in the world, may do very little to solve the suffering of vulnerable people. Corruption and armed thugs will hijack the resources, and soon it will seem as if your resources were never there at all.

Watching this happen over and over, I became interested in understanding the rule of law from the ground up, starting with my own hometown. In 2012, I began volunteering as an auxiliary deputy sheriff in Macon County, Illinois. I have lived in Decatur, which is located in Macon County, since 1992. And when our foundation expanded our research farm and ranch programs to southern Arizona, I also began volunteering in the Cochise County Sheriff's Office (CCSO).

Because of those experiences, when I hear about drug overdose statistics they are not abstract to me. I think about scenes like one in a cheap motel in Macon, Illinois, in the fall of 2015. My Macon County Sheriff's Office deputy partner and I received a call from dispatch and headed toward the scene, where an ambulance and another sheriff's vehicle had already arrived. We were responding to a 911 call reporting that a woman in a room of this motel had stopped breathing and was unresponsive. There was familiar evidence of heroin use in the room: a syringe, a spoon, and an electric razor cord used as a tourniquet. Paramedics were administering rescue breathing, but she was not reviving.

A man in the room with the victim had called 911. He admitted the thirty-five-year-old woman had injected herself with heroin in front of him. He told the deputies and detective that he was a recovering addict and that he had met the woman online and urged her to come to Macon so he could help her get into a drug treatment program. He said he'd picked her up at a bus stop, and, after they arrived at the motel, she produced a small foil pack containing heroin. She said she wanted to chase one last high.

After she shot up, however, she stopped breathing. He called 911 and stayed with her. The detective felt the man was telling the truth and released him. The paramedics took her by ambulance to a local hospital. My partner and I were assigned to stay with her body for another two hours until the coroner arrived. When we got back to post, the sergeant said the woman's mother had been tracked down in a town about seventy-five miles away. She said her daughter had left home abruptly and nobody knew where she'd gone. An officer had to tell that mother her daughter was gone forever.

These days I meet many individuals in my hometown who are trying to help family members struggling with addiction. They come from many walks of life—respected corporate executives, devoted soccer moms, and even law enforcement officers. In 2015 there were eleven identified heroin overdose deaths in Macon County, which has a population of just over one hundred thousand people. In 2016, that number jumped to fifteen heroin overdose deaths. By October 2017, eleven people were confirmed to have died in Macon County of heroin or other opioid-related overdoses, but it's important to note that in the same time period Macon County's ambulance service reported that EMTs administered the opioid overdose reversal drug Narcan to 118 people who might have died without it. In some cases, victims had heroin plus other illegal drugs in their system.

This is one county in central Illinois. I assure you that overdose numbers are skyrocketing across the United States.

America has long benefited from a strong rule of law, unlike those countries in Africa and Central America where at times I have struggled to keep my foundation's work from being derailed by corrupt and violent people. Working in law enforcement in two counties, one thousand miles apart, one along the border and another in the U.S. heartland, has opened my eyes to a dimension of America's drug problem that I want to share with you in this book. It's one that is threatening the fundamental stability of our rule of law.

Many Americans, including some politicians, think our nation's drug crisis and the security crisis happening at our southern border with Mexico are two distinct problems. Some people want to tackle one issue, but seem to care little about the other. From my experience as a landowner on the Mexico–U.S. border and in law enforcement, I know they are connected—and we must treat them as such. The flood of drugs cartels in Mexico are smuggling across the U.S. border by land, through our ports, and on our coasts is fueling a crisis impacting virtually every community in every state.

I don't believe it is an exaggeration to say that every single American is impacted by our insecure border. We tend to think of drug addiction and overdoses as community-based problems, and we tend to view drug dealing and related violence as "local" crimes. But federal officials routinely estimate that 90 percent of the illegal drugs smuggled into our country are coming from or through Mexico, where the drug cartels have assumed unprecedented power through violence and corruption at every level of government and law enforcement.[1]

The drugs come hidden in passenger vehicles driven through official ports of entry in San Diego or Nogales or El Paso.[2] They ride in the trailers of semi-trucks, stashed inside fake crates of soda and boxes of toys. They're loaded on carts driven or pulled through underground tunnels; they travel close to ocean beaches in small wooden paddleboats called *pangas*; they're packed inside "narco-torpedoes" carried by and shot from larger ships along the Pacific coast.[3] They are wrapped in bundles and catapulted and fired by homemade cannons over border fences in Arizona.[4] They come in the stomachs of couriers riding on airplanes, and they come on the backs of drug mules crossing harsh, dangerous deserts and wilderness areas. Once the drugs cross the border, they use our efficient highway system to reach customers in every community in every state.

Whether you live in rural Maine, in a Nevada resort town, or even on a Hawaiian island, 90 percent of the drugs Americans now spend $100 billion a year buying come from or through Mexico.[5] The cartels are infiltrating our territory and cornering the market for heroin and other dangerous drugs and spreading violence and death in the process. As you will learn, the profits from those drugs are destabilizing our entire hemisphere. The rule of law in America is under assault.

Our foundation's focus is on global food security, conflict mitigation, and public safety. We own research farms in the Midwest, Arizona, and Texas, and we own two ranches in Arizona where we have invested in land that preserves unique habitats and where we do research on soil, water, and grassland conservation. Almost from the first day we purchased our Arizona farm, which is about fifty miles north of the border, we realized drug smugglers and migrants were crossing our land on a routine basis. When we took possession of our ranch properties directly adjacent to the border, between cartel scouts watching us 24/7 from the Mexico side and the armed smugglers appearing in videos from wildlife cameras we had placed in remote parts of the property, we felt like we were operating in an active conflict zone in the developing world.

These experiences and investments of my time and resources have convinced me that border security is one of the most critical national security issues we face. Only the theoretical threats of war or a high-impact terrorist attack can compare to the overdose deaths and suffering the Mexican drug cartels will, without a doubt, deliver to our communities this year. On a regional basis, the cartels' activities have destabilized our friend and neighbor Mexico, and they exacerbate the suffering of Mexico's southern neighbors in the Northern Triangle countries of El Salvador, Honduras, and Guatemala. Those consequences also are a threat to our safety and stability.

My concern has motivated me to invite politicians, policy and security experts, military and law enforcement leaders, and other influential people to visit our properties in southern Arizona so they can see for themselves the reality and challenges of border security. I have rented helicopters so I can fly them above the terrain and so they can appreciate the variety of geographic features. They see the isolation of some areas and the congestion of others, and they see how all that must be factored into our border security equation. Many of them have encouraged me to share my insights and recommendations, and that is why I wrote this book.

As you will soon learn, "a wall" will not solve this problem. I will lay out a five-point plan for rebooting our approach to border security that involves changes we must make in how we view the border security challenge and how we command our frontline responders, the far more specific and appropriate uses of barriers and technology we need, some of the complex social factors we have to confront head-on, steps we must take beyond our borders to work with the Mexican government as a partner, and investing in building peace and stable livelihoods for the people of the Northern Triangle countries. Unless we take this comprehensive approach, we will not achieve the border security America needs.

Our tour begins near the U.S. border with Mexico, on the southwest side of Arizona's Huachuca Mountains on a cold January day in 2017.

Part I

COSTS AND CONSEQUENCES

I never feel like I can understand a complicated situation until I visit and talk with people who have to live with it every day. We're about to visit some remote and unusual locations, and you will see the complexity of border issues and the different points of view for yourself. But also keep in mind these incredible statistics—showing how the crisis impacts your own backyard:

- An American now dies of a drug overdose in the U.S. approximately every eleven minutes. Between 2002 and 2014, the rate of heroin-related overdose deaths increased fivefold to more than ten thousand people annually. Overall, deaths from drug overdoses, including methamphetamines, cocaine, and prescription opioids (often obtained illegally), topped fifty-two thousand in 2015, and as of October 2017 the CDC said that they exceeded sixty-four thousand in 2016.[1] The number of 2016 overdoses alone is about *twenty-one* times the number of Americans who died of terrorist-caused activities on 9/11, and *nine* times the number of U.S. military personnel who have been killed in the Middle East since 2001.[2]

- Drug overdoses now kill Americans at a rate that exceeds motor vehicle accidents and firearm fatalities.[3] Drug overdoses just in 2016 exceeded the total number of U.S. casualties for the duration of the Vietnam War.[4] Drug overdoses are now the leading cause of death for people under fifty.[5] In 2016, the number of overdose deaths from opioids alone—42,249—exceeded the number of fatalities from breast cancer.[6]

- Heroin use has increased across the United States among men and women, most age groups, and all income levels. Some of the greatest increases are occurring in demographic groups with historically low rates of heroin use: women, the privately insured, and people with higher incomes.[7]

- Federal, state, and community-based spending on drug control, including domestic law enforcement, federal criminal investigations, correctional costs, and prevention and treatment, exceeds $60 billion.[8,9,10]

- In 2011, the last year for which there are solid statistics, the direct impact of all illegal drug use on the U.S. healthcare system was estimated at $11 billion, and it is much higher now.[11] In November 2017, the White House Council of Economic Advisors announced that previous estimates that opioid abuse, alone, in 2013 had cost the United States $78.5 billion in healthcare spending, criminal justice costs, and lost productivity had dramatically underreported the true costs. For 2015, CEA estimates that the economic costs of the opioid crisis were $504 billion, factoring in fatalities from overdoses, heroin-related fatalities, and non-fatal costs of opioid misuse.[12]

- Roughly 70 percent of drug abusers are employed, and drug abuse costs American employers about $81 billion annually due to absenteeism, injuries, increased health care expenses, and lost productivity.[13]

Chapter 1

RED SHOES "WALK UP"

Along the U.S.–Mexico border, beautiful landscapes can hide deadly threats.

About seventy miles south of Tucson, Arizona, our foundation owns and operates Mission Oaks Ranch, a 2,200-acre property we purchased to help protect pristine wildlife habitats and research grassland preservation. MOR, as we call it, is one of my favorite places: It's a remote, unspoiled wilderness area of rolling grasslands, woodlands, and rock washes. Long operated as a cattle ranch, it also has unique archaeological and historical features including rock paintings from AD 700. The Spanish explorer Coronado passed through this area in search of the Seven Cities of Gold. Scenes from the musical *Oklahoma* and John Wayne movies were shot nearby.

When I woke up the morning of January 17, 2017, at MOR, I was excited that recent snow flurries had stopped and the skies were clear. People always think of Arizona as warm but MOR sits at about a mile-high elevation on the southwest side of the Huachuca Mountain Range. For several days, the snow had delayed construction projects I'd come to Arizona to work on. Finally, I could get back on a tractor with a box grader and finish building our new road.

I started early, and I was still working late in the afternoon when I heard my call sign over my two-way radio. Our ranch manager, Mark, said in a curt voice: "We've got a walk up." I shut off the tractor and hurried over to my truck to drive the mile back to the ranch house. I didn't like the sound of Mark's voice or his message. Mission Oaks is completely surrounded by federal lands and our nearest neighbor's house is a thirty-minute drive away. Mark would not have called me just to report that a deer hunter had stopped to ask for directions.

For all its beauty, the unfortunate reality is that Mission Oaks is located in a high-traffic drug-smuggling corridor. About 1.5 miles of our ranch parallels a sixty-foot strip of federal land separating us from Mexico. Mexican drug cartel operatives, many in camouflage and some carrying weapons, frequently cross MOR and other private and public lands in the San Rafael Valley. Every week our wild-life study cameras positioned in remote areas of the ranch not only capture images of mountain lions, bears, and coyotes, but also groups of sometimes twenty-five or thirty people, including drug smugglers carrying backpacks of methamphetamines, heroin, and other drugs. We know Border Patrol does not apprehend many of the smugglers we see on video because we sometimes see them again the same day or days later when the same individuals trigger the same cameras, traveling back the way they came but with lighter packs.

They move fast. Occasionally, some smugglers are armed, and a group may have one person at the back scratching out tracks with a leafy branch. They avoid making contact with anybody when they're headed north with their loads or heading back south again. Less often, groups that include women and teens appear on our cameras. After being apprehended, some have told law enforcement that they are migrants who have agreed—or been forced—to carry drugs in exchange for a cartel guide to help them cross the border.

The San Rafael Valley is not an easy place to try to enter the United States. The terrain is rugged. It takes many hours of hiking to reach highways, some of it through mountains. On the other hand, this remote and challenging topography makes it difficult for Border Patrol to detect and apprehend those who attempt to cross the border there.

Not surprisingly, smugglers' plans can break down. It's easy to twist an ankle or get dehydrated or overheated. Occasionally, trespassers will stop at local ranches and ask for food, water, or even medical assistance. If nobody is around, smugglers may break into ranch buildings and steal weapons or supplies. That motivates us all to stay alert. Several years ago a local rancher east of our ranch was shot and killed when he came across a drug mule returning to Mexico. We can't assume any visitor is harmless, and help could be an hour away. Our ranch hands and I carry holstered weapons when we work and travel around the property, hoping to never have to use them.

Empty, bleeding hands

When I arrived back at the ranch house, Mark was inside a covered porch standing over a shaggy-haired young man seated on a chair, his shoulders covered in a blanket. They came outside and we all sat on a short wall. What first caught my eye were the guy's cherry-red high-topped sneakers. Not exactly camouflage.

Mark said he was walking between two sheds when he heard a low whistle. Mark looked up and Oscar[*] walked toward him with his hands held up to show they were empty. They also were scratched and bleeding. It was cold outside but Oscar, who at about five feet tall looked like a young teen but actually was

---

[*] Oscar is a pseudonym. The first reference to every pseudonym will have an asterisk.

nineteen, had no jacket; he wore muddy jeans, the red sneakers, and a couple of T-shirt layers that were soaked with sweat. Oscar had been running and he was agitated and seemed afraid. He asked for help. Mark called me while he gave Oscar water and made him a sandwich.

Nobody on our ranch team that day spoke Spanish, but we called a friend who helped us translate. Oscar said he was from Honduras. He said he left in fear because of threats from gangs. He said he had been living in Mexico for six months, and then he decided to make his move to cross the border and find a place to live and work. After walking for several days, he said he was resting in a wash, the dry bed of a stream, when he saw a line of men walking past him carrying big backpacks. The men at the front and back were armed with long guns, likely AK-47s. He said he crouched in the bushes hoping they would just pass by, but the last man in line saw him and started shooting. Oscar ran toward the U.S. border.

It was plausible. Gang violence in Honduras is widespread and the country has one of the highest murder rates in the world.[1] That has motivated thousands of people to flee and try to find safety in the United States. In much of the border area near MOR, there are only four-strand, four-foot-high barbed-wire fences and low, anti-vehicle "Normandy" barriers separating the United States from Mexico. It would not have been difficult for Oscar to cross onto U.S. soil, reach a road, and follow it several miles to the gate of our ranch.

Mark and I exchanged looks. I knew we were asking ourselves the same questions: Was Oscar telling the truth, or even mostly telling the truth? Or was he a drug mule who'd become separated from his group? Was he a decoy for drug smugglers hiding nearby who might rob us or use the diversion to cross our land or steal a vehicle? Or could he be a member of a criminal "rip crew," thugs who lie in wait and steal drugs from cartel couriers?

Same routes, different journeys

As we talked with Oscar we were face to face with one of the most significant factors along the U.S. border today: Hundreds of thousands of people try to enter our country illegally each year. Among them, a small minority working for the ruthless, cunning, predatory Mexican drug cartels move among large numbers of vulnerable, poor people fleeing violence, looking for work, or hoping to reunite with family members. Both groups are committing a crime, but the former are a much bigger threat. When apprehended, the smugglers may tell the same stories as the migrants, and it's not always easy to tell them apart.

For many years we have pursued border security strategies and national immigration policies in the United States that have swung like a pendulum between the dominant issues of each of those groups. We hear extreme language on both sides, some demanding "open borders" for all...or President Donald Trump's supporters chanting "Build the wall" to keep out "rapists" and "killers."[2] Both positions are simplistic and unworkable. For many years, a lack of leadership from Washington has made border security one of the most volatile and controversial subjects in America, and it's made us all less safe. This issue is too important to be held hostage to politics and posturing, and I have become preoccupied with trying to understand and find answers to what I feel is America's most serious national security threat.

As you'll learn, I have invested a lot of time, energy, and resources to understand our border security crisis. I bring a law enforcement point of view, but I also come to this topic as a philanthropist whose foundation has spent hundreds of millions of dollars supporting development and humanitarian projects in countries that are overwhelmed by conflict and injustice, including Mexico and the Northern Triangle countries of El Salvador, Guatemala, and Honduras.

9

I've sat and talked at length with migrants in respite centers, with gang-affiliated murderers in jails and prisons, and with poor farmers who not only have to deal with challenges such as droughts and poor soil, but with violent gangs extorting money from them and stealing their crops.

I'm a photographer who has chronicled the dangerous and desperate journey of migrants trying to travel to the United States by hopping freight trains and paying *coyotes*.

I even consider these issues with the experience of a lifelong farmer. And make no mistake: Border security and immigration are connected to U.S. food security. It is concerning that U.S. agriculture relies on tens of thousands of undocumented workers to harvest our food. The rule of law applies to employers as well. It's also ironic that some farmers appear surprised that rhetoric that casts their workers as murderers and rapists has reduced that workforce and is resulting in crops that are rotting in the field.[3]

Confronted with the sudden appearance of Oscar on that January day at MOR, I felt like my worlds were colliding. Oscar seemed like exactly the kind of person our investments in development in Central America were designed to help. He said he wanted to be safe from the gangs and find work. And yet he had broken the laws of the United States, and so I had to call Border Patrol.

About an hour later as I watched the agent's vehicle drive away from MOR with Oscar in the back, I couldn't stop thinking about so many questions, starting with whether he was a criminal or a victim or maybe even both. What was the journey that brought him to our gate? What options did he have? Was he proof that trying to bring peace through development projects like ones we had sponsored in countries including Honduras is a failed idea? Or was he a good reason to double down?

I couldn't just shrug and put the incident behind me. As you'll learn, I would soon see Oscar again.

My road to the border

For most of my adult life, my preoccupation was agriculture. Farming, and also working for agriculture-based companies, is how I supported my family for many years. In the late 1990s, my parents' generosity paved the way for me to work as a philanthropist, and I focused largely on food security and livelihood development in Africa and Latin America. In 2013, I wrote a book about those efforts called *40 Chances: Finding Hope in a Hungry World*. I wrote in *40 Chances* about how I had tried to use my experience in agriculture to inform more realistic and effective programs to support global food security.

Those projects brought me to regions of the world where the extent of poverty and violence are unimaginable to most Americans. These areas often are chaotic, and many development efforts don't succeed. But that did not make me stop trying. By temperament and thanks in part to the encouragement of my father and mother, I'm a risk taker. When my parents provided my sister and brother and me substantial funds to create our own foundations, they reminded us that we were in a unique position. We would not have to focus on fund-raising or celebrating minor victories that appeal to donors but that rarely lead to significant changes. My dad in particular encouraged us to take on the toughest problems. In *40 Chances* I shared lessons many NGOs and charities can't easily talk about—what doesn't work and the mistakes well-meaning groups (including us!) have made that can make a difficult situation even worse. My desire was to help others avoid making similar mistakes.

These days my interest in border security has become more widely known, and people familiar with *40 Chances* sometimes ask me if I've "given up" on hunger. Not at all. We still support significant food security–related projects in Africa and Central America.

We advocate for good soil conservation practices around the world. But my thinking continues to evolve.

Clean water and food seem like the most basic human needs. Of course that is true for individuals, but I have learned over and over in countries such as Sierra Leone, Sudan, and El Salvador that a society will never reliably deliver those resources if another fundamental condition is absent: the rule of law. There is no point investing in agricultural systems or trying to develop markets when poor farmers are dodging bullets and avoiding landmines in their fields. Why plant seeds in the spring to grow crops you are unlikely to harvest because of the threat of violence and perhaps a need to flee? Why drill a well when, after you leave, a local thug can sit in front of it with impunity and demand people pay him to pump the water?

Both for humanitarian reasons and because conflict and suffering anywhere can lead to threats to U.S. national security, I care very deeply about vulnerable and marginalized communities around the world. To me, the goal of border security is not about keeping people out of the United States who seek asylum and protection from violence. It's not about turning away people who want to work and contribute to our society. These are policies we should discuss in an open, realistic way and make decisions based on the reality of our economic and social priorities and resources.

But we cannot have "open borders." We must create a system and a security strategy so that we can process the individuals we choose to let in through a legal, efficient, and safe manner. Safe for us and safe for them. We need to be in control of our own territory, and we need to protect the safety and property of U.S. citizens.

Demonstrating compassion for vulnerable people while defending the rule of law can be challenging. But I have seen firsthand the consequences for countries like Somalia or South Sudan, where there is no respect for the rule of law. The tools of democracy we take for granted like elections or respect for human rights become meaningless. I've visited Sudan several times to see if our foundation could provide resources to help with ongoing conflict. I once spent a hot, sleepless night in a shipping container being used as a field barrack near a government airstrip. For hours, I listened to the sound of Sudanese military planes and helicopters taking off to bomb the country's own citizens.

Today, the rule of law is crumbling in our hemisphere. In fact, right next door. On one hand Mexico is now the world's fifteenth-largest economy and one of the United States's largest trading partners. But even high-level Mexican government officials and business leaders admit that Mexico is now largely narco-controlled. There is no question that Mexico has suffered incredible bloodshed in recent years. The *Los Angeles Times* has reported that in 2016 there were 20,792 homicides in Mexico—a 22 percent increase over 2015, and 35 percent more than 2014.[4] By contrast, the population of the United States is more than 2.5 times the size of Mexico, but the FBI has reported there were 17,250 homicides in the United States in 2016.[5] For January through May 2017, the government of Mexico reported that murders were up 30 percent from the same period in 2016, according to *The Guardian*.[6] Corruption is rampant and Mexico's impunity rate is the worst in the Americas; it's estimated that fewer than 5 percent of *reported* crimes are successfully prosecuted. Cartel *sicarios*, or assassins, kill anyone who gets in their way. Rival gang members, honest police, and journalists are high on the list.

In mid-2017, I sat down with a group of undocumented Mexican farmworkers in Texas to better understand what is happening in that community. One woman who has been in the United States for a number of years said flatly, "I'm never going back to Mexico. It is too dangerous. My cousin [who she said had a legal U.S. visa] had not seen his mother in twenty years. He drove to Mexico and on the way back the cartel stopped him and pulled him out and said they wanted his truck. He said no, and they killed him and his wife and his two children." I had to remind myself: This woman is talking about Mexico—our trading partner, our ally, our neighbor.

Conflict and violence in the region extend well beyond Mexico. Excluding active war zones, forty-three of the world's fifty most dangerous cities are in Latin America and the Caribbean, which also are home to eight of the world's ten most dangerous countries.[7] It is no mystery why people are trying to get to the United States. If I found myself in a position where my family was hungry and gangs or cartels were threatening my children, I also might try to get to the United States at any cost despite a lack of legal options. At some point when you feel like you are standing on the roof of a burning building, just about everyone will jump.

But we need more than empathy and compassion to solve these problems. It doesn't make sense to respond to the collapse of rule of law in one country by ignoring laws in our own. As unfair as fate may have been to Oscar in Honduras, it also is not fair to U.S. citizens along nearly two thousand miles of border that they must live in fear because our current strategy to secure the U.S. border has turned their family's lands into dangerous drug trafficking corridors.

It's not fair that thousands of American families are burying loved ones who have overdosed on drugs criminals have smuggled over the border from Mexico, and then sold on U.S. streets.

It's not fair to all U.S. citizens who are bearing the financial and human cost of not just drugs but of violent transnational criminals who are deported over and over, and yet turn around and come right back and commit an array of crimes.

We have to face reality: Our appetite for illegal drugs and our failure to secure the border have had terrible consequences for American citizens and those threats are in many ways intensifying.

John Kelly, retired U.S. Marine Corps general and former secretary of Homeland Security addressed the U.S. Senate's Committee on Homeland Security and Governmental Affairs in 2015. He pointed out that on 9/11 three thousand Americans were killed by terrorism, but since 9/11 over half a million Americans have died of drug overdoses from illegal narcotics—"in my view murdered by narco-terrorists." General Kelly added, "These criminal cartels pose a direct threat to the stability of our partners and an insidious risk to the security of our nation."[8]

It's appropriate to be concerned about ISIS and global terrorism, but what about what I call slow-motion terrorism—the erosion of our communities by the poison of drug addiction and criminal activity? At a 2016 U.S. Senate hearing about the potent drug fentanyl, which is one hundred times more powerful than morphine, Senator Ed Markey of Massachusetts questioned whether our government was showing enough urgency in addressing this new and growing threat. "It's going to kill tens of thousands of Americans every year," he said. "There is no other threat to our country that even matches that!"[9]

I thought of the senator's prediction in August 2017, when I read about a vehicle that was transporting what experts estimate was $1.87 billion—yes, *billion*—worth of fentanyl. A truck and trailer, which appeared to be loaded with grocery supplies, was headed for the United States but was stopped and seized at a Mexican military checkpoint in San Luis Río Colorado, a city across the border from Yuma, Arizona. CBS News reported that the load included thirty thousand pills made with the drug, and 140 pounds of pure fentanyl.[10] The substance is so strong an amount equal to about three grains of salt can kill you.

The same month, a middle-aged Mexican couple were arrested in an apartment in Queens, New York, with suitcases packed with 141 pounds of pure fentanyl, which the DEA said was enough to kill 32 million people, according to the *Washington Post*. The couple, believed to be cartel brokers sent to arrange for the distribution of the drug to dealers in the United States, had flown in recently on Mexican passports. The *Post* also reported that narcotics agents seized 350 pounds of fentanyl in New York City in 2017, ten times as much as in 2016, and that Mexican traffickers are smuggling it across the border and then across the country.[11]

So that afternoon back at MOR, with all those concerns in the back of my mind, but also curiosity about whether Oscar was part of the complex web of drug trafficking or just a scared kid, I did what I always do when I'm frustrated that I don't know enough about something. I started to investigate.

Right to be wary

Our foundation helps support an Arizona nonprofit organization called the Florence Immigrant and Refugee Rights Project. The organization's mission is to provide free legal and social services to detained adults and unaccompanied children facing immigration removal proceedings in Arizona. Our foundation funds primarily go to helping Florence's work with children.

Given my advocacy for a stronger border, this might seem contradictory. I do not believe it is: I am opposed to illegal immigration because I am a defender of the rule of law. In the United States the rule of law also says everyone deserves a fair hearing. Our immigration courts are overwhelmed and backlogged. The individuals moving through them typically are very poor and can remain in detention for long periods with no resolution in sight. I've sat in those courts and watched the confusion myself.

Immigrants facing deportation have no right to a public defender because the deportation process is considered a civil offense, rather than criminal. While people who cross the border again after being deported can be charged with the federal crime of unlawful entry or reentry, that criminal offense is separate from the deportation process; it is only once the criminal case is done and the sentence is served that an immigrant faces the deportation process.

Immigration judges access interpreters on speed dial and they often do their work over speakerphones. People of all ages are in the deportation process. Children as young as three and four years old are forced to represent themselves in deportation hearings.[12] Many defendants do not speak English, and many are uneducated, unfamiliar with U.S. legal systems, and terrified. Some have been victims of violence in their home countries. Most cannot afford an attorney. As a result, some fall victim to unethical lawyers or people claiming to be lawyers in the United States who charge individuals and their families thousands of dollars, but do little to no work on the case, show up for court unprepared, or don't show up at all. Our support of the Florence Project is another way to reinforce the rule of law. It helps vulnerable people know their rights and navigate our system, and it keeps me up to speed on the consequences of the policies our government enforces.

I called the Florence team and gave them the details I had about Oscar. I asked if they could attempt to find him in the system and find out if it was possible for me to visit Oscar and speak with him. Within twenty-four hours, the team from Florence Project found Oscar and met with him. On the ranch he had given us a phone number for his aunt in Honduras; when the Florence advocate called Honduras to tell Oscar's family he was safe, she spoke to a man who was hesitant to offer any information. At first he just said Oscar's aunt was not available. Our contact from Florence explained to me, "He was wary, appropriately so. I think at first he thought I was calling to extort money. We hear of so many cases where individuals are kidnapped (by cartel operatives or smugglers)—the kidnappers call a relative and demand money before they will let them go."

Although Oscar told us he had been persecuted by gangs in Honduras, he declined to apply for asylum after he was told he could spend a year or more in detention before he would know if he had a chance of staying permanently in the United States. He told the attorneys he was without money to post bond, and his family was too poor to send any money.

Oscar signed his deportation papers, and ICE scheduled him for a flight back to San Pedro Sula, Honduras, one of the most dangerous cities in the world, especially for a person with no money and without family nearby. He also said he did not want to go to his hometown of Tegucigalpa, where his grandmother and aunt live. There, the Mara Salvatrucha gang, often called MS-13, dominates the area, and in the past gang members had threatened him.[13] He would have to figure out how to raise the bus fare to travel to where other members of his family lived in a rural village several hours from San Pedro Sula.

As he waited for deportation, Oscar was in custody in the federal detention center in Florence, Arizona. He agreed to speak with me, and I drove to Florence the next day. I spent a couple of hours with him talking about his life and the experiences that he said landed him at the front gate of our ranch. We sat in a small gray room on hard metal chairs. Oscar wore orange rubber shoes and a thin olive-green cotton uniform. He shivered in the air-conditioned room. His eyes were bloodshot and he appeared exhausted. I tried to learn as much as I could before our time ran out.

Threats, death, Guns n' Roses

We started by talking about the basics of his life. Oscar was just about to turn twenty years old. He had grown up in intense poverty. The gangs in Tegucigalpa require all homes to pay a "protection" fee, he explained, "and if you don't pay they will kill you." He did not want to join a gang, and he said he had seen many people, including kids, murdered by MS-13. He had tried two previous times to come to the United States, but both times he was apprehended in Mexico and returned to Honduras. He went to live in a rural Honduran village with his aunts where the gangs were not prevalent, but there was little work and the family barely had enough to eat.

The third time Oscar left to go north was in January 2016, a year earlier. He said he crossed Guatemala easily by bus, then he crossed into Mexico near Palenque, and he made his way northeast to Veracruz on the coast. There, he said he knocked on doors begging for food. He said he met a woman who took him in and paid him a small amount of money to work for her. She put him up for six months. During this time, he did not have a phone but he would sometimes use a friend's smartphone or computer in a house where he was staying to post updates to his Facebook account.

Oscar said his father came looking for him, and he traveled to Veracruz by hopping on and off freight trains. At this point in our conversation, Oscar began crying and could barely speak. He said that while traveling in Veracruz, his father had been killed when he fell beneath the wheels of a moving train.

Oscar was still determined to make it to the United States and said he kept riding trains and taking buses heading north. Eventually, he landed in Santa Ana, Sonora, south of Nogales not far from the Arizona border. Locals told him to walk east and north, and suggested he orient himself by lights and radio towers. He said he walked for seven days and when he arrived at our ranch he had not eaten for three days and had only drunk water from creeks and puddles along his route.

I asked Oscar about his goals and what he would like to accomplish in life. He said he'd once wanted to be an architect. He said he'd gotten good grades in school, but had to drop out after only a year of secondary school. He said he liked the band Guns n' Roses and the singer Shakira, and he laughed when I told him we had that in common.

I had many more questions for Oscar that we didn't get to. Several times we had to pause because the memory of his father, or the thought of his family back in Honduras, would upset him too much.

Still, even seeing his emotional display, I questioned parts of his story.

The Mexican cartels are very active on the south side of the border near San Rafael Valley and Mission Oaks. Was Oscar really on his own for seven days with no human contact other than the alleged shooting incident? Oscar had told us that once he finished the food and water he was carrying as he hiked to the border, he had thrown away his backpack. I thought that was odd. If it was empty it would be light, and he could potentially refill an empty container with water or find other objects he would want to carry. It is common for migrants to keep a change of clothes in a backpack and throw away their dirty traveling clothes after they cross the border to better blend in on the U.S. side. But Oscar had walked up wearing only muddy, sweat-drenched T-shirts.

When we parted in Florence, I wished him luck. I told him maybe I would come visit him in Honduras. I did not expect him to believe me.

In subsequent months, I worked with a small team of researchers on this book, and we checked in repeatedly with Oscar. And we also checked out other elements of his story. Eventually, I would travel to a tiny, impoverished village near Tegucigalpa and meet members of Oscar's family. Those efforts yielded some unexpected and interesting insights.

Over time, my interactions with Oscar contributed to my opinion that our border today is a place where the lines between not only fact and fiction, but security and humanity, survival and collaboration, fantasy and freedom, ambition and desperation, can blur—or even collide. It's so complex that it's not surprising to me that people of good intentions in government, in law enforcement, and in philanthropic circles sometimes advocate for strategies and policies that can create terrible unintended consequences.

It's not hard to feel compassion for someone like Oscar. But what do you do when hundreds of thousands of Oscars also feel they are out of options and are crossing our borders and to some degree providing cover for dangerous criminals who hide among them? Imagine how you would feel as a U.S. citizen if land that your family has worked for generations had turned into a conflict zone, a place where you never know when you might confront an armed smuggler in a remote area far from help. Many of my rancher neighbors in Arizona don't have to imagine that. As you'll soon learn, they live it every day.

Chapter 2

LIGHTS OFF, PISTOLS READY

Rural communities in the southwest U.S. border states, including Arizona and Texas, have seen the consequences of violence and poverty in other nations arrive on their doorsteps.

Our foundation works where many other foundations and NGOs can't or won't go, and we take risks that few others can afford to take. That's led me to visit more than 150 countries to see difficult circumstances firsthand. Almost inevitably, where there is poverty and hunger, there is violence. Years ago I traveled to the Guatemalan highlands, where we were funding an agriculture program run by an NGO active in this remote area. We stopped so I could take photographs of farmers working on the sloped fields of the region. I heard the sound of metal pinging, and the driver motioned me to hurry and get back in the vehicle. Some farmers were throwing rocks at us.

It turned out a drug cartel had convinced some of the impoverished farmers to cultivate opium poppies; I later learned the rock throwers thought we were part of a military group that had been eradicating their poppy crop. Not long after this, the cartels began hijacking NGO vehicles in this region and threatening the occupants with harm or death if they reported the crime. The narcos would then drive the vehicles, which carried special relief agency plates, and sail through police blockades.

We've supported initiatives in agriculture, water, and conservation even in intense African conflict regions including South Sudan, Sierra Leone, and the Democratic Republic of Congo (DRC). In 2016, while flying in a helicopter to visit a hydroelectric plant our foundation built in DRC, we heard a loud bang that jolted the helicopter. After landing, the pilot pointed to a dent and burn marks underneath the helicopter and said we had taken rifle fire from the ground, where armed rebel groups hide in the area's thick jungles.

Given these areas of interest for us, I'm also used to getting emails or phone calls from people facing violent crises. One of our partners in a development project in Congo wrote to us not long ago: "We have been in confrontations with militias for three days, continuously," and then he detailed the death of one national park ranger and the injury of another.

These dangers come with the territory, and the flexibility and willingness our foundation has to invest resources in these places is a point of pride for us.

Endangered species, endangered people

I was not always involved in such high-stakes situations, and what first brought me to Mexico and Central America was business, not conflict. I grew up in Nebraska and in the early 1990s I moved to central Illinois, where I bought farmland and also went to work for the giant Decatur, Illinois, food-processing company Archer Daniels Midland (ADM). One of my responsibilities was business development, identifying investments and acquisitions in Mexico. I fell in love with the people and the culture of Mexico and made lifelong friends there in business and government.

Around the same time, I became active in philanthropy. Initially, I was focused on conservation. When I traveled in Mexico and in Central and South America, I sometimes would extend my trips to photograph jaguars, birds, and other rare, often endangered species.[1] But as I wrote in *40 Chances*, everywhere I found animals to be endangered, I found people to be endangered as well. The connection was not coincidental. Nobody will starve to save a tree or an animal. I became aware that many people in our hemisphere were barely surviving. Poor farmers struggled with depleted soils, devastating storms, scarce or contaminated water, and few resources, and they were watching their children die from diseases related to poor nutrition. Over time, I shifted the primary focus of our foundation to helping people.

Many individuals in these countries told me their only option to escape misery and even death was to take dangerous journeys north through Mexico by train to try to reach the United States. While I knew there was drug smuggling going on, I was focused on photographing people who were trying to escape poverty and the violence that surrounds poverty. I was shocked to see mothers with young children, hopping on and off freight trains. They were making their way north to what they believed was their best and perhaps only chance to have enough to eat and a feeling of safety. While sitting a few feet from a set of tracks in Veracruz, I once asked a young mother how she reconciled taking such a dangerous journey north. She hesitated, then said to me, "My child will die at home, so it makes no difference if we die now. We are in God's hands."

One of my most memorable trips was to Altar, Mexico, in 2004. It's one of the key immigrant staging towns in the Sonora region about sixty miles south of the U.S. border. There, immigrants come and connect with guides, and they buy supplies like backpacks and food and water for the journey. Illegal immigration is an industry in Altar; migrants can rent rooms to rest in boarding houses and vans shuttle them right up to the border south of Sasabe, Arizona. The cartels control Altar now, and I could not safely make this trip today.[2]

Knowing my interest in these issues, a friend introduced me to a U.S. Border Patrol agent in Arizona who invited me on ride-alongs with him, so I also could photograph these groups after they crossed to the U.S. side of the border. I began visiting the border several times per year, and I would meet humanitarian and labor organizations working in various capacities in border areas. Our foundation made several grants designed to improve livelihoods in the migrants' home countries, where it was clear that most preferred to stay, or where they hoped they could return.

At the time, our foundation's primary focus was Africa. We had launched an ambitious plan to do large-scale agricultural research at our farm in the Limpopo region of South Africa; the work was aimed at developing better seeds and techniques to help millions of poor smallholder farmers. But the project became challenging: The Limpopo region is in an area with commercial farming, but we still had problems with delivery of fertilizer and other farming inputs, and maintaining and getting parts for farm equipment. But what finally forced me to consider other options was that violence in the region increased.

Around 2010 we began looking for land in the United States that could reflect African soils and climate so we could test and develop ideas and then send the best to Africa. We found the soil and water conditions we needed in Arizona. So in 2011, we purchased what we call our Apache Farm near Willcox, Arizona, where we planned to experiment with conservation farming techniques and with a variety of crops.

Smuggler in the cornfield

We had owned Apache for just a few months when I got a call early one morning from our farm manager. He told me that deputies from the Cochise County Sheriff's Office had chased a drug smuggler driving a pickup truck carrying 2,500 pounds of marijuana into a ditch on our property. The driver then bailed out and ran; the deputies and Border Patrol searched one of our cornfields for over three hours before they found him. This farm is more than fifty miles from the Mexican border.

Great, I thought. In part we came to Arizona to escape crime and violence in South Africa. So much for that plan. But this incident triggered my curiosity, and I began asking questions. For example, I learned that Border Patrol has access to any land they want to search for immigration purposes (although they cannot enter dwellings) within twenty-five miles of the border. However, within one hundred miles of the border they can pull over cars or question individuals if they have "reasonable suspicion" of an immigration violation. Inland, they staff both permanent and temporary checkpoints, and they monitor highways and major thoroughfares. Local law enforcement often complains that federal enforcement does not focus more on stopping the traffic at the border itself.

I also learned that the community was frustrated that Border Patrol didn't focus more attention on stopping illegal entry right along the border, because it led to more crime and damage inland. Law enforcement refers to all illegal border crossers, whether they are smugglers or economic migrants, refugees of violence, or people seeking to reunite with family, as "undocumented aliens" or UDAs. And there is no question UDAs sometimes commit burglaries as they pass through private lands; they also cut fences, leave gates open, and punch holes in PVC irrigation pipes to get water. The intent may not be malicious, but it costs ranchers time and money because livestock may escape or scatter and lose weight running around...or even die. When damaged pipes don't fill troughs, cattle can suffer dehydration.

In 2012, I became involved in law enforcement myself, first as a volunteer sworn auxiliary deputy sheriff in Macon County, Illinois (and then soon after as a volunteer in Arizona). I wanted to serve my community, but as I mentioned earlier, during this period of my life I was interested in understanding the factors that support the rule of law.

I had experienced the absence of the rule of law many times. In 1997, I visited Bosnia with an organization providing humanitarian aid for landmine victims, but I was arrested by police for no stated reason other than they did not like that I was taking photographs in public. I realized I had no rights, no reason to trust them to follow the law, no power whatsoever, and there was no "one phone call" to make. They eventually let me go after several stressful hours of uncertainty.

Obviously, issues arise in U.S. communities with law enforcement, but in general I believe Americans can and do view law enforcement as an institution that enforces the law and protects the vulnerable. That attitude is not the case in many parts of the world where our foundation's development projects have struggled because we could not depend on local law enforcement to protect the people we were trying to help. In parts of Africa corrupt actors or thugs have stolen resources we provided to communities, and sometimes police or military were more likely to be in on the crime than willing to help solve it. I wanted to understand for myself how American law enforcement was trained and managed in order to create the trust absent in other parts of the world. After certifying as an auxiliary deputy, I began working patrol shifts in Macon County, assisting with traffic stops, serving warrants, and responding to general calls, always with another deputy.

I didn't anticipate this, but the most dramatic insights for me have centered on the extent of illegal drug activity in my hometown and the surrounding area. Not just the overdoses that I have already described but also the impact on people you would not associate with illegal drugs at all. I learned grandmothers are becoming addicted to Mexican heroin because they can no longer afford prescription painkillers. Senior citizens as old as eighty-seven are being tricked into operating as drug couriers. When we serve a warrant at a drug distribution house, I see the secondary effects of drugs in our communities: hungry children whose addicted parents spend their money on drugs instead of food; the prostitution and other crimes that addicts (sometimes your neighbor) commit to fund their habits; the drain on public services that should be going to education or economic development that instead have to deal with drug-related problems.

We are so worried about terrorism overseas, but these foreign threats are killing our people and causing suffering in our communities every single day. What better way to bring down a country than to erode it from within by filling its communities with drugs and violence?

Armed scouts

As you can see, I was involved in a number of different activities in different parts of the country, and that helped me see connections between some of the dynamics at work. For me, so many of them led back to the border. Over the next few years our foundation purchased two additional properties in Arizona with boundaries that parallel six miles of the Mexico border. We bought a ranch that we call CR in the Naco, Arizona, area, and then MOR, which is thirty-five miles west of the Naco ranch. Later, we bought a farm in Texas with three-quarters of a mile of border along the Rio Grande.

On both of the Arizona properties we do conservation research and habitat preservation work, but we also get a firsthand look at smugglers who cross our border property on a regular basis. We began working with local sheriffs, supporting their efforts to protect their communities.

As I came to learn, the cartels have spotters, scouts, and operatives positioned around border areas, often hiding on high ground on private property. They tip off the smugglers to the timing of law enforcement's movements. They radio the drug mules about what routes they can take to avoid detection and where to collect the shipments and transport them across the U.S. border. Occasionally, Border Patrol has let us know when armed scouts are "laid up" on high ground around our ranches; they warn us to keep our distance because the scouts are armed and will "engage."

At CR, using binoculars we can see a spotter on top of a hill on the Mexico side of the border. There is someone there 24/7. One night two members of our ranch team were outside watching him just as it got dark and they realized somebody was throwing rocks at them from an area of dense brush behind our ranch house. Border Patrol agents nicknamed the area "Jurassic Park" because its thick brush is a habitat for Mojave rattlesnakes. Poisonous snakes don't faze the cartels. Clearly, one or more cartel-affiliated individuals had crossed the border with a clear intention: Just letting you know we're here and we're not afraid of you. We've had other incidents with suspicious footprints around our buildings and vehicles driving by that I have confirmed with law enforcement are likely members of the cartel putting us on notice.

Despite all that, I have come to love Arizona. The landscape is beautiful and the people are down to earth and make good neighbors. As a farmer I appreciate the challenges of producing crops and raising cattle in border areas, from extreme heat conditions, to poor soil quality, to lack of rainfall. I have great respect for what it takes to get up every day and make a living on the land. For the last several years, I have visited Arizona frequently and I've logged over 1,200 hours on patrol as a volunteer for the Cochise County Sheriff's Office.

I also appreciate that I signed up for whatever challenges we face on our ranches. We knew what we were getting into. It's a far different and more stressful situation when your family has owned and operated land in a region for generations—and suddenly your property and livelihood are overrun.

Malpai: *"There was a little something leading up to this..."*

In March 2016, I was away from Arizona when I received the following email from a neighbor, a border-area rancher who has become a good friend. She lives about forty miles east of our Naco ranch.

> Howard...My father and daughter just left the house with lights and their pistols. Lots of fires being started this afternoon...one just started on our south end. They are going to see where it is. I am sitting in the dark with the outside lights on...and inside off. The dog was barking like she winded someone, so I will sit quietly and wait to see if someone tries to come in the house thinking we have left.

I had to remind myself this email did not come from eastern Congo or some other conflict zone, it came from Kelly Glenn Kimbro, a U.S. citizen sitting in her own house. Kelly's father, Warner Glenn, is the owner of the 15,700-acre Malpai Ranch, which is adjacent to the Arizona-Mexico border. A few months prior Kelly had had a serious riding accident; among other injuries, she had broken her leg, and she was still using a walker. As I read her email, I had an upsetting image of her sitting inside in the dark alone and limited by her injury, not knowing what would come next.

The Glenn family has raised cattle on Malpai for generations. Warner's parents came to the area in 1896, and his late wife Wendy's parents also ranched in southeastern Arizona for decades. Warner Glenn, age eighty-two, and his family have been recognized by the Nature Conservancy for their work in preserving grazing lands for the good of both people and the environment.[3] The dining room table at their home has been a frequent meeting place for many thoughtful, committed ranchers trying to cooperate and thrive in this part of the country. Warner as well as Kelly and her husband, Kerry, and their daughter, Mackenzie, are determined to carry on Warner's legacy of responsible land stewardship and contribute to the health and prosperity of the community.

These are great people—hardworking, honest, optimistic, and courageous. They don't go looking for trouble. Unfortunately, as that email suggests, border-related trouble has found them.

During the first decade of this century, individuals who entered the United States illegally crossed southern Arizona ranches by the tens of thousands.[4] Malpai Ranch includes four miles of land right along the border, and the main house is five miles north of the border. From 2000 to 2012, Warner estimates they had about sixty people per day, but sometimes as many as two hundred people per day, hiking across their land, stopping to rest and eat, and then continuing on for miles to interstate highways to get picked up.

During those years, the bulk of the people crossing were not drug smugglers but economic migrants, entire families, sometimes children traveling without a family member. Most were from Mexico and, over time, more came from Central America. Many times, a late-night knock on the door would rouse Warner or the Kimbros out of bed to respond to an emergency reported by a frantic border-crosser whose child or loved one had become sick or separated from the group. One night a man whose wife had given birth outside on the cold ground of a cow pasture came to the door, and Warner got up, called 911 for medical assistance, and then went out with the man to bring blankets and water to the new mother and wait for help.

Malpai (which comes from the Spanish phrase *mal país* and means "bad land" because much of it lacks topsoil) is a beautiful ranch composed of rolling hills and pastures. Deer, mountain lions, foxes, coyotes, and many species of birds and reptiles share the land. It actually does have soils that support feed grasses, but it also has dry volcanic rocky patches that are hard on the feet of cattle and people alike. There is not a lot of shade on the ranch—much of the bushy vegetation is fairly low white thorn, mesquite, creosote, agave, prickly pear, and cholla cactus.

Just about every day, Warner saddles up his horse and rides ten miles or more around Malpai, checking on cattle, making sure troughs are filling up and pumps are working, eyeballing fences and gates to make sure all are secure. I've driven and ridden by horseback across Warner's property with him, and he is a devoted steward of this land. He has experienced a lot of seasons on Malpai, and he's constantly monitoring the state of the hardy desert grasses and plants that his cattle rely on as they fatten up in the spring and summer.

Warner explains that the groups crossing his land tend to rest during the heat of the day in the deeper washes created by run-off during the rainy season. They walk in those same dry creek beds during the night, which helps them navigate. The presence of people bothers and agitates the cattle, which also seek shade in the washes during hot days and may try to sleep there in the evenings. "When I come out in the morning and I see cattle bunched up and anxious, I know a group's been through in the night," Warner explains. "All that activity when they get spooked and run around takes weight off." And that takes money out of a cattle rancher's pockets.

The huge loads of trash left behind by migrants are sometimes reported in the media as an eyesore (which they are), but the impact is much more serious than that. Smugglers and migrants often carry salty food in plastic bags that they discard, and they throw away tuna and sardine cans that have sharp edges. Cattle smell the salt and they seek it out and lick and chew the cans, sometimes cutting their mouths and tongues and developing serious infections. They also sometimes will eat entire plastic bags, which can ball up in their stomachs, block their digestion, and kill them. Explains Warner, "I was out one day and I saw this cow standing there looking strange, not feeding or chewing. Uncomfortable. I walked up and I saw something was off with her mouth. It turned out she had chewed a tuna can and it had wrapped solid around her back teeth. It was stuck. She couldn't eat or swallow. If we hadn't found her and done something it would have killed her."

Warner Glenn and his family represent a unique way of life that is disappearing in the United States. Raising cattle is a tough way to make a living. Losing a single animal to a mouth infection or an intestinal blockage can cost the Glenns and Kimbros well over $1,000.[5] They are kind people with compassion for the less fortunate. But anyone would resent an outside influence that arrives uninvited, adds hours of physical work to an already big list of ranch chores, and destroys assets.

Warner and his family have always supplemented their ranch income by working as hunting guides in the local mountains. They are experienced trackers and they often travel on horseback, always armed. They know the territory like the backs of their hands. After 2012, Warner says the make-up of the people crossing the land began to change. There were fewer groups of migrants from Mexico and Central America. In their place arrived a more common group: a dozen or so young men that walked in single file, carrying large bales on their back, and occasionally guns. Drug smugglers. When the family is crossing the land or local mountain areas, they sometimes find cartel spotter posts, and even drug smugglers traveling on foot. The family does not engage. They call Border Patrol when they see people hiding or traveling over land where they don't belong.

Fire!

The number of economic migrants and refugees crossing in this part of Arizona has dropped in recent years.[6] Drug smuggling, on the other hand, has increased in the Border Patrol's Tucson sector.

There are fewer people overall, but those coming may be armed and they are determined. And smuggling teams have developed some techniques to create diversions to avoid being caught or to get provisions for their journeys. That's what Kelly Kimbro was concerned about the evening she sent the email.

Smugglers may organize a group of mothers and children (sometimes migrants from Central America they have kidnapped in Mexico) and send them in one direction to attract Border Patrol's attention and occupy their time, while smugglers go a different route. I have heard of many different diversion stunts, including a memorable one several years ago involving a commander in the Cochise County Sheriff's Office. He heard a knock on the door of his rural home. It was a young man, agitated, asking for water and food. He claimed smugglers had forced him to carry a pack against his will from Mexico and he just wanted to go home. The commander called dispatch and several deputies rolled to the scene. They found a big square pack covered in burlap stashed in the bushes a few yards from the commander's house.

They began a search of the nearby area for the rest of what they assumed was a smuggling group. But eventually a deputy took the pack and opened it. Inside were common grass weeds and hay compressed to look like a marijuana bale. The deputies realized the boy was a sideshow designed to draw patrols away from some other location where the drug mules were traveling.

It may be a crime to carry weed, but it's not a crime to carry weeds. All the deputies could do was hand him over to Border Patrol and go back to work. In the meantime, I'd bet good money the real load of high-value drugs made it to a drop-off point in Arizona and then was on its way to Kansas or South Dakota or New Hampshire.

But one of the most serious threats to rural ranchers, as Kelly expressed in the email she sent me, is that sometimes smugglers set decoy fires in the dry brush. This can have catastrophic consequences in wide open pastures and, especially when it is windy, ruin miles of fences and structures and harm or kill livestock. Ranchers and first responders rush to the fires to try to contain them, meantime the commotion may allow smugglers to cross the landscape without being caught or to enter and burglarize buildings owned by ranchers who've gone off to check on the fires.

Malpai Ranch is eighteen miles from Douglas, Arizona, the nearest town. In case of an assault or emergency, law enforcement is unlikely to be able to respond fast enough to help them battle whatever threat they are facing. That includes the Border Patrol agents who routinely patrol their land but have been unable to stop the smugglers crossing their property. The Glenns have to be prepared to face whatever develops themselves. By the time I reached Kelly by phone after she sent that email, everyone had made it safely back to the house and no intruders tried to break in that night.

Kelly followed up with more details in a subsequent email. She said two men had come into the Malpai barn area when the Glenns were not there, and based on their tracks, they "went in and around every vehicle and barn." When they found the footprints, Warner and Mackenzie followed the tracks for a quarter mile to make sure they left, but when the fires started they were concerned the two events could be connected. What's more, after the first fires were put out, she received a call from the foreman of a ranch south of Malpai in Mexico. He told her one of his ranch hands had reported to him that he'd seen a fire burning east of the Glenns' home. Again, this is everyday life on the border: Was it a friendly, helpful tip, or was the ranch hand somehow connected to the men who had cased the Glenns' property and might be waiting to see if the family took off east to find and fight that fire? This time there were no assaults or thefts, but imagine having to assess every situation with these concerns in the back of your mind.

Malpai's owners are just one family out of dozens of ranchers I know in southern Arizona who are concerned that as a nation we have lost control of a large area of our sovereign territory, sacrificing the safety and quality of life of U.S. citizens in the process.

How did we get to this point? It's not as if the U.S. government made a decision not to defend these lands. But there were two decisions at the federal level that put some difficult dynamics in motion. As you'll see in the next chapter, these actions created a lot of activity and a huge investment of tax dollars, but not necessarily a more secure border.

Chapter 3

STEPPING ON THE BALLOON

The federal government's response to increased immigration from Mexico in the 1990s has had long-term negative consequences not only for U.S. border communities but also, arguably, for the entire United States. Our policies have helped the Mexican cartels grow stronger and expand their businesses to other criminal activities such as human trafficking and weapons smuggling.

For much of the twentieth century, we don't really know how many undocumented people crossed over the Mexican border to the United States because the border was largely unsecured. There were official ports of entry (POEs), but along most of the border, fencing was minimal or nonexistent. Many people just walked across our southern borders near San Diego, California, and El Paso, Texas, which were near major highways and urban areas. In Arizona, the approximately seventy miles of the Tohono O'odham reservation physically straddles about 20 percent of the state's border with Mexico. Tribal members from the United States and Mexico (and many other people) freely traveled back and forth.[1]

The largest single group of migrants were Mexican,[2] although beginning in the 1980s civil wars, poverty, and natural disasters have motivated increasing numbers of people from Central America, the Caribbean, and other countries to travel north through Mexico and enter the United States. It was not difficult for many of those who crossed illegally to disappear into U.S. border communities. Some stayed there and settled permanently, while others moved on to cities and towns across the lower forty-eight states. Some moved from work camp to work camp, harvesting seasonal crops.

Some migrants went back and forth to Mexico frequently. After we purchased our farm along the Rio Grande in Texas, I was walking through the equipment sheds one day. The farm had not been worked for several years and everything was covered in a layer of gray-green dirt from wind and rain. But I discovered a bench piled with life vests that had been painted a dark green and also half a dozen deflated truck tire inner tubes. Not long after, I was speaking with a Mexican-born woman in her seventies who had worked in south Texas fields for decades. She remembered harvesting onions near our Rio Grande farm, and she said some Mexican workers would use the tubes to swim the fifty yards back and forth every day.

When did this situation, which I think was a normal element of the local labor economy, begin to change? The roots of today's security crisis were in the mid-1990s when the Mexican economy was depressed. The numbers of undocumented migrants streaming north to find work increased, and illegal immigration became a contentious political issue. In response, the Clinton administration launched Operation Gatekeeper, which strengthened Border Patrol manpower and barriers in high-traffic crossing areas south of San Diego (similar efforts took place in Arizona and Texas).[3] In some cases Border Patrol built double and triple fencing near POEs, installed light systems that turned night into day, and positioned sensors, all making it much more difficult for individuals to cross undetected.

BP could not afford to provide the same level of protection in rural areas. The agency figured that mountain ranges and deserts would be a deterrent to people crossing and make it easier to apprehend those who did. According to a 1994 Border Patrol Strategy Plan that laid out the Operation Gatekeeper strategy, "with traditional entry and smuggling routes disrupted, illegal traffic will be deterred—or forced over more hostile terrain less suited for crossing and more suited for enforcement." The report also noted: "Illegal entrants crossing through remote, uninhabited expanses of land and sea along the border can find themselves in mortal danger."[4]

To put this strategy into perspective, the New York Police Department (NYPD) has about 36,000 uniformed officers. At the time Operation Gatekeeper was implemented in 1995, there were only about 4,400 Border Patrol agents protecting almost two thousand miles of the U.S.–Mexico border. (As of May 2017, Border Patrol had about 16,500 agents deployed along the southwest border, according to government auditors.[5]) After you break the total number into three shifts, take into account vacation, sick time, specialty teams, administration, command, and monitoring, in many locations you have a handful of agents covering long stretches of border. So it's not surprising that while the strategy reduced illegal crossings near ports of entry, elsewhere the flow of migrants exploded.

In the years since then, Border Patrol has seen their apprehension numbers both rise and fall; 2016's 408,870 apprehensions along the southwest border are well below the 1.28 million when Operation Gatekeeper began. Subsequently, several administrations have used apprehension statistics as a proxy for the amount of traffic attempting to cross the southwest border—implying that fewer attempts mean security improved dramatically. Along the sixty miles of the San Diego sector, BP notes that annual apprehensions dropped from over 560,000 in 1992 to fewer than 32,000 in

2016.[6] Those numbers may be accurate, but the security argument is far from clear.

Apprehension numbers just tell you the absolute minimum number of attempted crossings—in the same way that in a soccer game the number of goalie "saves" reported would represent the minimum number of shots the other team attempted. If a goalie makes increasingly fewer saves, is that because your team is getting better and opponents are taking fewer shots? Possibly. It may also be that the number of shots has doubled or tripled and many are flying right by the goalie. A more insightful number would be the *percentage* of shots the goalie is blocking. If it's 100 percent, your team is in great shape. If it's 10 percent, they're probably losing the game.

On the border, we don't know the number of people attempting to cross every day. Even the DHS acknowledges this as the "denominator problem."[7] We know the areas where large numbers are attempting to cross at any given time, but the activity moves around. BP keeps a count of apprehensions and "gotaways," but we don't know the total number of individuals who attempt crossing. We do know that in the same period of time when the reported apprehension numbers were steadily dropping, people like Warner Glenn were seeing scores of people crossing their ranches every day.

After we began buying Arizona properties in 2011, I heard Obama administration representatives repeatedly claim the border was as secure as it had ever been. And yet we had evidence of dozens of drug smugglers crossing our two ranches every week. It's possible that the dropping apprehension numbers meant the border was more secure than it had been, but from my perspective seeing those videos of guys in camo (some with rifles) crossing our ranch and knowing other ranches had the same experience, did not suggest the border was more secure.

In 2013, the Center for Investigative Reporting (CIR) published an article on border security that discussed an experimental radar technology called Vader that can spot people on the ground from an elevation of twenty-five thousand feet.[8] According to government documents obtained by CIR, from October to December 2012, remotely operated aircraft detected 7,333 border crossers during its Arizona missions.[9] Border Patrol agents reported 410 apprehensions during that time. Critics have said that the technology needs to be fine-tuned: there might be apprehensions that occur outside of the drone's range, for example. But CIR also noted that during one week sensors showed 355 people on foot on the U.S. side of the border in Arizona, and "Border Patrol agents caught 125 of those, about 35 percent, while an additional 141 people evaded apprehension and 87 more turned back south to Mexico."[10]

What soccer fan would be content to know how many shots a goalie is blocking but not the score of the game? Maybe it's impossible to get a reliable estimate of total border crossing attempts. Personally, I combine my observations of the traffic crossing our ranches with the growing number of heroin and other opioid addiction rates and overdoses, and I know the "score." We're losing.

Mortal danger

East of San Diego all the way across Arizona, the land is harsh: little water, rocky terrain, snakes, scorpions, coyotes (the wild animal variety), bears, mountain lions, and extreme temperatures. Few roads or landmarks mean it is easy to get lost. Oscar's physical condition when we met him after a week in the desert was not unusual: He was dehydrated, hungry, exhausted, and bleeding from cuts on his hands. During winter, temperatures hit freezing at night at the Mission Oaks elevation. At the point where Oscar happened to stumble on the road that led to our ranch, even

41

ignoring that he'd been shot at, he was, in the words of that memo, in "mortal danger."

Before Operation Gatekeeper, migrants used to gather near borders and they would just take off running toward unsecured areas near U.S. border towns or swim across the Rio Grande after the sun went down. However, once urban areas were reinforced, a new danger evolved from an animal that had lurked around borders for a long time: human *coyotes*.

Border-crossing guides have existed for decades in Mexico and Central America. According to a Mexico City–based Jesuit priest our foundation knows who has spent many years working with migrants passing through Mexico, "When I started working in migration *coyotes* tended to be local community members that had been to the U.S. several times and knew the routes and therefore offered their services for a fee. They were locals and well known by community members. Most of them were honest."

The Operation Gatekeeper–style strategies changed that dynamic. In fact, in a twisted way it helped "professionalize" human trafficking. As the feds predicted, it was hard to navigate mountain and desert routes, and more people were traveling to the Mexican border from Central America who did not know the region at all. They needed help. The price *coyotes* charge rose over the years from a few hundred dollars to thousands.[11] Unscrupulous guides new to the business would make one deal at the start of the trip and then ask for more money later. Often, they would lie about the distances and hardships. *Coyotes* more frequently abused the women in their groups. "Rape trees," on which rapists hung bras and underwear as trophies, appeared on the landscape. Migrants who sprained an ankle or got tired or sick were told to find shade— and then were left behind, sometimes with no water. Adds the priest: "Practically all of the smuggling routes in Mexican territory are controlled by different cartels, and the *coyotes* have to pay steep taxes to move through that territory or they just simply hand over the 'goods,' which in this case are the migrants. The people that I have met that have been the most brutally tortured by organized crime were those whose *coyotes* refused to pay the cartels for the right to pass through their territory. They do some horrible things or sometimes even kill them."

Still, people kept coming. As the barriers and fortifications near cities and towns became more secure, by the year 2000 huge numbers of people were crossing in the harsh desert areas. And many were perishing. According to Border Patrol, more than seven thousand migrants have perished along the U.S.–Mexico border since 1998.[12] Warner Glenn, my neighbor John Ladd, and most other ranchers with property along the border have found the remains of migrants who've become lost or were left behind. The San Pedro River runs adjacent to John's ranch, and in early 2017 he found the body of a migrant who drowned in a flash flood there.

Stacks of bodies

For years I have been familiar with the work of the Pima County Office of the Medical Examiner in Tucson, Arizona, and its forensic anthropologist Dr. Bruce Anderson. Dr. Anderson's team has examined and cataloged thousands of remains recovered from Arizona border-area deserts, including more than one thousand that still have not been identified.[13] Since 2001, they've arrived at the rate of about 160 per year. After collecting DNA and detailing any possible identifying features, the remains are released to the counties where they were found; most counties in Arizona cremate unidentified remains.

I've visited the Pima County morgue and seen the shelves of unidentified corpses inside plastic body bags stored five rows high. On one of my visits, the office was processing and storing so many bodies it had to lease a refrigerated van to handle the overflow. Often the bodies recovered from desert areas are severely decomposed and they lack any identification documents. They span all ages, children to elderly. In the desert in the summer a body can become unrecognizable within a few days. Some of the body bags on the shelves are almost flat; the remains within consist of just a few dry bones because water, wind, and animals have scattered the rest. It's hard to describe the heavy, sickening smell of death in a room full of refrigerated but unembalmed bodies. After leaving the morgue I felt like the scent was attached to my own skin for hours.

Originally, our foundation supported Dr. Anderson's work directly, but now we support it through a nonprofit called the Colibri Center for Human Rights that works with the medical examiner's office to identify these remains and provide closure for families regardless of the origins of the deceased. For example, we funded an international geographic information system (GIS) initiative in Pima County to link data from missing person reports to postmortem reports. We agree with Anderson and Colibri that respect for the dead is one measure of a civilized society.

Is it civilized to view the "mortal danger" of the desert as a deterrent? Should it give us pause that before Operation Gatekeeper funneled immigrants to the desert, there were only about twelve bodies per year recovered along the border? People debate these questions. Some say yes; it's not our fault that people have unrealistic expectations about how difficult it is to cross. Others point to the bodies the desert claims as evidence that we should find a way to open our borders to anyone who wants to come.

I reject both of those arguments. This tragic loss of life reinforces that treating illegal border crossing as a victimless crime and being inconsistent in enforcing immigration laws drives people to make terrible, deadly decisions. A porous border creates hope. It sets the stage for the lies of cold-hearted human traffickers telling poor migrants that they can buy a guaranteed path to a brighter future. Enough succeed that others are inspired to try.

Red flags

As the Jesuit priest explained, over time the cartels took over the traditional *coyote* routes through Mexico to the United States. Today, they not only abuse and extort migrants traveling through Mexico, but they continue to traffic and threaten people after they arrive in the United States.

The drug cartels also soon realized that the odds of drug smugglers getting caught in remote areas were much lower. By using young, experienced smugglers in good physical condition—whose energy they may further fuel by providing them with crack cocaine and methamphetamines—they also began to move large amounts of drugs through remote and rugged U.S. counties. They developed complex systems of routes and scouts and technology that enable a seemingly limitless supply of human "mules" to find routes unlikely to be detected by Border Patrol. If Border Patrol staffs up in one region, they just move to another. If agents are gathered in one spot, scouts radio the mules to patiently wait until they disperse or they adjust their routes.

The complex natural landscapes provide smugglers a tactical advantage. As an experiment, we once took four men wearing camouflage and sent them to an area of rocks and low vegetation typical of CR, our Naco ranch. I went up on a hill and took photographs of them, first with them sitting near vegetation, but not hidden; then I called down on the radio and had them lay flat and hold up bright red flags. Even when you see exactly where the flags are, it's nearly impossible to find the men in the photographs (you can see for yourself in the photo insert in the middle of the book). Even if BP spots and closes in on a group moving across the desert, sometimes they can disappear just by diving into a wash or under a creosote bush.

According to the Drug Enforcement Administration, the Sinaloa cartel is dominant in smuggling in southern Arizona, but at least six different Mexican cartels have sophisticated smuggling operations in Texas. These groups routinely bring heroin, fentanyl, methamphetamine, cocaine, and marijuana over the border and then they transport the drugs throughout the country using routes and distribution cells managed or influenced by Mexican transnational criminal organizations. The DEA has estimated that Mexican criminal networks transport the bulk of their drugs through POEs in passenger vehicles and tractor trailers. In addition to using drug mules to physically carry drugs overland, they also employ tunnels under the border, cargo trains, and small boats. In some cases the cartels even drop drug loads from ultralight aircraft.[14]

Border security is often compared to stepping on a balloon—you eliminate border crossings in one place and they expand somewhere else. In this case, diverting refugees, economic migrants, and smugglers to rural areas created new opportunities for criminals to exploit. But it did something else, too: It created a more fearful atmosphere in U.S. communities along the border. Break-ins increased, as did concern about armed smugglers crossing private land. The increase in traffic in general made local law enforcement's job more difficult. "The adverse effects of the drug and human trafficking organizations operating in Cochise County not only have significantly diminished the quality of life of county residents, but also placed unbearable strain upon the budgets and resources of private and government agencies in the county," Sheriff Mark Dannels of Cochise County told the House Subcommittee on Maritime and Border Security in 2016.

Sheriff Dannels knows this all too well. And as an example of direct threats to his community, he pointed me to the case of a single drug smuggler you will meet in the next chapter. This individual's impact on the innocent citizen he assaulted will be lifelong, and the financial burden of his actions on the taxpayers of Cochise County and the state of Arizona is substantial.

Chapter 4

AN EXPENSIVE JUGGLING ACT

An insecure border puts an unfair burden on law enforcement in border communities.

Each year, more than fifty thousand generally law-abiding visitors travel to the southeast corner of Arizona to see Chiricahua National Monument, which is about ten miles east of our Apache Farm. Hikers enjoy viewing the tall rock spires called hoodoos, caves created by ancient lava flows, and acres of rock pinnacles that appear to balance on small bases. The twelve-thousand-acre park sometimes is called the Wonderland of Rocks.

In late August 2013, a Mexican national who was in the U.S. illegally was hiking through the park. Rocks figured into his visit as well. He picked up a football-sized chunk of compacted pumice and ash and smashed it into the head of a sixty-year-old park employee named Karen Gonzales. The perpetrator surprised her from behind while she was cleaning a public restroom. He hit her so hard the rock split into a dozen fragments. Then he left her in a pool of blood, stole her keys, and drove off in her National Park Service (NPS) vehicle.

This was a vicious crime, and the effort to bring the man who committed it to justice took more than three years. The crime was solved by a combination of solid detective work by the Cochise County Sheriff's Office, integrated law enforcement databases shared by federal and local agencies, and luck. It also was aided by a federal immigration detention system so backlogged that five months after he'd been picked up on a charge unrelated to his assault on Karen Gonzales, the perpetrator was still sitting in an Arizona facility waiting to be sentenced for another immigration offense.

Our foundation team followed this case because it offered some important insights into the consequences of an insecure border. It's important to point out that there is no evidence that economic or refugee immigrants as a group, documented or undocumented, commit more serious crimes than U.S. citizens. Studies from the libertarian Cato Institute,[1] the justice reform group the Sentencing Project,[2] and others suggest that immigrants are incarcerated for serious crimes at a lower rate than native-born citizens.

That said, let's also be clear: The Mexican drug cartels are among the most ruthless and well-organized criminal networks in the world and there is no question the cartels regularly send UDA drug mules through Chiricahua National Monument. The cartels recruit, train, load up, and at times provide armed escorts for the mules, and they give them instructions to meet up with drivers at drop-off points to take their drug payloads further inland.

In this case, a previously convicted drug smuggler named Gil Gaxiola committed a heinous, violent crime. And we will never know how many times Gaxiola carried drugs into the United States on the cartel's behalf. We do know that before he was arrested in the Gonzales case, he had committed other felony crimes in the U.S. in both Arizona and Idaho, and he had been deported several times. The human and financial costs to the victim and the taxpayers of Cochise County, Arizona, of the federal government failing once again to keep Gaxiola out of the country, were extraordinary.

"You have to talk about terrain"

In a conference room in the Cochise County Sheriff's Office in Bisbee, Arizona, Sergeant Tal Parker, head of special operations and investigations, talked to our team about the case. He unrolled several card table–sized topographical maps. On one, the region around Chiricahua National Monument is highlighted, and red lines identify known drug-smuggling routes. "When you talk about the border," said Parker, who spent twenty-three years in the U.S. Marine Corps disarming bombs all over the world, "you have to talk about terrain."

Chiricahua Monument's location and natural features make it a favorite of drug mules. After crossing the border, first smugglers head north through desert for forty miles, and then ten or more miles through the park, and then another ten miles or so to Interstate 10, where they deliver their payloads to a contact in a vehicle and then they turn around and hike back to Mexico. This is a 120-mile round trip that is hot in summer, cold and snowy in winter, and it demands hiking through canyons and up and down mountains. But the area is also hard to patrol, and there are many caves and other hiding places. Chiricahua has natural water springs, which smugglers traveling long distances appreciate so they can refill water jugs (a hiker can lose half a gallon of water per hour in 100-degree temperatures, but a gallon of water weighs more than eight pounds). In the late nineteenth century, the famous Chiricahua Apache leaders Cochise and Geronimo and their warriors holed up in these and nearby mountains when they battled new settlers and the U.S. Army.[3]

Parker turned to a thick notebook of evidence and photographs, including some images from the Cochise County Sheriff's Office motion-sensitive game and trail cameras hidden throughout the park near known smuggling routes. From these cameras, officials know many groups of backpack smugglers cross the park each month, usually in groups of five to twenty. On August 21, 23, and 24, 2013, cameras caught images of a specific group of six drug mules carrying large packs of marijuana heading north. Near the north boundary of the park, Border Patrol was alerted to that group and tried to apprehend them on August 26, but they scattered and four escaped. On August 27, a trail camera caught three of the four headed south again. That left one unaccounted for.

By the morning of August 28, 2013, Parker said the missing mule made his way to a picnic ground and parking lot in what is called the Faraway Ranch Trailhead, which serves as a visitor center on the west side of the park. Seasonal park employee Karen Gonzales helped maintain park facilities. On the morning of August 28, 2013, Gonzales pulled into the parking lot near the trailhead. She took some cleaning supplies out of her park service–issued silver Dodge pickup, but left her purse and cell phone in the truck because the area does not get cell service.

As she worked cleaning the handicapped stall in the ladies restroom, she would later testify, Gonzales realized that she was not alone. She turned and saw a man behind her holding a large rock. He then brought it crashing down on her head. He did this repeatedly as she struggled to fight him off.

Gonzales tried to run away, but her assailant grabbed her and she fell right outside the restroom. He dragged her by the hair back inside, leaving a blood trail. Eventually, he removed her truck keys from her pocket and drove off. Gonzales lay on the floor, unconscious and bleeding.

Around 11:30 a.m., Karen Krebbs, a naturalist who was studying bats in the park, hiked into the area and ate lunch at a picnic table. She walked to the ladies room, saw blood, and discovered the wounded Gonzales, but had to run a mile to the closest ranger station to get help. National Park Service employees raced to the scene and radioed for a medevac helicopter, which eventually took Gonzales to University Medical Center in Tucson.

When Parker arrived, he was surprised at the amount of blood at the scene and the violence of the act. A large rock used in the crime had shattered into a dozen smaller fragments, which filled eight ziplock evidence bags. "Some of the rock pieces traveled as far as the stall at the other end of the wall," according to Parker's report. Gonzales eventually would need 150 staples to close the gashes in her head.

CCSO issued an alert for law enforcement to look for the silver Dodge truck with government plates, and they had the phone company ping Gonzales's cell phone around 3:30 p.m. That activity showed it was forty miles away in Douglas, Arizona, near the border, where it was found around 8:30 p.m. In the driver console, investigators found a McDonald's food bag with a drink cup and straw and a receipt from Burger King from 1 p.m.; in the back of the vehicle they found a pair of jeans with bloodstains. Parker's team collected the evidence and shipped it off for DNA analysis.

DNA doesn't lie

If this were a TV crime show like *CSI*, when Parker and his team arrived at work a day or two after handing over the samples to be processed, they'd learn whether the DNA produced a "hit." But as any police or sheriff's office in the country will attest, those time frames are a fantasy. Crime labs are so backlogged, DNA evidence can take months or even years to analyze and check against databases. In August 2016, Parker told us: "I just received DNA analysis on another case…that happened in 2010."

In the meantime, Parker and his colleagues pursued other clues and evidence. They used the receipt time stamp to check video cameras in the area, including McDonald's, Burger King, and the local Walmart. They also picked up an image of the stolen truck on a government security camera that showed the vehicle headed east into Douglas at 12:56 on the afternoon of August 28. In each video, there appeared to be a dark-haired man, alone. The case attracted media attention, which sometimes can make law enforcement's job even more difficult, as officers must investigate tips that don't pay off. For example, a government informant in Mexico said there was a man in Agua Prieta who had a wad of cash and was telling people that something had gone very wrong on his last drug mule run. The situation turned out to be unrelated to the assault.

But the DNA results came back five months later, on December 30, 2013, and they cracked the case open: Analysis showed the blood on the jeans from the Dodge pickup belonged to Karen Gonzales. Meanwhile, "unknown male DNA" from the waistband of the bloodstained pants and also from the straw in the McDonald's cup matched the DNA from the rock fragments from the scene of the crime.

The lab investigator ran the male DNA through the National DNA Index System (NDIS), and not only did the database turn up a match, but she learned the man was already sitting in federal custody in Florence, Arizona. He had been arrested in Douglas for illegally reentering the country the day after Karen Gonzales had been assaulted.

Consider the resources, personnel time, and expenses that this crime in Chiricahua cost the community just to this point. Begin with the cost of the NPS emergency response, the medevac to Tucson, and the medical bills for Karen Gonzales. Add in the time of multiple CCSO deputies and Parker in investigating leads, from the multiple surveillance and game cameras to tracking down false leads. Several other law enforcement agencies, including U.S. Customs and Border Protection (CBP), which is the parent agency of Border Patrol and also includes CBP officers who enforce customs, immigration, and agricultural laws and regulations at U.S. ports of entry, and the Douglas Police Department invested time in looking for the vehicle and suspects. There were more than a dozen DNA tests of blood and other evidence, which can cost about $1,200 each.

The extraordinary impact of just this one individual, who it turns out had entered the country illegally time and time again, becomes clear. Before the case was over and the perpetrator convicted, Cochise County would spend at least $500,000, Sheriff Dannels estimates.

Many aliases

The suspect had been apprehended by CBP in the Douglas area on August 29, 2013; it was the day after Karen Gonzales's assault, but he was apprehended for an immigration violation. He was turned over to ICE, then booked into a detention center in Florence under the name Horacio Rodriguez. However, after the DNA analysis brought him to Parker's attention, authorities discovered that his real name was Gil Gaxiola, who was born in 1981 in Guaymas, Sonora, Mexico. Previous illegal entries to the United States had brought him into custody of CBP multiple times, going back to 2007. He had used four other aliases in addition to Gil Gaxiola and Horacio Rodriguez. He previously was convicted of felonies in Idaho for drug trafficking, and he had been convicted of felony possession of burglary tools in Maricopa County, Arizona. He had served multiple prison sentences and been deported multiple times. At the point when Parker was notified of the NDIS hit, Gaxiola was scheduled for a sentencing hearing for felony reentering in U.S. District Court.

Parker rushed to Florence to meet the man he'd been chasing for four months. He obtained Gaxiola's fingerprints and another DNA sample, and Gaxiola waived his Miranda rights and agreed to an interview. Gaxiola claimed he had not been in Arizona prior to his apprehension on August 29 and that he had just crossed into the United States that day. When told his DNA had been linked to the assault on Karen Gonzales, Parker's partner wrote in the case report that he "noted (Gaxiola's) facial expressions changed…his eyes swelled and they became red and watery. I asked him if he had anything to say about that. He stayed quiet and appeared to want to say something. But then he said he wasn't there." They asked him again about Chiricahua National Monument. He repeated that he was never there.

Three days later a lab confirmed Gil Gaxiola's newly obtained DNA also matched the DNA on the drinking straw, the waistband of the bloody jeans, and a handkerchief found in the stolen Dodge truck.

Deliberate delays

In February 2014, Gaxiola was transferred to the Cochise County Jail near Bisbee. He was charged with seven criminal counts: attempted first-degree murder, attempted negligent homicide, armed robbery, three separate counts of aggravated assault, kidnapping, and one count of theft of means of transportation (that is not a minor crime in a state with sparsely populated deserts and hot temperatures; by itself, it carries a twenty-eight-year sentence).

During his five months in federal detention waiting to be sentenced for felony reentry after deportation, U.S. taxpayers paid at least $20,000 to keep Gaxiola in custody (based on 2014 average immigration detention costs of $160/day). But the next phase of his journey, which the citizens of Cochise County, Arizona, paid for, is when the meter really started running.

Gaxiola was given a court-appointed lawyer. By August 2014 that lawyer had negotiated a plea deal of twenty-eight years, and Gaxiola was given thirty days to accept the offer. It seemed like a good deal for him: If convicted of all charges against him, he could serve ninety-four years in prison. But at the end of thirty days, he rejected the offer and fired his lawyer. So, his case sat on the shelf for months until a new lawyer was appointed and got up to speed on his case. Gaxiola was held for trial without bond.

By the fall of 2016, after many other delays, Gaxiola had been involved in nineteen different hearings, including two "Rule 11" competency hearings ($42,000 each) evaluating him and restoring him to mental competence to assist in his own defense.

Trading pants?

The trial finally began in March 2017, nearly four years after the assault. By then, however, many things had changed—including Gaxiola's story.

Gaxiola took the stand and suggested an entirely new theory for what had happened that August day. Reversing the initial story he gave to Sergeant Parker at Florence, Gaxiola now admitted he was at the scene of the crime. But he now claimed he had been a victim himself.

Gaxiola told the jury that he had been part of a group of immigrants who had paid a *coyote* in Agua Prieta, Mexico, to take them over the border and reach the interstate near Chiricahua. He detailed health problems for his family in Mexico that meant he needed to find work and send more money home. He claimed he was headed for a job in construction set up by a friend in Phoenix.

After crossing the border, he said the group began hiking inside the park en route to a vehicle pick-up point. Then, he claimed, he slipped and fell fifteen meters down a rocky slope and badly injured his leg. He said it immediately swelled and then became infected. He said the group helped him to a cave that had some kind of water source in it, and they stayed there for a couple of days. Gaxiola said he went in and out of consciousness due to the pain and due to painkillers the leaders of the group gave him, but they abandoned him while he slept.

We sent a researcher to the courthouse during the trial, and she observed Gaxiola's testimony. She reported that Gaxiola was very composed in the courtroom. His head was now shaved; he wore conservative dark-rimmed glasses, and he wore a suit and tie. Preparing to answer questions, she said he would press his fingers and hands together thoughtfully. Gaxiola claimed that after the immigrant group left him in the cave alone, he fashioned a cane from a branch and began heading south. He said he used his walking stick to catch and eat a snake raw as his hunger grew unbearable. He said he cried out loud to God to help him. Finally, resting near a spring, he heard voices, two men talking. But one of the two men jumped him, pushed him to the ground, and interrogated him. The man said he was going to take him back to Agua Prieta, where he would offer him to a cartel smuggler to carry drugs. "Finding you is like finding three hundred dollars on the ground," he said the man told him. In the meantime, Gaxiola claimed his new traveling companions said he would have to help them smuggle the marijuana bales they were carrying.

Gaxiola testified that "the leader" asked him to exchange pants because his own had holes and were dirty. That was the defense explanation for how Gaxiola's DNA was on the waistband of the bloody jeans found in the truck. Gaxiola also claimed the leader asked to see Gaxiola's phone and as the leader swiped through his family photos, Gaxiola became so afraid of what the man might do to his family that Gaxiola picked up a rock and started tossing it and juggling it to calm himself. He asserted it was that same rock that the leader, now wearing Gaxiola's pants, used to assault Karen Gonzales.

Gaxiola then claimed that after assaulting Gonzales and taking her keys, the leader and the other smuggler and Gaxiola climbed into the Dodge truck, along with the bales of marijuana. He said they drove to Douglas, where the other two men took the marijuana and left him. He said they previously told him: "Look, man, everything you've seen or heard, don't say anything or you'll go to Hell."

On March 17, 2017, the jury found Gaxiola guilty of seven of eight counts against him. On April 17, the judge sentenced Gaxiola to a total of seventy-six years in state prison, to be served consecutively.

Prison safer than freedom

Gaxiola's violent outburst in Chiricahua not only angered Cochise County residents, but it very likely infuriated the Mexican cartel bosses he worked for as well. Several officers involved with the case have said they thought one reason he was trying to stall and prolong time to his eventual trial was in hopes that the cartels would lose track of him or forget about his crime. As extreme as cartel violence is in Mexico these days—beheadings, group executions, and other horrible methods of torture have become common—it's also true that the cartels frown on their people committing violence in U.S. border communities. It's bad for business. When the cartels rely on a productive, efficient smuggling route like Chiricahua, the last thing they want is for a low-level drug mule to commit a high-profile, violent crime that focuses more law enforcement energy on that area and, at least for a short time, makes it more difficult to use as a smuggling corridor. As Karen Gonzales later told a reporter for the *Willcox Range News*, "If he had just asked me for the keys to the car, I would have given them to him."[4] Instead, thanks to Gaxiola's senseless violence, Gonzales suffered terrible injuries. She now walks with a cane and is living on her disability income.

"This defendant should never have been in the U.S. at all, and Karen Gonzales and Cochise County had to pay the price for the lack of border security," said Sheriff Dannels. Gaxiola now will serve his time in the Arizona Department of Corrections, and a new meter will begin running. The cost to the state of Arizona's taxpayers to punish him for this crime, if he serves his entire sentence and not including any special medical or psychiatric bills, will top $1.8 million (assuming no inflation in incarceration costs).[5]

There are many more people like Oscar, poor, hungry, and desperate to improve their lives, streaming over our borders than there are psychopaths like Gil Gaxiola, who talk about praying to God and yet nearly beat an innocent person to death. But one of the most difficult elements of border security today is the outsized threat of the minority of individuals like Gaxiola. They have not only committed a first civil violation in crossing our border, but repeated criminal entries after deportations, and sometimes repeated felonies, including violent crimes and drug trafficking on behalf of the cartels. In 2015, 15,715 people were convicted of reentering the country after being previously deported, according to the U.S. Sentencing Commission.[6] We don't know what percentage of all who tried to cross after a previous deportation were apprehended and convicted. But that is the dangerous revolving border door that represents a safety threat to all Americans and is sometimes masked in "local" crime statistics.

Chapter 5

SANCTUARIES AND "SLAM DUNKS"

Previously deported, "revolving door" criminals are not just committing crimes in border areas. They are straining our justice system, and they are infiltrating and disrupting immigrant communities across the nation. It's unfair when local law enforcement has to pick up the slack—and then gets accused of releasing dangerous criminals.

As the case of Gil Gaxiola dragged on, the mounting bills were like salt in the wounds of Arizona's Cochise County Sheriff Mark Dannels. Dannels's frustrations go well beyond that case. In the same month Gaxiola was sentenced in Bisbee, Arizona, Border Patrol agents in Tucson Sector arrested two previously deported UDA Mexican nationals with prior sexual assault charges—both committed against children.[1]

What sheriffs and police across the country realize is that Dannels's concerns have become their concerns. It's not difficult to find cases where a perpetrator's history resembles Gaxiola's.

- In February 2017, police in Bridgeport, Pennsylvania, said an undocumented Salvadoran, who previously had been deported after felony convictions for assault, stabbed and murdered the mother of his six-year-old daughter. The child was recovered after a high-speed chase triggered by an AMBER Alert.[2]

- Also in February 2017, a Los Angeles woman named Sandra Durán was killed after a car driven by an undocumented immigrant fleeing the scene of another accident slammed into her. The man, a Mexican citizen who had already been removed from the United States five times and who had been convicted of multiple felonies, was charged with gross vehicular manslaughter while intoxicated.[3]

- In September 2017, the *New York Times* reported that a sixty-five-year-old woman in Portland, Oregon, was raped by an undocumented Mexican named Sergio José Martinez. Martinez had been deported to Mexico twenty times and in 2017 alone had been arrested ten times.[4]

Who can blame communities where these crimes occurred for being outraged? The question is, are we aiming our outrage in the right direction?

Define "cooperating"

In San Francisco in 2015, the murder of a thirty-two-year-old woman named Kathryn Steinle made headlines and triggered a national conversation about how we treat UDA criminals. Steinle was walking around a tourist area with her father when she was shot by a Mexican national named José Inéz Garcia Zárate.[5] Garcia Zárate was in the country illegally. He had seven previous felony convictions in the United States and he had been deported from the United States a total of five times, most recently in 2009. Most of his priors were drug crimes, including felony heroin possession.

Prosecutors argued Garcia Zárate aimed the gun at Steinle, and they charged him with murder in the first degree. The defendant's attorneys argued that Steinle's death was a horrible accident. They noted that he did not know the victim, and they claimed Garcia Zárate picked up a gun that he found on the pier. The gun previously had been reported stolen, and his lawyers said it accidentally discharged (the bullet did ricochet off the ground before it hit Steinle in the back and lodged in her aorta). On November 30, 2017, a jury acquitted the defendant of all charges except illegal possession of a firearm by a felon.[6]

However, during the months leading up to the trial, the focus was on the fact that a few months before the incident took place, Garcia Zárate was in custody in San Francisco County Jail. He had been serving time for a criminal immigration violation in federal prison, and then ICE turned him over to the San Francisco Sheriff's Department because of a two-decade-old drug warrant. But ICE had requested, via what is called a "detainer," that Garcia Zárate be returned to their custody when the drug case was finished. That's where the story took a turn.

San Francisco is a self-proclaimed "sanctuary city," and the sheriff said he was prohibited from honoring that detainer. When the county finished with Garcia Zárate (it's common for a district attorney to decline to prosecute drug charges that old), the jail released Garcia Zárate without coordinating with ICE to take custody.[7] When this detail became known, many were outraged. On the 2016 presidential campaign trail, Donald Trump specifically cited the Steinle murder as a reason federal funds should be cut off from any and all sanctuary cities that didn't honor ICE detainers.[8]

When I first read about the Steinle case and related stories about sanctuary cities, I also was angry. How did we become a country that tolerates violent offenders who've been repeatedly deported coming back and inflicting terrible harm on innocent victims? These examples seem like such overwhelming evidence that we need to enforce border security to keep U.S. citizens safe. When it comes to sanctuary cities, I thought, *Why would cities promote local law enforcement not "cooperating" with federal law enforcement? Aren't we on the same team? Shouldn't we prioritize justice for victims above perpetrators? Shouldn't we do our best to protect our communities from known criminals?*

I discussed these questions with my friend Chuck Wexler, who is executive director of the Police Executive Research Forum (PERF). I was intrigued by a column he had written suggesting that a number of top U.S. police departments were not happy with the political rhetoric criticizing sanctuary cities and calling for immigration sweeps.[9] I respect Chuck and I took a step back to examine my own assumptions. I reached out to law enforcement and organizations working with undocumented populations, and our foundation team researched the issues.

Much of the rhetoric around sanctuary cities is ill-informed and overly simplistic. ICE detainers are far more complicated than a Left versus Right debate. As usual, reality often does not make for good sound bites, and therefore it can be difficult to understand what's going on from politicians and from media accounts. As you'll read, one remarkable reality today is that deportation seems to represent a more significant fear to people who are not a high-level threat to our society rather than functioning as a deterrent to violent criminals who cross back and forth over the border as easily as many of us cross state lines. We need to listen to local law enforcement and follow their recommendations designed to keep their communities safe. And we need to stop kidding ourselves that just deporting criminals will make communities safer.

Protecting the "fish" who help police

Sanctuary city advocates and activists often talk about the tradition of protecting people running from persecution or even slavery. The idea of "sanctuary" for the oppressed has religious connotations and a long history. But in terms of federal, state, or local policy the term is too vague to be operable. It can refer to a given community's general, welcoming sentiment or to a set of specific policies that expressly prohibit law enforcement from working closely with federal immigration agents. What at least some sanctuary advocates seem to want are no limits on immigration levels. I understand their humanitarian impulses, but as I hope this book has already shown, this kind of thinking in today's world is naïve and dangerous.

That said, law enforcement must maintain good communication and relationships of trust with undocumented community members in support of public safety. Local law enforcement's top priority must be apprehending dangerous, violent individuals. Confusion in an immigrant community about whether local police also are operating as federal immigration enforcement can have serious and negative consequences. As a major city's deputy police chief told me, "Gangs will tell people, if you cooperate with police we will make your status known and you'll be deported. The dead fish is the one who opens its mouth."

And yet that confusion has developed from both extremes. Police say liberal activists sometimes scare immigrants with horror stories, such as that their children will come home from school to find the house empty and their entire families deported. They may warn immigrants not to trust police, or even open the door when police are investigating a crime against their neighbors.

Meanwhile, some law-and-order advocates want to ignore federal law and have police or sheriffs stop and question individuals suspected of being UDAs. Former Maricopa County Arizona sheriff

Joe Arpaio, who called himself "America's toughest sheriff," bragged that he told his deputies to detain anyone they encountered in any situation whose right to be in the country was not clear. He eventually lost his position as an elected sheriff and in July 2017, he was found guilty of criminal contempt of court for defying a judge's order that he stop those immigration round-ups.[10] In August 2017, President Trump pardoned Arpaio.[11]

Now, let's face facts: Fear of deportation is a logical consequence of being in a country illegally. We have had a porous border for a long time, and millions of individuals have entered illegally; even more have entered legally but then overstayed their visas and are now living here in violation of immigration rules and are susceptible to deportation. There may be more than 11 million people whose status and fears make them vulnerable to threats and manipulation.[12] We can debate how we got here, but this is where we are.

Whether or not we attempt a larger, comprehensive immigration reform agenda, regardless of what federal policies are pursued in coming years, the sheer volume and distribution of the undocumented population means the vast majority are going to be here for a very long time. Communities will not be safer if immigrants retreat further into the shadows because predators exploit their fears. In the climate Arapaio's order promoted, you can see why an undocumented woman who may have just been raped may be afraid to reach out to a law enforcement officer to ask for help or to report the crime. Or why a farmworker forced to live in subhuman conditions will be afraid to report the abuse for fear he or she will be deported.

What is the right trade-off that promotes public safety and security that is consistent with the rule of law?

"Es mejor," perhaps, but not right

Among sheriffs of border areas and law enforcement leaders in the Midwest, I don't know any sheriffs or police chiefs whose priority is to target suspected UDAs. I think the Joe Arpaios are a very small minority.

But I have seen firsthand the fear of authority among undocumented individuals. In 2015, I sat in the kitchen of Elisa*, forty-two, a sweatshop seamstress in Los Angeles who works 8 a.m. to 6 p.m. six days a week sewing garments for which she may be paid twenty-five cents apiece. She has no breaks or lunch hour, and no benefits whatsoever. She fled Guatemala in 2005, leaving a daughter behind, and she has since had two more children. She told me that growing up in Guatemala, she was hungry every day, eating edible weeds when other food ran out, and she came to the United States so she could send money back to her family to feed her daughter. Her current job means she can put food on the table for her two sons. Compared to Guatemala, *"Es mejor, es mejor"* (It's better!), she said.

We communicated through an interpreter, but it was clear Elisa would never complain or ask for more money or benefits or better conditions because the owners of the company would fire her and hire someone else. If she went public, she was certain her illegal status would be used to deport her. Elisa is not the only lawbreaker here; her employer could face federal penalties. But I suspect only one of these lawbreakers is living in fear and poverty.

In 2017 in South Texas, I sat around a table of farmworkers; none had valid documentation to work or live in the United States. There was a woman in her seventies who said she'd been deported dozens of times over the course of her life, but just came right back. We met in the yard of the dilapidated house where she was living; wall boards and window casings were hanging off rusty nails. Her bathroom sink had fallen off the wall, and her toilet appeared

66

to just drain into the dirt below her house. I had to step carefully to avoid falling through open holes in the floor. Like the others around the table, she said she would never consider moving back to Mexico because the cartel violence has become so extreme.

As we talked, I heard other comments suggesting that illegal immigration wasn't the only gap in the rule of law in the area. The workers said that to accommodate local farmers, Border Patrol selectively enforced immigration law. The workers said BP ignores hundreds of workers going into the fields of big farms during harvest season, but then when the harvest is completed, BP will stop and detain people they would see walking on roads or in nearby towns. I cannot say how accurate this is or how often it occurs, but with the large numbers of farmworkers present in the area, inconsistent enforcement seems likely.

I had many questions, and Chuck Wexler set up a meeting for me with law enforcement leaders from Los Angeles. LA has one of the largest undocumented populations in the country—in total LA and Orange counties combined have roughly 1 million undocumented residents.[13] I also rode along on a patrol shift with Lieutenant Craig Heredia of the Los Angeles Police Department (LAPD), who commands the Gang Impact Team; I spent several hours on a helicopter rapid response airship, and I spoke with members of the gang team about the issues of undocumented individuals in their community. It's clear to me that every single day involves trade-offs and judgment calls prioritized to achieve optimal public safety.

Crazy riders and table taxes

On the ride-along we passed sidewalks in the city's Rampart area that were crowded with vendors selling everything from tortillas to secondhand shoes. These are not licensed, legal stands. There are no health and safety standards. Food and drink for sale sit in the hot sun. But the people who run the stands are poor and doing what they can to feed their kids.

The lieutenant explained that just as they do in San Salvador or Tegucigalpa, local gangs prey on these vendors for a "table tax" or extortion money if they want to keep operating without trouble. If you're police, do you shut the vendors down for operating without a license? Or do you develop relationships with the vendors and possibly get their help in maintaining order by tipping you off to gang activity? These are trade-offs; sometimes enforcing the letter of the law is at odds with maintaining public safety. It is not always an easy choice.

"Right here we're surrounded by 18th Street gang," Lt. Heredia said, pointing out some graffiti as we drove near MacArthur Park, an open area with a large lake in the middle; people were sitting on blankets and walking around. Heredia explained that many of the people sleeping on blankets were drug addicts. The local gangs split up the turf to sell drugs or hang out. "On the southwest corner it's the Crazy Riders and then northwest are the Wanderers," he said.

Lt. Heredia is a twenty-two-year veteran of LAPD. Every day he and his team confront violent gang members, and the walls of Rampart station post mug shots of individuals of interest who go by names like Wicked, Tick, and Menace. But Heredia says he was trained in a community policing style that dates back to the 1970s in Los Angeles. It's an approach that has been maintained through both liberal and conservative administrations. Officers never focus on immigration status when they are on patrol, and they do not want to be involved in federal immigration enforcement. His comments reflected the point of Chuck Wexler's editorial column. "We want victims to call us, and we want witnesses to show up for court," Heredia explained.

No patience for criminals

Other officers from Heredia's team joined our conversation, and one noted that some gang members are UDAs, but many are U.S. citizens. A twelve-year veteran sergeant said that in his opinion, "If you removed every undocumented person in Los Angeles tomorrow, I doubt the crime rate would change much at all." The other officers nodded. Added a detective: "The vast majority [of undocumented people in LA] are here looking for a better life, trying hard to provide for their families. Only a small minority are committing crimes. We have a good relationship with our community, but sometimes I think outside agitators come in and stir things up" and claim police will be enforcing Trump administration policies and immigration sweeps. LAPD does not want that, he says. "We have enough real crime [other than illegal immigration] to deal with today."

At a meeting with senior law enforcement leadership from both the police and sheriff's department, it was clear to me that they are as frustrated about the sanctuary city debate as I am. Their focus is on public safety, not politics. First of all, although it's often referred to as a sanctuary city, when I spoke with them Los Angeles had never officially adopted that designation. The police and sheriff's department resent suggestions that they are eager to release dangerous criminals from their jails or actively shelter anyone who has broken the law. "We have no patience for criminal aliens," said First Deputy Chief Michel Moore. "We do not stand in the way of [their apprehension by the federal government]. We do not interfere or discourage that."

But Moore believes: "It's misguided to use local law enforcement as a federal force extender. The vast majority [of undocumented residents in LA] are not significant criminals. Grabbing Mom and Pop and Grandma is not going to have any impact on public safety," he explains, "but it puts us at odds with the community." Adds Arif Alikhan, director of the LAPD's Office of Constitutional Policing and a former official at the Department of Homeland Security, "To me the term 'sanctuary' means we shield criminals, and the LAPD does not shield criminals from enforcement of the law. We operate consistent with the law to protect the public and abide by the Constitution. Moreover, we can't have 500,000 people in LA not talking to LAPD. That's half a million potential victims."

Sheriff Jim McDonnell of LA County agrees: "Predators tell their victims not to go to the police because they'll be deported."

Deputy Chief Moore pointed out that evading taxes also undermines the rule of law, but local law enforcement is never called upon by the federal government to enforce the tax code. Consequently, nobody worries that reporting a robbery will trigger an audit. On the other hand, when armed ICE agents do general sweeps for immigration violators, members of communities with undocumented people understandably think they are aligned with LAPD. Then, "when we're at the door investigating a murder and trying to find a witness, [the residents] think we're a ruse," Moore says. "It's only a matter of time before the community begins to push back and may physically attack ICE, then we're called in to protect ICE and then we become the enemy."

Look past the red herring

We spent some time talking about the ICE detainers that were part of the issue in the Steinle case. These are giving sheriffs headaches across the country, but it's a red herring to focus on sanctuary cities, because there are very specific legal issues involved in how and when undocumented offenders get released. Sheriff McDonnell helped me understand what he faces as the administrator of LA County's jail system, which has seventeen thousand inmates. I think it might be helpful to unpack the typical steps that occur when an undocumented person is arrested.

Let's say Mr. X is arrested in Los Angeles for breaking into an empty parked car. He is taken to LA County Jail and booked and fingerprinted. His information, by law, is automatically available to the federal government. For our purposes, we'll say ICE's database flags Mr. X as a Mexican citizen who was deported a year ago and therefore has returned to this country illegally. He has committed a federal felony and is eligible for deportation again.

Mr. X is in jail. ICE sends the sheriff who runs the jail a "detainer request."[14] It typically says: When Mr. X is ready to be released, please give us notice and hold him for at least another forty-eight hours so an ICE agent can come pick him up.

The first unfair accusation is that sheriffs "ignore" detainers and deliberately "release known alien criminals into communities." That makes it sound like sheriffs prioritize immigrants' issues over public safety, which is unfounded and false. The decision to release a prisoner is the result of the legal process, not the sheriff's preference.

Mr. X will be released for one of several reasons. First, it could be the district attorney declines to prosecute the case for lack of evidence. Or, the case may have been settled by either a plea bargain or a trial. Maybe Mr. X negotiated or was sentenced to thirty days in jail or a year in jail, and his time has been served. Or, the DA is going ahead with a trial, but a judge has granted bail and Mr. X has posted it (there is some evidence suggesting that the existence of an ICE detainer reduces the chance of a judge granting bail, but it still happens).

Detainers have always been voluntary. For years, many sheriffs have "honored" the ICE detainers and held the prisoner for forty-eight hours or even longer. Others have stuck to the forty-eight-hour limit, and still others have not honored the detainer and just released the prisoner. In San Francisco, one point of controversy in the Steinle murder case is that the sheriff had the option, even under San Francisco's sanctuary ordinances, to alert ICE in advance of an individual's release so they could immediately take custody.

The ordinance said the sheriff could honor detainers only for those with prior violent felony convictions and pending charges, but it was the sheriff at the time who had told his department not to cooperate with ICE at all.[15]

Beginning in 2014, a series of court cases had discouraged many sheriffs from honoring ICE detainers and created liability concerns for others.[16] To understand that, as well as the legal basis for why police not only don't but *can't* arrest for most immigration violations, we have to look at both some technicalities of immigration law and the practical consequences of an overloaded justice system.

A status, not a crime

Federal law 8 U.S.C. 1325 describes improper entry to the United States, whether by evading inspection at a port of entry or using false credentials, and it establishes the *first* apprehension for that act to be a misdemeanor crime.[17] In California and many states, this kind of misdemeanor is considered "completed" at the scene, which means law enforcement cannot make an arrest unless an officer witnesses the act taking place.

There are other misdemeanors in this category. For example, a police officer cannot come arrest you for the misdemeanor crime of public drunkenness because your neighbor reported that last Thursday you were staggering down the street drunk. If an officer doesn't witness this misdemeanor crime, he or she won't act unless someone with credible proof files a complaint and then a judge must issue a warrant (unlikely for minor offenses). However, if a witness reported to police that you stole a car last Thursday, which would be a felony, law enforcement could investigate and find enough evidence (perhaps the car in your driveway) to arrest you for suspicion of felony grand theft.

In the immigration context, that misdemeanor designation

means that if caught in the act (such as a Customs agent realizing a person's visa is forged), the offender can be fined and even imprisoned for up to six months and then deported—or just deported. But Alikhan explained to me that if the person evades detection at the border and is in the country, "Being undocumented is a status, not a crime." In other words, if Oscar had made it past our ranch and joined his friends or family, he would have undocumented status; he could be deported by ICE—but he could not be arrested for criminal misdemeanor entry.

Overstaying a visa, meanwhile, is not even a misdemeanor; it violates civil immigration law, but it is not a crime to remain in the country. LAPD and other law enforcement agencies are not "ignoring criminals" as another unfair comment sometimes puts it, because, in fact, many undocumented residents have not committed a crime police can legally arrest them for.[18]

If you illegally reenter the United States after being deported, however, the stakes go way up. You have now committed a felony. This crime is most commonly charged if the person is caught near the border by Border Patrol. If the person is convicted, the penalty is two years in federal prison or a fine, or both. According to Pew Research Center, in 2014 (the most recent year for which statistics are available) half of the 165,265 total arrests made by the federal government were for immigration-related offenses, versus 28 percent of those a decade earlier.[19] And two-thirds of all federal arrests in 2014 occurred in five federal judicial districts along the U.S.–Mexico border.[20] In a separate report, Pew also reported that the number of unlawful reentry convictions rose twenty-eight-fold to over 19,000 between 1992 and 2012.[21] In the same period, the total number of annual federal convictions doubled in size to nearly 76,000, and the share of the federal prison population that is Latino grew from 23 percent to 48 percent.[22]

Large shifts in these federal activities impact budgets. Charging these crimes and incarcerating people is expensive, especially because in the United States a criminal charge triggers significant rights for the accused. Defendants have the right to counsel and to a trial (although most will choose a plea bargain). Multiply that by hundreds of thousands of border apprehensions and ICE detentions every year. It's even driven a procedure called Operation Streamline, where large groups of people, sometimes forty at a time, are tried simultaneously and a single public defender might represent fifty clients a day.[23]

Because of the overwhelming number of these cases, especially if a returning deportee is apprehended by ICE some distance from the border, U.S. Attorneys almost never charge these felonies. Instead, ICE is encouraged to use what are called "administrative" remedies from an immigration judge—such as reinstating a prior removal order. It's much less complicated and expensive than charging the felony, and people can be deported very quickly.

Let's go back to Mr. X. The detainer request triggered by ICE learning that he was in custody is an administrative warrant from a special immigration judge or an ICE agent, not a judicial warrant based on probable cause that Mr. X has committed a felony. This is an extremely important distinction. Beginning in 2014, lawsuits involving ICE detainers prompted rulings saying that for a sheriff to continue holding someone, including a UDA such as Mr. X, without a judicial warrant violates that individual's civil rights.[24] The courts consider it an unlawful arrest under the Fourth Amendment—and the sheriff could be liable for civil damages.

Several sheriffs have said to me that even they did not realize the ICE detainer requests were not equivalent to judicial warrants until these lawsuits surfaced. But sheriffs who had held offenders— particularly violent offenders—for ICE now say they cannot take on the civil liability of holding these prisoners beyond their release dates.

I strongly oppose the idea of criminal aliens being released, but I understand the courts' rulings. No other law enforcement agent is empowered to detain people beyond an original arrest for probable cause; our system gives judges that power to make sure arrests and detentions are lawful. I think about my experience in Bosnia, and another time I was detained in DRC by "secret" police. I was at the mercy of those officers, who seemed to operate with no checks on their power or authority. As a result, I support the need for checks and balances in our criminal justice system, but it doesn't mean I always like the outcome.

It's time to stop blaming sheriffs and police for this situation. At minimum, ICE should have a process for a UDA with a violent criminal history to have a judge issue a felony arrest warrant (for violating the deportation order). That removes the liability from sheriffs and will lead to more efficient cooperation.

However, because of a lack of judicial system capacity, ICE will likely resist any change. And U.S. Attorneys will protest that they don't have the resources to prosecute all those additional felony cases. Today, federal prosecutors focus on cases that cops often call "slam dunks," the most serious crimes where charges are supported by strong evidence that was collected by the book. For cases that don't meet that standard, such as a drug bust of a load below a certain number of pounds or street value, they may end up accepting minimal pleas or even seize the drugs but then just deport the offender. "If we prosecuted every case with a ten-pound bag of marijuana, we'd run out of beds for murderers," notes Paul Charlton, a former U.S. Attorney in Arizona, who is now in private practice in Phoenix. He adds, "It's resources, not a lack of desire to prosecute. People become prosecutors because they want to prosecute."

We risk our lives, you let them go

While that makes sense, you can also understand the response of a retired BP chief who told me: "It sends a signal that agents are risking their lives to apprehend illegals in an environment where most of the people are set free or suffer no consequences for breaking the law."

Local jurisdictions have the option of picking up some of the slack, but at a price. In Yuma, Arizona, Sheriff Leon Wilmot was frustrated with the lack of prosecutions and began pushing his county DA to prosecute drug smugglers under state drug laws. From October 2014 through December 2016, Sheriff Wilmot says that the Yuma County Detention Center housed a total of 241 undocumented criminals on charges of drug transport and identity theft. After the U.S. Attorney's office deferred prosecution, just the detention cost of these prisoners (23,684 days) was $1.8 million. And that did not cover court costs, cost of prosecution, major medical expenses, or the public defender's costs. Sheriff Wilmot billed the Department of Justice, but never received any reimbursement. He feels prosecution creates a deterrent that discourages future smugglers from crossing in his county, so he has no regrets. Still, "You have to get politics out of law enforcement," says Sheriff Wilmot. "If you want to come here, you should do it legally. We're a nation of laws."

That is the critical point. The detainer issue can and should force us to confront how serious we are about enforcing existing immigration law. In early 2017, the Trump administration focused on shaming sanctuary cities and counties and sheriffs, and it even published lists of sheriffs who weren't cooperating with ICE detainers.[25] But in some cases sheriffs had alerted ICE to a detainee's imminent release. The problem was, ICE did not have the manpower available to take custody—which I'm told happens with about two-thirds of prisoners for which a detainer has been issued. The sheriff could not hold the person without risking civil liability and would have to take on the actual costs of the extended custody, for which the department would not be reimbursed.

Strained resources

In 2017, a Decatur police officer I know well pulled over and approached a car with a mechanical breakdown on the side of Interstate 72 in Illinois. Five young men had been traveling in it, and he called me in my role as an auxiliary deputy sheriff to back him up.

After I arrived we spoke at length with the men. Two said they were from Guatemala, and three from Mexico. A couple of their IDs were suspicious: One was issued by the Guatemalan consulate but carried a U.S. address. The Mexicans said they came from Michoacán, and we talked about how dangerous it is there today and they said that was why they left. One man told me they had driven to Illinois from California, where they'd been picking strawberries; another man said he'd been deported twice in the last six weeks from the Tucson, Arizona, area. In other words, he volunteered that he had committed at least one federal felony reentry offense.

The driver gave the DPD officer permission to search his vehicle, and the officer put his canine to work; the dog alerted to the presence of drugs, but after a thorough investigation the officer could not find any drugs. The officer called ICE to report the individual who appeared to have violated the federal immigration statute. The ICE agent said, take photos of the men and let them loose, adding that ICE didn't have the manpower to respond to calls like this unless the suspect has committed a more serious crime.

Since he could not find any drugs, the police officer had no probable cause to suggest that the men had violated state or local laws, so he had to let them go. I couldn't help but think, *What if these guys commit some serious crime tomorrow or next month?* They're not supposed to be in this country, but ICE has refused to pick them up. People will blame the Decatur Police Department for letting them go.

Remember Sandra Durán, the Los Angeles woman who was killed by the repeatedly deported driver? LA law enforcement officials have pointed out that local law enforcement did honor detainers from ICE for this prisoner, and in the past ICE had taken custody of him and deported him. *The problem is he kept coming back.* The victim's fiancé was later quoted at a public event saying that if LA was not a sanctuary city, this tragedy would not have happened. But in fact, LA is not officially a sanctuary city and LA County is not a sanctuary county, and the key reason this individual was in a position to commit this crime was lack of border security. My heart goes out to the victim's family, but you also can see why local law enforcement resents shouldering the blame in these situations.

Focusing on sanctuary cities is a distraction. We need to listen to local enforcement agencies who are focused on public safety, not political rhetoric. We need to ask, What policies work best to keep a given community safe? We need ICE to figure out a constitutional method to issue legal, criminal warrants for dangerous felons so that local law enforcement can comply. Right now, sheriffs are caught in an impossible position.

Second, we must do what Sheriff McDonnell suggested when I asked about the most important actions we can take to prevent the cycle of deportation and repeat offenders: "We've got to secure the border."

Even if sheriffs turned over all undocumented inmates from their jails to ICE and even if ICE deported every one, because of our porous border many would come right back. Kathryn Steinle's assailant had been deported five times already. What if the San Francisco sheriff had honored the detainer and ICE deported him? Garcia Zárate might have already made a round trip in the period from being deported to when he fired that shot on the pier in San Francisco. ICE detainers are dysfunctional, and the border is not secure. The bottom line is: Secure the border or these revolving-door crimes will continue.

Chapter 6

DRUG CARTELS AND DECATURS

The reach of drug distribution fueled and managed by Mexican cartels extends into every corner of our country. Cartel operatives even grow drugs on U.S. soil.

America's bus stations are like watering holes on the African savannah. Small herds arrive at predictable times. They get off the bus for a bathroom and food break and may briefly mingle before some individuals depart and others get back on the bus and move on. Predators like pimps and drug dealers also gather, because they know they can find vulnerable travelers, runaway teens, and drug customers in bus stations. And cops know bus stations are a place to find predators and smugglers moving drugs, money, weapons, and sometimes even people.

In August 2013, Chad Larner, a detective in the Decatur, Illinois, police department, and his partner, Detective Jason Hesse, made a routine stop at the Pilot Travel Center, a Greyhound bus depot in Macon County, Illinois. As a sworn auxiliary deputy I've worked with Detective Larner, and he is a professional and highly skilled second-generation cop.

He makes it his business to stop by the bus station several times a week and meet the 11:25 bus, which will continue on to Chicago, two hours and twenty minutes north. Larner calls it "Good old-fashioned community policing—Hi, I'm Chad, welcome to Decatur, where you from?" He'll board the bus, or sometimes mingle with passengers stretching their legs outside.

Despite his friendly manner and conversation, Larner is not that interested in the weather or the Cubs; he has significant training and experience in what is called Advanced Highway Criminal Enforcement. He is an instructor for the El Paso Intelligence Center of the Drug Enforcement Administration. He specializes in what is called mass transit interdiction, or apprehending and arresting criminals who are on the move. He arrives with a smile. The goal is to strike up a friendly conversation with a traveler who has attracted his suspicions. If he has a reason to believe something is off, he will then convert to a question: "Based on my observations and my encounter with you, I am asking permission to search your luggage."

On that 2013 day, most passengers had already exited the bus, but as Larner walked down the aisle of the passenger compartment, he spotted a red and black backpack in an overhead luggage compartment. The backpack appeared to be brand new, no signs of dirt, frays, or tears. There was a handwritten Greyhound Bus tag affixed bearing the name Enrique Vaughan, and an address in Yuma, Arizona.

Decatur is a long way from Yuma, and the brand-new backpack attracted the detective's interest. He exited the bus and went to the side where the driver had opened the undercarriage compartment. When he poked his head inside the hatch, he immediately smelled something strong—"Like a perfume or a scented lotion," he explains. A smell like that from bags puts him on high alert: Drug smugglers often use masking odors, intense smells designed to hide the smell of drugs from law enforcement and particularly canine units. There is a lot of debate about what, if anything, will throw off a good drug-sniffing dog, but it's common for drug smugglers to spray their contraband with fabric softener or perfume, or smear them with thick substances like Vaseline or axle grease.

In the hold he found two more pieces of luggage for "Enrique Vaughan," also in new condition, both from Yuma, and the tags stated all were headed for Chicago. They were similar in size, shape, and color.

The detectives walked over to several passengers standing outside the bus and began talking. A man walked up eating some food he had purchased inside. Larner said hello and introduced himself. The man said he was "Enrique."

Larner says not all smugglers react the same way to this kind of attention. Some hang back and look nervous. Some will actually run. Some put on a false confidence. Larner asked for his bus ticket and the man produced it, hands shaking. "I've had guys I eventually arrest come right up and start talking to me in these situations," Larner explains. "They're paranoid carrying these drugs. When they see police arrive they start thinking: 'Did somebody tip them off that I was coming?' It just depends on the person what they do."

After providing quick and clear answers to questions in English about his name and where he was coming from, Enrique suddenly reverted to nervous one-word answers. "Work," he kept repeating as the officers looked at his ticket. What kind? Larner asked. "Asbestos." He said he'd never been to Chicago before. Larner asked if he had any more bags under the bus. One, the man replied. Larner already knew there were two. Enrique then changed his answer and said he had two bags under there. Larner asked if he had packed his own bags or if someone else packed for him. He said he'd packed them himself, then the detective said his chest began to rise and fall, and he showed signs of stress.

Larner asked, *"Puedo buscar?"* (Can I search?)

"Yes," the man replied.

Larner walked to the luggage and picked it up. It seemed unusually heavy, despite its pockets being mostly empty. "Here he was going off to a job, and there was one jacket and a blanket in one of the bags, and this was the middle of summer. It didn't add up." Enrique said he'd purchased the luggage himself in Mexico. Larner examined the seams and could see that the lining had been restitched by hand. Enrique denied that he'd resewn it. Between the smell, Enrique's nervousness, and altered stitching in the luggage that seemed too heavy for what appeared to be in it, Larner determined he had probable cause to search further. He asked Enrique if he could search between the lining, even cutting it open. Enrique nodded yes, but as the detective began slitting the luggage he walked away. Larner immediately found a flat, duct-taped package that had been slipped between the bag's lining. He called to Enrique to put his hands behind him, and Detective Hesse handcuffed him.

Larner transported the luggage and suspect to the Law Enforcement Center in Decatur, and there they met DEA Special Agent Richard Dollus and an interpreter. Ultimately, they determined that Enrique was a UDA transporting $1 million worth of cocaine—over eighteen pounds of it—in the lining of the luggage.

Relentless pursuit

Larner calls this bust an act of "divine intervention." Having already traveled over twenty hours from Arizona, Enrique Vaughan-Montano (his full name) was just a couple of hours from his destination. Smuggling, Larner sighs, is just too easy. "The only way to be successful at interdiction is just to be relentless, every single day. Yesterday I was on the interstate and I must have stopped thirty cars. Didn't come up with anything. Stopped one guy with $10,000 I think was drug money on his way to Springfield. We let him go and I called ahead to alert their police to look for him and follow him. We lost him. That's the game. Sometimes you don't win. But sometimes you find a murderer. Criminals like public transportation. They can blend in to a crowd. You're not going to have a bus or a train or an airplane pulled over and be found out the way you could be in a car."

You recall that Vaughan-Montano said it was his first trip to Chicago. Detective Larner had probable cause to search his cell phone and could see that Vaughan-Montano made calls the previous week from Chicago. Larner went back and reviewed videotape from the bus station. Sure enough, the previous week on a day when Larner had not visited the bus station, there was Vaughan-Montano dressed in the same exact clothes, getting off the bus for a quick pit stop. The cell phone he was carrying only had records going back a week. We can only imagine the volume of drugs this one man may have moved over time.

These days most drugs are coming over the border from Mexico, then following every major highway throughout the country. Chicago is a key hub city for drugs that are then shipped out east or west, or even up to the northern border states like Minnesota and North Dakota.

Most of Enrique Vaughan-Montano's trips to the Midwest appear to have been brief. Not this time: He accepted a plea deal that means he'll spend fifteen years in an Illinois state penitentiary.

Sniffing the U.S. mail

Detective Larner recently called me with news of another shipment of drugs he'd seized in Decatur. He knew I'd be glad to know he was aided by Leeroy, a trained Malinois canine our foundation donated to the Decatur Police Department's K-9 unit. But the bad news is this case spotlights a weakness in our "virtual" border.

The case involved two boxes shipped via the U.S. Postal Service (USPS) from Sierra Vista, Arizona, to an abandoned house in Decatur, Illinois. When the boxes hit Springfield, Illinois, a U.S.

postal inspector became suspicious of them. Problem one, explains Larner: "USPS is supposed to verify that a sender address is legitimate. They did not. A bogus address out of Sierra Vista was supplied by the sender." When the inspector realized that, he contacted the Decatur Police Narcotics Unit. "They contacted me and requested that my K-9 sniff the boxes. K-9 alerted to both boxes. We drafted federal search warrants off the alert, opened the boxes, and found sixteen pounds of cannabis."

DPD and the postal inspector organized a controlled delivery "sting" of the boxes. They sent undercover police in a vehicle to observe the abandoned house where the postal inspector, posing as a mail carrier, dropped off the boxes on the front porch. A man came from inside and picked up the boxes. Shortly afterward, two men came running out when they realized the package had been emptied of its contents, and the undercover team arrested them. They were both repeat drug offenders in Illinois.

The packages of cannabis contained distinct markings—one batch had a Southwest-style cow skull, another a bird graphic. Sierra Vista is very near our ranches in Arizona, and I showed a photograph of the markings to a customs inspector from Naco, Arizona, at a law enforcement luncheon when I was in Arizona. He identified one of the markings as one he had seen on packages of drugs he had confiscated coming through the Naco POE in the past. The investigation is ongoing, but the first electronic sweep revealed that an IP address in Mexico was clicking on the delivery link to track the boxes.

Detective Larner and I talked about his frustrations with the USPS. Local law enforcement can get state and local warrants to track packages shipped using private shippers like FedEx or United Parcel Service, but they need a federal warrant to search the U.S. mail. The result is that the USPS "is moving more narcotics around the country every day than anybody can even wrap their heads around."

Detective Larner says USPS inspectors are certified law enforcement, but they don't participate in DEA task forces or cooperate much at all with federal agencies. They are chronically short-staffed. And they can only work in concert with local law enforcement when they obtain a federal warrant, which is more time-consuming and difficult to obtain in part because of the explicit protection of the U.S. mail from government included in the Fourth Amendment to the U.S. Constitution.[1]

Legislation has been introduced to try to make it easier for law enforcement to investigate drug shipments in the U.S. mail.[2] With the growing threat of fentanyl and carfentanil being ordered online, that can't come soon enough.[3] In New York, Customs and Border Protection agents looking specifically for fentanyl have begun using canines, special laser detectors, and x-ray machines to target "high-risk" mail coming through the JFK international mail facility, which handles one million pieces of mail per day, or about 60 percent of all international mail coming into the United States. According to *USA Today*, a CBP official said that as of September 2017, they had seized sixty-four packages containing fentanyl for the year to date, compared to eleven in all of 2016. Most of the high-risk mail comes from China and Hong Kong, according to CBP.[4]

We have to constantly adjust our technology and tactics as the threats change. It's difficult, it's expensive, and it requires constant vigilance, but the magnitude of threat these substances represent is extraordinary.

It's not hunting season

As I mentioned in the introduction, one of the biggest surprises I experienced after becoming involved as a sworn auxiliary deputy in Macon County is the extent of drug use in Decatur, Illinois, my own hometown. As these examples show, right in my hometown border security failures arrive daily by public and private transportation, and even U.S. mail.

As we researched background on these cases, we kept running across intersections of cartel-related crimes in other Decaturs. For example, a friend of mine who works on a special Midwestern task force for the DEA told me about a series of raids yielding thousands of marijuana plants cartel-affiliated growers were cultivating in remote timberland areas of Decatur County, Iowa, and other Midwestern areas in 2013.[5]

These wooded acres are often near farmland and have few people around except for the occasional hunter during deer season. Especially in large counties with a limited number of sheriff's deputies to patrol rural areas, cartel-affiliated marijuana growers will look for properties near a water source like a creek or pond. Several men will move a tent and some cooking supplies into a secluded area and set up a camp. They will clear a space underneath trees, from which they will shave off limbs ten or twenty feet up to create room to move about and plant, but they are careful to keep the operation hidden from air surveillance. They bring in irrigation pipes and gasoline pumps, and sacks of fertilizer, and in some camps law enforcement has found knives and hatchets. In six months, they can grow and harvest a crop and then be gone.

A break in this case came during a normal traffic stop of a van with two men inside wearing full camouflage suits in June (not hunting season). Police also could see large black plastic bags covering something in the back. They tracked the van to a house rented to a man and his girlfriend, and then they discovered the pair had ties to a family known to drug agents as cartel related. The drug task force obtained a warrant to place a surveillance camera observing the house from a block away, and in the middle of the night an agent placed a tracking device under the van.

Three days later, the owners swapped the van for a truck, so the agent had to track down the van, remove the tracker, and replace it under the truck.

But it was all worth it: The agents monitored the truck driving out to a remote spot and returning every few days for groceries and supplies. They finally prepared a raid on the field and a sting operation at the house and arrested four undocumented individuals with ties to the Mexican cartels. One was deported immediately, and the other three pled guilty in federal court and served two years before they were deported.

As we researched local news accounts of these busts, we Googled "Decatur" and "drug bust" and "cartel," looking for local news stories and more details. These searches not only provided more references to these cases, they generated a long list of results of drug-related incidents in Decaturs all over the country. It turns out there are more than a dozen American cities and towns named Decatur as well as counties we found in Georgia, Tennessee, Iowa, and Indiana. It's challenging to find a Decatur that *hasn't* had a significant drug bust or cartel-related activities in recent years.

A sample:

- In 2017, Georgia Bureau of Investigation in Decatur, Georgia, said it was investigating fifty overdose deaths in Georgia believed to be the result of a super-opioid combination of heroin, fentanyl, and carfentanil called "gray death" on the street.[6]

- On April 4, 2017 in Decatur County, Tennessee, a DEA task force arrested two men who claimed to be from Texas transporting $13 million worth of fentanyl.[7]

- In Decaturville, Tennessee, in May 2017, a drug task force team arrested a mother who had $21,000 worth of meth, $27,000 in cash, marijuana, and a handgun under her pillow. Local law enforcement said she appeared to be a "major drug distributor."[8]

- In 2015, a man who said he was an enforcer for a Mexican drug cartel pled guilty to nine counts of murder in California. In addition to multiple murders in California, he'd been charged with murdering two Florida men over the theft of ten kilos of cocaine, and also a Decatur, Alabama, roofing contractor who was found in a field, shot five times.[9]

Collateral damage

I'm also certain that in each of those counties, cities, and towns called Decatur, you will not only find crime stories about drugs and cartel activities, you will find the same tragic stories I have heard in Illinois. In 2017, Indiana state officials released statistics for the 2012–2015 period that showed the drug overdose death rate in Decatur County, Indiana, was the second highest of Indiana's ninety-two counties, at 37.96 out of 100,000 population.[10]

In all these places you'll find the indirect impacts of an insecure border, including children who have lost parents to overdoses or who have been taken away from their drug-using parents and placed in foster care.

You will find treatment programs that don't have the resources to treat everyone who needs help.

You will find heartbroken parents like good friends of mine, who never dreamed they would be spending their retirement years talking to other parents of heroin addicts in Decatur, Illinois, and surrounding towns about the best ways to help their children without destroying the rest of the family's life. These families get together and share their stories, and they realize how much they have in common. "I couldn't keep a teaspoon in the house," one mother of an addict who was living in her house told me. Her son was taking them to cook heroin. "It took me so long to admit where they were going."

You will find addicts so sick with craving for heroin that when they read in the paper about a particularly strong batch of drugs that has prompted overdose deaths, they will seek out the dealers they think sold that batch to see if they can get some for a more intense high. A twenty-three-year-old woman once told me she craved heroin so badly she would kill to get it.

You will find people in positions of authority in law enforcement whose own family members and friends are using and buying drugs. A young police officer I know has a sister who has been in and out of rehab several times, and it tears him apart that he can't figure out how to help her get clean permanently. A detective on a mail delivery sting I was part of in Decatur discovered that the "addressees" of drugs ordered online were three high school kids— including his own son's classmate.

You will find detectives like Chad Larner, who can't believe the federal government is not better at securing the border and cracking down on narcotics shipped through the USPS.

You will find local cops who know that residents of their communities are working for Mexican cartels in some capacity, whether it's dealing on the street or helping launder money by making cash deposits in personal bank accounts. Maybe you will find a postal clerk who conveniently forgets to verify the sender's address on packages leaving the state.

We must stop treating these situations as local or community issues. As you are about to read, the stories are being repeated over and over across America, and sheriffs and police officers say the pressure is intensifying.

Chapter 7

WHAT ABOUT DEMAND?

Without question, America's appetite for drugs contributes to our insecure border. But can we impact demand fast enough to save tens of thousands of lives?

I view the basic drivers of America's drug epidemic and related criminal activity through the lens of border security, but I realize some people view it through another lens. They believe it is America's appetite for drugs that should be our focus. Without demand, they say, without millions of people willing to part with billions of dollars to buy illegal drugs, the cartels would stop smuggling drugs into our country. That would stop overdoses, drug-related violence, devastated families, and many other negative social consequences that we have today.

Without a doubt, lowering demand would reduce the widespread harm to our country resulting from drug use. In fact, in part 3's recommendations you'll read a compelling argument against buying illegal drugs that I heard from a young Mexican man. It's one that I hope every person who uses illegal drugs today and every young person thinking of trying drugs will take to heart.

The problem is that observation about demand is just an observation. It's not a strategy. We've been trying to figure out demand for a long time. I don't know what approach works to keep people from trying and using drugs. I doubt we'll come up with one fast enough to prevent many deaths if we just shift our attention to prevention. And don't forget: The people profiting from America's addictions and drug use are not just going to give up if drugs that currently bring them huge sums of money are legalized; they will adapt, and they will continue to prey on anyone they feel they can exploit.

Can't arrest our way out

There is a law enforcement angle on demand that I believe is critical: focusing on getting drug users into treatment instead of jail so you can disrupt the endless loop of nonviolent drug offenders constantly going in and out of the criminal justice system, at great expense but for little benefit.

These days you hear police chiefs and sheriffs all over the United States repeat the phrase "We cannot arrest our way out of the overdose problem." In April 2017, our foundation cosponsored a conference on the national opioid crisis organized by the Police Executive Research Forum and held at the New York Police Department headquarters. Police chiefs and sheriffs from small towns and rural counties and big cities alike shared stories of the tidal wave of opioid overdoses in their communities. They talked about the kind of incidents many of us have seen on television or online: A man and woman overdosed, slumped in the front seats of a car while their young child sits strapped into a car seat behind them. A little girl in a supermarket trying to shake her mother awake after she collapses in an aisle.

These leaders relayed how the extent of the drug addiction problem, particularly heroin and other opioids, was overwhelming their resources. I attended the conference and heard the concerns among senior law enforcement leaders about what lies ahead in the opioid epidemic. PERF produced a report from the meeting featuring the comments of many attendees. The sheriff of Hennepin County, Minnesota, Richard Stanek, said, "In my county, we had a 39 percent increase in 2016 opioid-related deaths, which generally matches the national trend of opioid deaths being about three times the homicide rate." Police Commissioner Richard Ross of Philadelphia said, "We've had saves [meaning interventions] where the Fire Department and the police are both using naloxone to save two different people in the same car at the same time."[1]

Most law enforcement leaders have accepted a basic fact: Once a person becomes addicted to opioids, they need treatment to overcome it. You can't shame people or punish them enough to overcome the chemical dependency. And with such powerful drugs on the street today, many will die. Police Chief Terrence Sheridan of Baltimore County reported: "The people who are using these drugs can't get out of it...We had a man who overdosed twenty times, and he died the twenty-first time...He would resist medics and police because they said they were 'ruining his high.' That's what we're dealing with."

I had lunch not long ago in Decatur with a woman who shared with me some of her family's struggles with her son's heroin addiction, an addiction that eventually killed him. After multiple overdoses and multiple rehab visits, she caught him using again. She said she was exhausted and furious. She shared the sad memory of a yelling match where she finally said: "You are a piece of s—." And she said he looked her in the eye, and with no anger or defensiveness, but defeated, and he said: "Mom, I know I am a piece of s—. I can't stop."

Addicts like her son or like my late cousin Billy are in the grip of a disease. They are continuing to use not because they are evil or bad people. They are addicts. They would like to be free of the addiction, and they can't do it alone. I've seen firsthand that opioid addiction takes hold of, and sometimes kills, good people. Parents feel helpless, and addicts think they are beyond help. The same mom told me, "I felt like I was walking around with 'Bad Mother' written on my chest like in *The Scarlet Letter*. His addiction was a sickness, and it made me crazy."

I support first responders carrying naloxone to save lives—in fact, our foundation has donated the treatment to first responders in Illinois, Nebraska, and Arizona. I hope that the lives we save can be turned around. That will mean getting people into treatment, probably multiple times. That's how difficult this is.

Too late to legalize

There is another way to approach the drug epidemic and impact demand for illegal drugs that some believe would create a safer, less lethal economy around drugs: legalizing them. I do not agree. Even though efforts to legalize marijuana have gained momentum around the country, I think that is a dangerous trend.

If you legalize and regulate drug sales and tax them, the argument goes, you cut the most violent and bad actors out of the profits and they will go away. There is no point smuggling drugs across the border anymore. And besides, marijuana is no worse for you than alcohol, so why are we so hypocritical about this?

It's not just about whether marijuana is more harmful than legal alcohol use, although its health and safety impacts are important. In Colorado, with some of the most liberal rules for personal use of marijuana in the nation, some studies show communities are seeing higher rates of teens using marijuana, more visits to emergency rooms and poison control centers for THC-related overdoses—including children—and more impaired driving resulting in higher deaths.[2]

Also important is that in Colorado law enforcement leaders believe legalization has created a shield for the cartels to expand U.S. growing of marijuana and transport it more easily.

I had dinner with a group of Colorado sheriffs who walked me through what they are seeing in their communities. Colorado now allows individuals to buy marijuana in licensed dispensaries and also to grow limited amounts of marijuana in their homes. They said there have been more armed robberies at homes of people growing more than the legal limit who are selling marijuana themselves and have cash around. They say more transients are traveling to Colorado to access marijuana, which can lead to more street crime, an observation reflected in local media coverage of Colorado's crime rates.[3]

But they also told me that the legal marijuana industry is masking the activities of cartels. Once you allow individuals certain rights to possess, transport, and grow marijuana, it changes the game for what represents "probable cause" that a crime has been committed to allow for a search of a vehicle or a residence. A driver may be stopped by police for a traffic violation, for example, and the car smells like marijuana. The driver says he came from a party where marijuana was being smoked legally and the smell is on his clothes. Where marijuana is legal, the law enforcement officer cannot use the presence of the smell as supporting a search of a vehicle; in this case it's harder to argue probable cause unless the stop was for dangerous or impaired driving.[4] The driver could be a drug dealer with one hundred pounds of marijuana—and for that matter another five kilos of cocaine—in the trunk about to be smuggled across state lines. But now, the deputy or officer cannot legally search.

In Colorado in 2017, an appeals court ruled that the alert signal from a dog trained to detect multiple drugs, including marijuana, was not sufficient to justify the search of a vehicle driven by a person over age twenty-one without the driver's permission. According to the Associated Press, the judges said that in Colorado, where use of marijuana is legal for adults, the dog could be alerting to a substance that is legal. Therefore, the search would violate the driver's reasonable expectation of privacy.[5]

I also thought about this recently on a traffic stop I made in Illinois. The driver was a woman who had failed to signal when making a turn. When she lowered her window, marijuana smoke literally billowed out of the car. When the smoke cleared, I realized she had two young children strapped in car seats in the backseat. Marijuana use and possession have been decriminalized in Illinois, but many are pushing for full legalization. Active smoking while driving would no doubt still be illegal, but what about smoking in a small space before pulling onto the roadway? And how can the law protect innocent children from the unintended consequences of this mother's secondhand smoke?

Sheriffs have told me about individuals with known ties to cartels who arrive in Colorado communities and buy houses with cash and then set up "grow houses." But even if they suspect this is happening, law enforcement cannot easily get a warrant to search the premises and make sure growers are within legal limits. One Colorado sheriff told me he believes the cartels are trafficking people to work in these grow houses, sometimes in exchange for helping someone cross the border illegally.

These so-called "pirate grows" produce volumes well in excess of legal limits, then sell it privately or drive it out of state. The *Denver Post* reported in 2016 that in one day, police conducted raids on thirty grow houses believed to be part of a pot trafficking organization. Separately, two intruders were killed in two separate break-ins to grow houses.[6]

Criminals respond to developments that cut their profits by committing new kinds of crimes. It's what criminals do.

I know that some counties strapped for cash welcome the tax revenues legal marijuana sales are generating. At a recent conference I attended, sheriffs and police officers from states with liberal marijuana laws who clearly did not believe that was a good thing sarcastically advised their colleagues: Advocate for taxing legal sales as high as possible because your community is going to need it for drug treatment and the costs of dealing with additional criminal activity.

I find it alarming when I see campaigns advocating for legalizing marijuana, especially the use of the term "recreational." It seems to minimize the impact of these drugs. From my experience in law enforcement, I feel the evidence is so clear that drug use both directly and indirectly is doing serious harm to our country. Framing these legalization campaigns as if we're just voting to approve a new golf course or a theme park seems wrong and self-defeating.

Pill mills and suspicious pharmacies

If you think regulating drugs ensures fewer negative impacts, pay attention to the skyrocketing opioid epidemic. Many experts have documented that patients who started with legal, prescribed, regulated opioid painkillers and became addicted, then switched to heroin when their doctors cut them off or they could no longer afford the pills. Some addicts originally were workers injured on the job, victims of auto accidents, or even young athletes with sports injuries who started taking opioid-based pain medication like Vicodin or OxyContin for a legitimate pain condition and end up addicted.[7]

Regulators, among others, dropped the ball. In some regions of the country crooked, unethical doctors set up "pill mill" storefronts and essentially sold prescriptions for opioid pain relievers. In West Virginia, unethical prescribing of legal opioids was ignored by drug distributors, state regulators, and pharmacies who filled enough orders between 2007 and 2012 for every man, woman, and child in the state to have taken 433 pills, which was revealed in a Pulitzer Prize–winning investigative series by the *Charleston Gazette-Mail*.[8]

Lawsuits are starting to pile up. Ohio is one of several states suing five pharmaceutical companies that make opioid painkillers, claiming that they minimized the addiction potential.[9] In Everett, Washington, the city has filed a lawsuit against Purdue Pharma, claiming the company should be accountable for "supplying OxyContin to obviously suspicious pharmacies and physicians and enabling the illegal diversion of OxyContin into the black market."[10] In 2007, Purdue and its executives paid more than $630 million in legal penalties and admitted Purdue had marketed the drug inappropriately and misrepresented its risk of addiction.[11]

Today's opioid crisis began with the increase in legal opioid prescriptions in the early 2000s, then both legitimate patients and other users turned to illegally produced opioids created in Mexico and China and smuggled into the United States. In fact, I'm told the Mexican drug cartels realized the opportunity developing as they watched the pharmaceutical companies develop their customers' "legal" addictions. They rushed to take them over with smuggled drugs. Journalist Sam Quinones investigated this situation in his 2015 best-seller *Dreamland: The True Tale of America's Opiate Epidemic*. Quinones says Mexican drug dealers pushed heroin into the same territories where drug companies were aggressively promoting opioid painkillers like OxyContin roughly a decade ago, and that created "catastrophic synergy, and presaged the transition from pills to heroin that would happen in the rest of the country years later."[12] Greg Burns, the assistant chief of police of Louisville, Kentucky, told PERF in 2017: "When we started to crack down on the prescription drug pill mills, that's when we started to notice the heroin problems shoot up, because it was relatively cheap, and the pills are so expensive now." During 2016, he added, "We used 688 doses of Narcan" for 480 patients.

To me some of the most concerning risks of legalizing drugs are the unintended and unforeseen consequences.

For example, as the Mexican cartels have watched states legalize marijuana, not only have they moved into growing marijuana in the United States to undercut legal sales with cheaper product, but they have switched tens of thousands of acres of marijuana fields in Mexico to poppy production to make heroin.[13]

The long-term safety impact of legal marijuana is not fully understood, but it is likely not positive: Young children now have access to a drug that society increasingly says is acceptable but that is known to alter brain activity.[14] Cigarettes may be legal, regulated, and taxed—but they also created widespread health problems that kill people and that we spend incredible sums treating, by some estimates ninety cents of every ten dollars that is spent on healthcare. And then we spend millions on ad campaigns trying to convince both kids and adults not to smoke.[15]

When there is more marijuana in circulation, we are seeing situations where people, including teenagers, are at a party and handed a joint they do not realize is laced with fentanyl.[16]

People debate whether marijuana is a so-called gateway drug that leads to more serious drug use. To me the issue is not whether marijuana triggers a craving or desire to experiment with other drugs; it's that drug dealers are marketers out to make a profit. People selling marijuana are often also selling more dangerous— and more profitable—drugs and have an incentive to expand their business. When your judgment is impaired from any substance, including alcohol, prescription pills, or marijuana, you will make decisions you might not make when sober. I was involved in a traffic stop once as an auxiliary deputy sheriff where we came upon an individual who was passed out in his vehicle. Later, I talked with him at some length. I asked how he got involved with using drugs. He said he began with marijuana, and the drug dealer he bought his marijuana from finally convinced him to try heroin.

In terms of other practical consequences, I think about businesses that employ heavy equipment operators or delivery truck drivers. When marijuana is legal and may stay in your system in detectable levels for days or weeks after you use it, you can't create an easy test to determine if an employee is a hazard on any given day.

Don't dare drug test

A lot of the energy in the legalization debate has the broader effect of minimizing the overall threat of drugs. I think it's going to become more and more important how we frame the larger threats of substance abuse in our country. In 2017, I thought about this when we met with the private equity owners of a U.S. company with a manufacturing plant in El Salvador that I had visited a few months prior. It is a model program where management has worked with local churches and recruited workers from the ranks of former gang members. The workers get a second chance; the company gets good workers and is profitable. In New York, the company's investors told me the company's management is so pleased with their Salvadoran operations that they are moving all the company's manufacturing there from Pennsylvania.

That's good news for El Salvador, which needs to develop a growing, legal economy to offer young people an alternative to gang life. But what got my attention was when they said a key driver for this decision to move the jobs out of the country is the extent of drug use in the communities near their U.S. plants. "Turnover has become one of our biggest issues, and that has to do with drug use. We would like to drug test; we now cannot do drug testing because we could not put a full shift on the assembly floor if we did." They said workers are unreliable and often just don't show up on a Monday morning. The *annual* turnover rate in the factory in El Salvador, he said, was equivalent to the *monthly* turnover rate in their factory in Pennsylvania. These investors have positions in small-scale manufacturing operations across the United States. They said this workforce challenge was not unique to Pennsylvania, and that it seemed to be endemic to the ten- to fifteen-dollar-an-hour labor force, a reality that the *New York Times* found to be true in 2017.[17] These investors are considering moving other manufacturing jobs from other companies they own to El Salvador as well.

Who could have predicted that one consequence of failing to stop the Mexican cartels is that a U.S. company can find a more reliable workforce in one of the most violent countries in our hemisphere than it can in Pennsylvania?

The imminent threat of heroin and opioids demands that we take action today to stop the lethal agents crossing our borders. We don't have time to debate or experiment with whether the free market and social engineering might lower demand. It's possible that the severity of this overdose crisis alone will play some role in the future of discouraging people from trying these drugs, but right now we need to take a hard look at our physical defenses and figure out how to better deploy people, tools, and barriers on the front line.

Chapter 8

TOO MUCH, TOO FAST

Customs and Border Protection is America's frontline law enforcement agency, and many dedicated officers risk their lives every day to protect our borders. But the agency is still coping with issues that arose after 9/11—and undermine its effectiveness.

The boat pilot and two Border Patrol agents holding automatic weapons and wearing armored vests all gave a thumbs-up, and we pulled away from the wooden dock in Mission, Texas. The dock is located within south Texas's ninety-six-acre Anzalduas Park. The uniforms and firepower were a dramatic contrast to the many bikers and joggers we could see enjoying themselves along the shore that summer afternoon in 2016.

Just a hundred yards or so away, several dozen picnickers on the Mexico side of the Rio Grande were holding a twilight cookout. I could see tables full of food, children laughing and playing in shallow water, adults wading in the Rio Grande. Some called out to us in Spanish (with a few using one-fingered gestures for emphasis).

Our boat's female commander, an eighteen-year veteran of Border Patrol, steered us to mid-river. She yelled "Coming up!" and hit the throttle. We took off and a few minutes later we slowed to a stop by Anzalduas Dam, which creates a bridge over the Rio Grande. The commander pointed downstream to a raft in the water with several people in it. "The water's too low right now; we can't get a boat in there. They know that." She radioed to agents on land to try to intercept that raft on the bank. We turned and headed back upriver.

The Rio Grande delineates more than 1,200 miles of the U.S.–Mexico border, including a serpentine, 320-mile stretch in the Lower Rio Grande Valley where we are traveling tonight. This border between the United States and Mexico in Texas is a dramatic contrast to the mostly dry, desolate, and rocky Arizona desert borderlands. Along much of the Rio Grande, development and farmland extend right to the shore.

At times, the banks are full of people and the river full of boaters. In fact, the commander explains that one smuggling ploy is for groups on the U.S. side to host a picnic near the riverbank in Anzalduas Park. After Border Patrol boats pass by, an individual may quickly swim or paddle a raft across from Mexico and immediately join the party on the other bank. "We've had situations where there is a family reunion T-shirt everybody is wearing, and they have one ready to immediately hand to whoever has crossed over." Sometimes, legal U.S. residents will ride a bike to the park, wait for a contact to cross, then hand over a helmet and biking outfit to a person who crossed the river illegally. The U.S. resident later just walks out.

The agents point out other features along the bank that create ready hiding places. The vegetation the agents hate most is Carrizo cane, an invasive weed species that grows in dense clumps and can grow thirty feet high. Its structure tends to trap heat and makes using thermal detectors ineffective when trailing a suspect. Worse, "You just get stuck in it," one agent explains. "And down by the banks when you're in the middle of it you're not sure if it will hold you, so you can fall down into a hole or the river." Rattlesnakes, ticks, and Africanized killer bees also live along the banks. The boat commander said she was once stung by bees thirty-two times during a pursuit.

We pass several elaborate homes believed to be owned by drug cartel kingpins. Sometimes, there will be parties on the broad patios and docks as BP passes and the "guests" will throw rocks or bottles. It's common to see fishermen anchored in small watercraft or sitting on banks. Some are spotters. There is one inlet where the agents often see an alligator. "The rumor is he loves donuts and spaghetti," the boat commander says, grinning. As if that isn't bizarre enough, there is a Mexican zoo along one bank where zookeepers take full-grown tigers on chains down to the river to play in the water.

The agents can't afford to get caught up in the sideshows: Mexican drug cartels are using this river 24/7 for drug and human smuggling, and a pleasant summer evening can quickly turn deadly. The patrol boats cruise all night with their running lights off so as not to be a target for snipers along the dark banks. "Sometimes you're using night vision goggles and you see somebody on the shore using night vision goggles on you," the commander says. It's not unusual for migrants to attempt to cross the river who are not strong swimmers or who may be tired from days or weeks of travel. Drowned corpses sometimes wash up on shore downstream.

At night, a struggling swimmer may pop up out of nowhere in front of a patrol boat's bow. If the commander throttles back too fast to avoid hitting the person, the engine may stall. Big problem: Now, you've got a rescue and you're stalled in the water and cannot maneuver. "We like to have three agents on board for that reason. We're out here like sitting ducks," she explains, adding that "Dispatch calls us every hour on the hour" to confirm the agents' safety.

The middle of the river technically is the border, but Border

Patrol does not attempt to interfere with anyone while they are in the water. But given that BP boats can't be everywhere at once, it's easy to see how one crossing strategy is to pretend to be paddling around as a recreational boater or kayaker, waiting for a patrol to pass before paddling to shore and jumping out and disappearing into the brush.

The complexity of the Rio Grande river ecosystem and all these human activities are why talking about building a "wall" along our borders (and by wall I am specifically referring to a tall, solid barrier) is impractical or even impossible in many locations. You can't put a barrier in the middle of the river. The fingers of land created by the serpentine nature of the river, and the complex flood plain dynamics, mean in some spots you'd have to build a wall well inland of the border, effectively surrendering significant U.S. territory to the south side of the border. South Texas residents fought previous attempts to build walls across private property, and the government eventually reinforced levees as a compromise.[1] I've flown over these structures in a helicopter and the need to let farmers and landowners cross to the river side of their property creates many gaps and openings.

I came away from my evening on the river with a new appreciation both for the incredible challenges of the diverse landscape and communities along our borders, and for the demands on Border Patrol agents. But that is one side of a complex situation that, unfortunately, has another.

Open gates

In chapter 3, I discussed how the consequence of the federal government doubling down on securing the border near urban areas was a strategic shift that drove huge numbers of people to attempt to cross the border in rural areas. But there was another major event that triggered significant changes for our frontline agents protecting the border: 9/11.

In 2000, 1.6 million individuals were apprehended along the border, and another 2 million may have successfully entered the country illegally.[2] The next year, after 9/11, federal officials assessed our vulnerabilities and realized that a total of 7,458 miles[3] of our borders with Canada and Mexico patrolled by fewer than ten thousand agents was a serious security threat. With urgency and good intentions, the government reorganized the border security mission and put it under the umbrella of the new Department of Homeland Security. Among the billions of dollars of measures designed to boost our defenses, it created resources to hire thousands of new Border Patrol agents, bolster our physical barrier defenses, and invest in surveillance technologies.

The problem is, in the rush to action, Washington never really settled on what a definition of border security would be. Former military analyst and border expert Sylvia Longmire discussed the issue in her 2012 book *Border Insecurity: Why Big Money, Fences, and Drones Aren't Making Us Safer*. In the wake of 9/11, "The US government spent over $90 billion on border security efforts without having a truly objective way to measure success—or acknowledge failure."[4]

What does that mean? We talked about the apprehension rate as a flawed metric. How significant are total apprehensions when we don't know how many people are making attempts? But beyond that, is it our priority to stop all unauthorized entries to the country right at the border, or within a certain number of miles of the border? How should law enforcement engage with local landowners in high-impact traffic areas? Should we treat all undocumented people making a crossing attempt as equal threats, or should we prioritize drug smugglers and other criminals? Should we look for options for those fleeing violence to find legal and orderly ways to enter the country?

Some use the military term "situational awareness" or "operational control" at the border, suggesting that we will be secure when we know what is going on and can respond in a meaningful way to threats. Senator Heidi Heitkamp from North Dakota has said to me, "I don't think anybody knows what that actually means, because everyone has a different idea or way of defining that term—if they define it at all—so whose definition determines when we've reached 'operational control'? We need agreement on what these terms mean and what actual quantifiable metrics we will use to make that determination."

To understand how this confusion developed, more history is in order. The new Department of Homeland Security brought together Immigration and Customs Enforcement (ICE), the U.S. Coast Guard, Customs and Border Protection, the Federal Emergency Management Agency, the Secret Service, and others. The idea was all these agencies had a stake in keeping us safe from terrorism and should be managed under the same department. The U.S. Coast Guard retained responsibility for our maritime borders, but the activities of Customs, ICE, and Border Patrol were reconfigured. Border Patrol and ICE, for example, used to be housed within the Immigration and Naturalization Service, but in the new DHS, BP and Customs were joined together under CBP, while ICE was separate.

"All kinds of stupid things"

The point of the reorganization was to support better collaboration and effectiveness. Instead, the changes created some difficult dynamics that plague border security today. "Congress failed to articulate a coherent mission and did not perform the oversight it should have during DHS's first five years. Because it wasn't properly managed in its infancy, DHS is now a teenager and all of the organizational and morale problems are magnified," says Senator Heitkamp, who sits on a Senate committee that oversees DHS. "DHS employs thousands of great Americans who want to serve their country. Their greatest impediment is Congress's failed leadership."

Senator Heitkamp is not alone in her frustration. In a 2015 report, then-Senator Tom Coburn, ranking member of the Senate Homeland Security and Governmental Affairs Committee, noted that despite spending nearly $61 billion annually and a total of $544 billion since 2003, DHS was "not successfully executing any of its five main mission areas." Among other consequences of those failures, the report said: "The nation's borders remain unsecure."[5]

I will recommend in part 3 some high-level command and organizational changes. For now I want to drill down on one particular consequence of 9/11: Huge budget increases landed on southwest border stations; the agency had doubled the size of Border Patrol agents along the southwest border to around eighteen thousand agents by 2011.

On the surface, how could that not be a good thing? More agents along the border should mean faster response and a higher apprehension rate, and be a deterrent to those with criminal intentions, including terrorists. But from my own observations and many conversations I've had along the border with community leaders, local law enforcement, Border Patrol leaders, and Washington policy experts, that's not how it played out. The surge of hiring overwhelmed the agency's management capacity; the growing strength of the National Border Patrol Council, BP's union, complicated strategic deployments; and poorly vetted candidates meant internal corruption increased.[6] What's more, relationships with the border area residents and Border Patrol became and have remained strained for well over a decade.

The sudden, large budget increases were a mixed blessing, observes a former BP sector chief. "We used to be driving around with cardboard on the floor of our vehicles to keep the dust out. The vehicles were falling apart. Then, we went from mainly hiding in the brush to apprehend people, to standing up as a deterrent." The discipline of prioritizing threats and needs was lost. He explained that after 9/11 there was internal pressure to spend the newly designated money quickly before other agencies might try to compete for it in the next budget cycle. According to the chief, "All kinds of stupid things happened. I walked into one station and the place looked like a bunker with towers made out of boxes of paper everywhere. What happened was the chief had been told to spend $100,000 in two hours or he would lose it, so he bought a semi load of paper."

Despite all those new resources, this former chief explains that the effect of that huge staff increase was like trying to paint just one wall in your house—it makes everything else look bad. "You focus on hiring agents, but you don't have mission support—you don't have vehicles and mechanics to work on vehicles. You create a new station in a town that doesn't have enough housing for the agents you want to send there, so now you've got guys commuting 1.5 hours each way." This happened in remote Ajo, Arizona, where the Department of Homeland Security's inspector general said CBP wasted millions of dollars. Says the chief: "We tried to move four hundred agents in. There was no housing to handle that."[7]

Some believe one of the most serious consequences of this expansion was flawed hiring, a conclusion reached widely by government analysts, think tanks, journalists, internal affairs groups, and oversight bodies. I want to be clear that I know and respect many Border Patrol agents and chiefs. I believe the majority to be hardworking law enforcement officers who risk their lives to protect us. But I do believe the following issues to be fair criticisms.

First, there was so much pressure on BP to hire so many people quickly, standards were not as high as they should have been. BP had trouble finding enough applicants to fill the slots they had open. A GED was the only educational requirement to apply for BP, and many recruits were young and had no other law enforcement experience. Some were fresh from highly stressful military deployments in the Middle East, and they had difficulty transitioning into law enforcement. Military conflict is about neutralizing an enemy. Law enforcement is about public safety, and it's also about respecting civil rights, such as waiting to initiate a search or apprehension until you have probable cause. Some hires had trigger-happy temperaments and reacted with excessive force—for example, shooting multiple rounds at young people armed only with rocks.[8]

Being a Border Patrol agent can be a lonely, high-stress job. Many agents found themselves in small towns in remote locations where their spouses were stranded with little to do, and where they had to travel miles for schools and medical resources. Hours of boredom sitting and driving in the desert punctuated by bursts of high-adrenaline danger is a difficult combination. Chiefs have confirmed to me that for some agents that stress and isolation can contribute to alcohol abuse and sometimes family violence.

According to one former high-ranking BP official, as some minimally qualified agents moved up the ranks into management, their lack of education, experience, and training undermined their success. For example, they did not follow uniform procedures sector by sector. In complex operations demanding cooperation and coordination, Border Patrol leadership sometimes clashed with other agencies led by more highly trained individuals, such as military officers who've attended War College, U.S. Attorneys, and FBI agents with advanced degrees. That reinforced a defensive posture in the entire organization and a reputation for not cooperating. A retired sector chief told me: "Nobody fails the BP academy. We need to up the standards."

Border Patrol developed a reputation for defensiveness and closing ranks. A longtime border expert told me that posture has undermined Border Patrol's credibility in ways that are both unfair and avoidable. "If you look at something like officer use of deadly force, Border Patrol's numbers are not out of line compared to a big city police force," says the expert. That appears to be true: Between 2004 and 2014, for example, an *Arizona Republic* investigation reported that Border Patrol agents killed forty-six people in the line of duty, including fifteen Americans.[9] The *Washington Post* reported that the Los Angeles Police Department, with roughly half the personnel of Border Patrol, had forty-seven fatal shootings between January 2015 and June 2017.[10] I also would point out that the former head of U.S. Border Patrol Mark Morgan told a Congressional committee in 2016 that Border Patrol agents were among "the most assaulted law enforcement personnel in the country." According to CBP, 38 BP agents have been killed in the line of duty since 2003.[11]

Unfortunately, the border expert continues, "The union and Border Patrol respond defensively and don't feel they have to explain anything, or release agent names. And so they don't make that argument effectively. Look, this is dangerous work and there are individuals who engage agents with lethal force. But you can't just say 'you have no right to question us.'" In doing that, Border Patrol is ignoring a standard that is expected of all other law enforcement.

In 2013, the Police Executive Research Forum released a report about deadly force in CBP. It made several recommendations for changes to the training of agents. A big source of conflict has been rock-throwing at agents while they are in pursuit of a suspect or suspects; agents also have fired on vehicles when they feared the driver was going to use the vehicle itself as a weapon. PERF's recommendations involved tactical changes to how agents approach both these situations. They also recommended that CBP investigate all incidents involving deadly force by agents whether or not an injury resulted, as that had been an area of lax reporting.[12]

Bad hires

One of the most serious consequences of weak vetting was corruption. Coburn's 2015 report specifically noted that DHS was grappling with "potentially widespread corruption" within its workforce along the southern border.

In the hiring surge, some Border Patrol agents were hired who had close connections to or even worked for drug cartels. Scores of corrupt agents have been charged with crimes. In a recent high-profile case reported by the *Washington Post*, Border Patrol agent (and Iraq war veteran) Joel Luna, whose younger brother was born in Mexico and considered a "commandant" in a cartel, was on the job for six years in Texas before his cartel connections were exposed. According to prosecutors, Luna used his position with BP to help his brother's cartel move illegal weapons and ammunition south and drugs north. Eventually, he and his brother were charged in the murder of a Honduran man prosecutors say threatened to expose Luna's cover. In January 2017 Agent Luna was found not guilty of the murder, but he was found guilty of aiding organized crime; his Mexican-born brother Eduardo was convicted of killing the Honduran man by beheading.[13]

In June 2017, a seventeen-year BP veteran agent and supervisor stationed in Douglas, Arizona, near our ranches, was arrested for making false statements on a questionnaire. The *Arizona Daily Star* reported that he wrote on a federal disclosure form that he had made a total of two visits to Mexico between 2011 and 2016, when an investigation showed it was more like 1,200 times, and further investigation showed he actually lived in Mexico with his wife and came to the United States to work his shifts. In July, a grand jury indicted him for lying to law enforcement and concealing funds from authorities, when investigators discovered he'd made $70,000 in cash deposits in a "structured" series of small deposits to avoid federal reporting regulations. The agent also claimed he had never been charged with a felony, but investigators discovered he had been charged with three felonies in Florida in 1996, including retaliating against a witness and aggravated battery.[14] He eventually pled guilty to charges that would send him to prison.

BP is not the only agency dealing with corruption issues. ICE agents and Customs officials also have been accused of corruption, including helping cartel smugglers and human traffickers make their way through POEs without being searched or stopped. According to a former investigator for ICE, customs inspectors who staff ports of entry have the power to wave through thousands of vehicles and tractor-trailer rigs in a day. "You have families who have lived in these areas for hundreds of years on both sides. Let's say a guy who works for CBP at the POE has an uncle who's a smuggler. Customs guy is staffing lane 8 today; uncle gets a call to drive through lane 8. No inspection. Thousands of pounds of dope sail through."

Even some individuals with no criminal ties when hired can be tempted by the promise of easy money from the cartels for looking the other way or even helping smuggle drugs and people. As Longmire points out, the temptations on the border can be overwhelming: "Narcotics officers working in other parts of the country consider seizures of a few pounds of cocaine or methamphetamine to be a big deal," she notes. "In places like Texas and Arizona seizures by CBP, Border Patrol, or sheriff's deputies working on border highways are measured in *tons*, with cash values over a million dollars. Cartels who successfully recruit these officers for their payrolls are handing over tens of thousands of dollars in bribes, expensive cars, and jewelry on a regular basis."[15] There are internal affairs teams within BP that investigate corruption, but as the former ICE agent explained, "These are difficult investigations and IA doesn't have enough people to handle all the cases."

Lie detectors

In 2012, Border Patrol began the use of polygraph tests for new recruits to try to identify those with connections to criminal organizations or who had committed crimes. The head of Border Patrol told the *Los Angeles Times* in 2017 that 65 percent of applicants fail those tests.[16] But a number of experienced chiefs have told me that among agents hired prior to those tests being implemented in 2012, there are still agents in the ranks whose integrity is questionable.

One of the most dramatic commentaries I've read on this subject is from James Tomscheck, who until 2014 served as the assistant commissioner at U.S. Customs and Border Protection (CBP), and headed the Office of Internal Affairs. A forty-year law enforcement veteran, Tomscheck wrote in an article that was printed in the online blog *The Hill*: "From those decades of experience, the cases that most disturb me are people who applied to work at CBP—the country's largest law enforcement agency—and admitted in the screening process to committing serious criminal offenses, including drug smuggling, rape, and infanticide, or confessed to seeking employment as infiltrators paid by transnational criminal organizations or cartels."[17]

Tomscheck was writing to oppose pending legislation in 2017 that would have eliminated polygraph tests for some law enforcement and military applicants (who would not necessarily have taken polygraph tests in their previous positions). Tomscheck added: "We would not have caught hundreds of these applicants without a polygraph examination. Indeed, CBP maintains a lengthy roster of near-misses that summarizes hundreds of these egregious admissions by applicants. Even so, nearly two hundred CBP agents and officers have been arrested for corruption since October 2004."

It's important to point out that corruption is not confined to Border Patrol, ICE, and federal agents along our southwest border. In Texas, there are counties where one elected sheriff after another has ended up in jail when their ties to drug smuggling and cartel activities were unearthed, and there have been deputy sheriffs, police officers, and politicians charged and convicted of the same offenses.

Local consequences

Accusations of corruption undermine any law enforcement agency's reputation and relationships. But ranchers in Arizona have other concerns and complaints about Border Patrol's presence in their communities. When our foundation first bought land in Arizona, I have to admit I was surprised by the anger and negative view of BP so many ranchers seemed to have. I had assumed they would be grateful for BP's presence.

Many concerns involve what ranchers consider abuse of their private property. The area directly adjacent to the border barriers near our ranches in Arizona is government land, and BP patrols the gravel road next to it. However, BP has the right to travel onto private property (although not to enter structures) in pursuit of suspected criminal trespassers. Ranchers told me BP agents were often arrogant and disrespectful of private property and ranch etiquette. If you're not familiar with ranch life, a simple act like leaving a gate open after you pass through is a big deal. Cattle or other livestock may escape and become injured or mingle with another herd. Ranchers also resent when agents riding quad runners on patrol behave more like joy-riders. They ride fast and tear up pasture land, creating new roads and ruts that mean topsoil is lost when it rains. Over time and thanks to complaints from ranchers, many agents become educated to these issues and change their behavior, but BP agents are rotated frequently and there is significant attrition. Ranchers have to start all over again.

Another common complaint is that BP sends too many agents to staff inland checkpoints instead of stopping smugglers and illegal border crossers right at the border. BP uses a layered strategy called Defense in Depth that means there are roadside checkpoints as well as permanent checkpoints well inland of the border. Today, by law, only authorized federal agents can actually stop and detain individuals suspected of immigration violations. I think the inland checkpoints represent a solid approach, especially when K-9s are used, but I also think it's a fair question to ask if you need only fully authorized, armed agents in large numbers at these locations, or if at least some of the duties could be handled by other categories of BP personnel.

There is no question that checkpoints push agents into a difficult, sometimes combative relationship with citizens and legal residents who must also pass through these checkpoints, sometimes several times a day. Members of local communities resent that they sit in a line of cars, and then a new, rookie agent asks them for their citizenship or spends time giving their ten-year-old truck a once-over.

It's also true that BP checkpoints create significant security issues and expense for their communities. For example, there is a major Border Patrol checkpoint located along Highway 281 in Falfurrias, Texas, seventy miles north of the border. It sits within geographically large (nearly one thousand square miles) but sparsely populated (8,500 people) Brooks County.

Human traffickers transporting UDAs and sometimes drug smugglers often tell them to get out a few miles before the checkpoint and hike around it. Meanwhile the driver, often a legal resident, drives through. The meet-up point may be many miles away. The terrain is rolling pastureland and mesquite with few landmarks. The UDAs may have a jug of water, but in the heat of summer, temperatures top 100 degrees and many of the travelers are already stressed and dehydrated.

Ranchers and hunters find many of their bodies later. Since 2009, the office of Benny Martinez, the Brooks County sheriff, has recovered more than five hundred bodies in remote areas. "We estimate that we recover less than half of all those who perish," he testified before the U.S. Senate in 2015, and he says the county spent $700,000 for body recoveries from 2008 to 2014. He and his deputies must respond to each discovery and arrange for a coroner and other logistics—and that takes time and money that is in short supply in Brooks.

I've met several times with Sheriff Martinez, who is a low-key, compassionate career lawman. He also explained to me the consequences of cartel members recruiting scouts and helpers to move people and drugs around the checkpoint from within his community. Members of the Zeta cartel have personally threatened Martinez.[18] If he didn't have the federal checkpoint in his county, the Brooks County Sheriff's Office could focus more time on the safety of the people who pay his salary.

Tense encounters

During my frequent visits to our Arizona ranches, I admit I've had my own frustrating experiences with BP. I have been stopped numerous times while driving on a road that cuts through the middle of our ranch. I have been blinded at night by BP agents shining their floodlights directly into my eyes as I drove on the public road. One of our employees was stopped by three Border Patrol agents for "speeding" on a nearby county road (federal agents have no authority to enforce state traffic laws). At CR, a Border Patrol agent once drew her weapon on a local rancher who leases grazing rights on our land.

In areas where we own property, I've had productive conversations with the local command about these incidents. And I often talk with agents I meet near or on our ranches. I've had many discussions with local leadership about topics such as their interest in putting sensors or cameras on our property, as well as the level of smuggling activity in the area. We try to give Border Patrol a heads-up when we see suspicious activity, or when we are going to be doing something on the ranch that might appear unusual to them. We appreciate it when they do the same for us, and they have.

I believe most agents are trying their best. I spent many hours with the BP agents who let me ride along years ago in order to take photographs along the border, and I appreciate what agents are up against. This is a tough, dangerous job. If they are in hot pursuit of drug smugglers, you can imagine why, for example, they don't stop to close gates. And they may end up miles from the gate if they are involved in an apprehension. Still, when your livelihood is based on keeping your cattle safe and on your own land, that open gate is not just a nuisance.

I've also spent time with BP's special Border Search, Trauma, and Rescue (BORSTAR) unit, which is a highly trained group of agents who conduct tactical medical and search and rescue missions. To say they operate in hostile environments is an understatement: Temperatures in the desert can reach 115 degrees or more in midsummer, and BORSTAR teams have saved thousands of migrants attempting to cross rocky, dry areas full of rattlesnakes, scorpions, coyotes, and other threats. They also respond to distress calls from hikers or other civilians or law enforcement. They stand ready for a range of interventions from supplying water to a disoriented and dehydrated migrant to staffing the rescue of an individual from a canyon by helicopter airlift.

My impression from speaking with both BP and community members in both Arizona and Texas is that Border Patrol sectors are highly dependent on a given sector chief's investment in building good relationships. For example, I'm told BP chiefs and agents in the Yuma, Arizona, sector have had an excellent relationship with the community and a team attitude, and are highly respected by local law enforcement. They share local resources, such as practice shooting ranges, and they meet regularly with farmers, local tribal representatives, police, sheriffs, and residents.

In Border Patrol stations, the commanding officer is called the "patrol agent in charge" (PAIC). All the PAICs I have worked with in Arizona are excellent individuals, and I hold them in high regard; however, with hundreds of agents to oversee and bureaucrats far from the border who impose policies that can be impractical with negative consequences for U.S. citizens, it is a difficult balancing act, one you cannot always get right. In the sector where our ranches are located there are quarterly meetings between local ranchers and BP, usually with other government officials from other agencies or the U.S. Attorney's office. I have attended these, and sometimes they are productive, but I've also seen the government guests antagonize the ranchers.

In terms of relationships between local law enforcement and BP agents, the picture seems to be mixed. Local law enforcement generally also would like to see more agents deployed directly on the border so they can stop UDAs from infiltrating their counties. Some agents seem to work well with local police and sheriff's deputies, others are seen as aloof and uncooperative.

There is a federal program that I feel has been a big benefit to border area law enforcement. The Operation Stonegarden program makes federal grants available to local, state, and tribal law enforcement groups who can buy special equipment and also pay their officers and deputies to help federal law enforcement under the direction of Border Patrol.[19] The way it works is that a sheriff's deputy, for example, is eligible to work a Stonegarden shift before or after a normal patrol shift. The officer will phone in to report for duty with BP, then again to check off duty. The deputy may be told to patrol an area where BP suspects migrants may be moving, or to back up an operation in progress. These kinds of operations improve communication and, I think, offer long-term value to both law enforcement organizations and border security.

Border Patrol in Arizona has a particularly challenging situation with the Tohono O'odham Nation, whose territory, culture, and traditions predate borders between Mexico and the United States. Traditionally, members of the nation have the right to cross the U.S.–Mexico border on reservation land because it owns the land on both sides, but over the years relations with the U.S. government and, by extension, Border Patrol have been strained. BP has been accused of using excessive force on reservation members when agents encounter them near the border. But it is well known that both migrants and drug smugglers cross the nation's land (the majority of unidentified immigrant remains in Arizona are collected there), and the complicity of tribal members paid by cartels to assist in those crossings has attracted scrutiny.[20] A member of the tribe's legislative council told author and border expert Todd Miller in 2012 that perhaps 30 percent were involved in helping smugglers.[21] On the other hand, special groups of Native American trackers from the Tohono O'odham Nation called Shadow Wolves have worked successfully with Border Patrol and ICE to track smugglers on tribal lands.[22]

In the Rio Grande Valley sector in Texas, former chiefs say the pool of applicants for BP includes more individuals who have some familiarity with ranches, which tends to make for better relations. In Texas, I'm told BP has more informal and frequent get-togethers, such as standing weekly coffee sessions, where ranchers and agents and leadership can talk about issues—maybe before they get so highly charged. This requires valuable time and adequate staffing, but strikes me as worth that investment.

Mixed missions

Rapid hiring of poorly vetted applicants, the lure of corruption, and the challenges of trying to enforce federal law using tactics that border area residents resent all have made Border Patrol the target of criticism. And the job of responding to that criticism and representing agents charged with a difficult mission over vast amounts of territory has been taken up by a very aggressive union, the National Border Patrol Council (NBPC), which has represented Border Patrol agents since 1967.

Because of what I see as a conflict between BP's unusual dual law enforcement and national security mission, I think collective bargaining agreements are an obstacle to Border Patrol being more effective. "How do you deploy personnel in an emergency when the union rep is looking over your shoulder?" asks one law enforcement veteran in Arizona.

The first issue involves flexibility. Former chiefs and supervisors have told me that union rules put strict requirements on the transferring and deployment of agents, such as how much notice they must be given before a transfer takes place, compensation for travel, specified rotation schedules off the actual border, and other tactical changes.

Remember that "stepping on the balloon" phenomenon: BP may deploy agents to one area with heavy traffic, but overnight the traffic there will disappear and shift to a region miles away where staffing is thin. This creates a need for fast reactions and flexibility in command. The challenge is when the negotiated regular rotation of BP agents through different assignments based on seniority and other factors takes priority over sending the most qualified teams to respond to a given threat on a given day.

For example, during 2014 tens of thousands of unaccompanied minors streamed across the Rio Grande in Texas,[23] but the agency was accused of being slow to redeploy needed personnel from other areas to respond to the huge wave of people arriving. In terms of drug interdiction, near our Mission Oaks Ranch, a forward operating base has sat empty for at least six years because the union overtime and travel rules have made it too expensive and cumbersome to staff. The facility has deteriorated and become unusable because it sat unoccupied for so long.

A former BP sector chief told me he believes a real challenge for management is that the union prides itself on "belligerence." I have to agree that the union's public commentary often is aggressive and personal in attacking the agency's leadership.[24] When I testified before a U.S. Senate committee in 2015, a Border Patrol agent who has a leadership position in the union asserted that agents were pressured to misstate the numbers of people crossing to make apprehension rates look better or face "retribution." These are strong charges, which require evidence to back them up. That doesn't make the claim wrong, and I've heard stories that suggest that during the Obama administration there were reporting policies that did have this effect. But even when the union has reasonable concerns, this kind of inflammatory language does not appear to be aimed at solving problems.

Corruption has to be one of the most critical issues for a force whose work has national security implications, but the union's public statements can be difficult to reconcile. For example, NBPC claims that "As long as the Border Patrol continues to place priority on the quantity of recruits rather than the quality of recruits,

121

corruption within the Border Patrol will continue to be a problem."[25] However, the union has given its full support to the Trump administration's proposal to increase BP's ranks dramatically: "Adding an additional 5,000 agents will be a logistical challenge, but will have a tremendous impact on border security," the union stated in a press release.[26] And yet at the same time the union opposed a recent effort to add additional internal affairs investigators.[27] I'm not arguing against the need for additional resources or manpower by any means, but we've staffed up the wrong way once, with the negative outcomes former assistant commissioner Tomscheck reported. The union could be more helpful if they provided specific recommendations to help resolve existing problems.

Unions can serve an important purpose, but given the imperatives of defending the U.S. homeland, their presence in DHS has always been an issue. The Bush administration initially tried to remove civil service designations and collective bargaining rights from all entities it moved into DHS. In support of that, Senator Phil Gramm of Texas famously said on the floor of the U.S. Senate in 2002: "Do we really want some work rule negotiated prior to 9/11 to prevent us from finding somebody who is carrying a bomb on a plane with your momma?"[28]

Walmart greeters?

Some reasons the atmosphere between many border community residents and Border Patrol has been strained for a decade or more originate far from the border. Though my argument for improved border security is intended to be bipartisan, we can't ignore the impact of past political decisions and messages.

After enjoying support and increased resources from the Bush administration, Border Patrol chiefs and agents blame the Obama administration for creating morale problems. They say it sent a mixed signal when the president signed executive orders such as the Deferred Action for Childhood Arrivals (DACA)[29] designed to protect "Dreamers" and in general deemphasized apprehending immigrants who have been in the country for long periods of time. Asks one former Border Patrol chief: "How can the president do something illegal? They say: 'The kids are dreamers. They deserve a life here.' Well, OK, but our job is to keep them out. They say 'You put them in jail mistakenly and we'll have your badge.'"

He continues: "The Border Patrol agents are trying to do their jobs, but we have to pull agents off certain areas because it's a political shitstorm. We have to say 'We love the enthusiasm, but stay off [specific highways]. There may be guns and money coming, but if you pull over a car driven by an illegal with an eighteen-year-old kid in it who came here at age two, all hell breaks loose.' By the time they got done broiling us in the press, we said it is not worth it. We'll just sit on the border and get the new ones." Other chiefs and agents have expressed similar frustrations to me.

More and more refugees from Central America cross the Rio Grande and immediately surrender: They claim persecution in their country of origin and request asylum. In 2015, the Department of Homeland Security reported that there were 61,000 pending asylum applications by year-end 2014,[30] and while 40,000 cases were completed during the year, by the end of 2015 there were 108,000 applications pending.[31]

This has impacted Border Patrol agents' daily activities in a way many resent. Applying for asylum complicates the nature of an apprehended person's interaction with Border Patrol.[32] BP turns the person over to U.S. Citizenship and Immigration Services (USCIS), which is obligated to ensure that they receive a "credible fear" interview in a timely fashion. Obviously, apprehended smugglers may also request asylum and try to blend into the refugee ranks. If captured, some will spin a fictional story designed to at least win the right to be released while they wait for the slow asylum process to grind on. Then, they can disappear.

It's no wonder BP struggles with these categories of UDAs. The issue is not just trying to sort out who is telling the truth; it's about the time and procedures that must be followed that agents believe distract them from a more important mission. As we drove along an area of thick vegetation near Anzalduas Park, agents explained to me that they will sometimes turn a corner and find a dozen or more women and young people just waiting to surrender and request asylum. As BP agents process the group, radio for vehicles, and wait for support, "Ten feet away, a cartel drug smuggler is hiding in the bushes waiting for us to drive off, then he gets away," complained one agent. In 2016, the vice president of the National Border Patrol Council told Fox News that federal policies about the processing of immigrants had reduced BP to "glorified Walmart greeters."[33] I have heard agents complain that they feel like babysitters.

Those resentments surface in different ways. Some agents and supervisors get frustrated. An Arizona sheriff's deputy told me after making a stop of an undocumented juvenile who was transporting drugs, he called Border Patrol to come get the suspect. He says he was told to seize the drugs and impound the vehicle, but as for the driver, Border Patrol said: "Take him to McDonald's and let him call a friend to pick him up."

These are the stories that make the rounds in a small community, and the upshot is the federal government—whose face is that young agent alone in his car driving along your ranch road—may be seen as unconcerned with the rule of law. Or, you may have the opposite sentiment from local residents who, again, blame that agent who patrols near their land for the excesses of others. In 2016, the *Arizona Daily Star* published a photo of a large sign some ranchers near St. David, Arizona, made and displayed on their property: BORDER PATROL: THE MEAN GREEN UNIONIZED KILLING MACHINE, it read. SHOOTING UNARMED CHILDREN ADVANCES THE MISSION? THESE KILLERS PROTECTED BY THEIR UNION.[34]

In Arizona, many ranchers are deeply cynical of the federal government's commitment to border security. For one thing, the 2010 murder of rancher Rob Krentz by an illegal smuggler crossing his property has left a deep and painful wound.[35]

The thirty-five-thousand-acre Krentz ranch is not far from Malpai, and in 2005, Rob Krentz told local television reporters in Arizona that undocumented immigrants crossing his land had done millions of dollars in damage, ranging from cutting water lines to ruining fences to creating weight loss in constantly agitated cattle.[36]

Two years later, in March 2010, Rob Krentz left his home and radioed his brother that he saw an illegal immigrant who appeared to need help. He was later found shot dead next to his dog, who also was shot dead. Officials think a drug smuggler he confronted on his own land shot him. Signs of the perpetrator led to the border, but he was never found.[37]

The Krentz case triggered an outcry in Arizona, where ranchers who felt they'd been ignored began talking to the press and politicians about how unsafe their communities had become. Rob Krentz's murder is the case that brought so much national attention and political controversy to Arizona when, that same year, the governor later signed SB 1070, giving state law enforcement expanded rights to check on individuals' immigration status and several other states followed suit.[38] The law's constitutionality eventually was only partially upheld by the U.S. Supreme Court.[39]

There have been other violent incidents, including a New Mexico ranch hand who was kidnapped by smugglers, and his truck was used to transport drugs to Arizona.[40] In 2017, a Border Patrol agent was kidnapped in New Mexico and later found by the side of the road with severe injuries.[41] Also in 2017, law enforcement in southern Arizona was tipped off that cartel operatives were actively looking to assassinate individuals who had acted as informants to U.S. law enforcement agencies about cartel activities.[42] There was at least one suspicious, execution-style murder near Douglas, Arizona, that may have been linked to this organized effort.

Those cases made headlines, but you'd be hard-pressed to find any ranch owner in our region of southern Arizona and New Mexico—or along the Rio Grande in Texas for that matter—who has not had some kind of experience with drug smugglers or had to develop habits and security measures designed to protect property and lives from criminal trespassers. Not long ago an equipment installer for a telecommunications company we had worked with on all of our properties was arrested for smuggling drugs for a cartel and eventually convicted and sentenced to five years in prison. This man knows the details of all of our properties and people who live on them, and he could identify all of our vehicles if the cartel wanted the information.

One day a rancher we know was driving on his property, and he had a tire blow out. He got out of the truck and said he swore and became angry when he realized somebody had put a spiked plank in the road. He did not realize some smugglers were nearby and observed this. A couple of days later, they left a brand-new tire at his farm with a note in Spanish explaining that the spikes were meant for Border Patrol.

Although he supports and cooperates with Border Patrol, this is another insight to the murky world of the border. The cartel wants to maintain a low profile; the rancher wants to make his living as his family has for decades without violence or trouble. Would you accept the tire? Would you report the incident to Border Patrol, knowing that the cartel knows precisely where you live and where your children go to school?

To be fair, Border Patrol understandably gets frustrated when communities expect them to provide a high level of security so that they feel safe, and yet some people within those communities constantly criticize agents for trespassing and being heavy-handed—or they don't report UDA activity to Border Patrol. More agents on the border will not necessarily solve all those issues. Unfortunately, it reminds me of that joke about the guy who goes to a restaurant and says he has two complaints: The food is terrible and the portions are too small. I believe Border Patrol chiefs recognize that mistakes have been made in the past and they understand why frustration runs high. But as one former chief in an Arizona sector told me, echoing Longmire's point about definitions, "Every single person you talk to—including BP agents, local law enforcement, and ranchers—defines [security] differently. A rancher will say he doesn't want anyone to ever cross his property. OK, well, that level of protection would cost a billion dollars. You can't have that."

Warner Glenn and Kelly Kimbro invest in developing good relationships with Border Patrol. Kelly frequently reaches out to new agents and helps them understand ranch etiquette, as do some other ranchers. And when she took the terrible fall in the mountain range, she credits Border Patrol for airlifting her out and possibly saving her life. It occurred miles from any road, and several agents hiked in to reach her. As the light was disappearing at dusk, they arranged for a helicopter from El Paso, Texas, to get her airlifted to a hospital. This is how communities are supposed to work.

After the election of Donald Trump as president, morale improved among the ranks of Border Patrol. The Border Patrol's union was an early and vocal backer of Trump, and one of his early executive orders was to increase funds for Border Patrol to hire more agents, among other resources. "On a scale of one to ten I'd say morale right now is an eleven," a Border Patrol chief told me in the spring of 2017 after Trump took office.

Our personnel challenges on the border are significant. We need to settle down the politics and inflammatory commentary and focus on real solutions. In part 3, we'll talk about changes in those areas that I think we have to consider. But in the next chapter, we'll talk about a tool that is essential to support border security, but cannot deliver it alone: fences, walls, and other barriers.

Chapter 9

BARRIERS

Used appropriately, barriers are an effective tool to support border security, but they are not *the* solution.

In late 2016, I stood on a remote spot of desert about thirty miles southeast of the town of Yuma, Arizona, on the southern edge of 1.9 million acres of federal land called the Barry M. Goldwater Complex. This vast pilot training range is a barren expanse of flat, fine sand and sagebrush and is the nation's second-largest military reservation. It's used to train military personnel day and night in bombing and field maneuvers.

I was facing Mexico. To my right, an anchor brace and heavy steel pole marked the beginning of a fifteen-foot-tall border fence that stretches west for about as far as the eye can see—more than thirty miles to the commercial POE in San Luis, which is surrounded by more elaborate double and triple fencing. The fence along the bombing range is not a solid wall, but it is constructed of heavy steel mesh and concrete-filled steel pipe supports. It is challenging but not impossible to climb, but almost impossible for a vehicle to knock over. Plus, the height of the supports is staggered to discourage would-be crossers from trying to build a ramp over it. Precise construction costs are difficult to obtain, but government sources suggest it was more than $3 million per mile (and closer to $5 million per mile in some areas).

To my left, a huge sand and jagged rock formation juts up out of the desert floor forty or fifty feet to a high point where a stone monument marks the dividing lines between the United States and Mexico.

And below me around my boots, on sandy ground on a moderate rocky slope where all those miles of sturdy fence end once the terrain changes, there were plenty of footprints and a few discarded water and soda bottles.

Yes, despite the many miles of that expensive fence, undocumented individuals just walk around it.

Some might consider that ironic. One person who doesn't is Sheriff Leon Wilmot of Yuma, who is standing near me and who brought me out here to show me this spot. He feels that in terms of return on investment, this barrier has been a huge success. Since construction began in 2007, it has eliminated the illegal vehicle traffic in this area. And the sheriff says it does not need to be replaced by a big, solid concrete wall.

The fact is, a wall would not stop those footprints. A solid wall also would have to stop at the large rock formation to my left, one of many small mountains extending for miles in that direction. This is a location, one of countless others along the U.S.–Mexico border's nearly two thousand miles, where the terrain and geography dictate that a barrier is a valuable tool in border security, but cannot alone deliver security.

I confess: I didn't want to write this chapter about whether we should build "a" or "the" wall to improve border security. It was frustrating to me to listen to Donald Trump's campaign rhetoric in 2016 about some "big beautiful" wall that Mexico would pay for. At first, I thought that talk was mostly symbolic and just meant to signal that he was focusing on improving border security, which I support.

But focusing on the wall became a way for Trump to insult Mexico, which is the opposite of what the United States needs to do if we are ever going to achieve border security. Talk about making Mexico pay for it was unproductive and ridiculous, and it set back years of progress between our countries. We will never secure the border without the support and cooperation of the Mexican government. Period.

Trump's rhetoric also made the challenge of border security seem simple, and one reason I'm writing this book is to debunk the idea that there is anything simple about it. The challenges around our border go back a long time, and they are complex. The stakes are enormous, and we must unwind some of the bureaucratic and command gaps undermining it today. But there are no simple fixes.

Constant references to the wall tend to swamp the national conversation about border security. And I want to lay out the specific reasons I and every person I know and respect who knows anything about border areas, regardless of their politics or views on immigration, do not believe a wall can solve our security challenge.

Variable terrain

Our foundation's two properties along the border in Arizona and in Texas have unique geographic features and thus unique challenges of security. I have invited many people involved in border issues and policy, from U.S. senators to U.S. Army generals, to visit and tour these ranches so they can better understand the situation on the ground. That's one reason why, in April 2017, I was invited to provide a written statement to the U.S. Senate Homeland Security and Government Affairs Committee, which was holding hearings about barriers and border security.

There already are about seven hundred miles of different types of barriers along the U.S.–Mexico border, some of which have been here for many years.[1] Mostly, they are not walls (high, solid barriers with no or limited visibility to the other side); these structures are different kinds of fences designed to discourage or slow down individuals crossing by foot or vehicle. On our land at CR near Naco, Arizona, there are eight different kinds of fences and barriers along the four and half miles that run parallel to the border. Some are fifteen feet high or taller and challenging to cross. Others are ten feet or less, and a motivated person could climb over them fairly easily. At Mission Oaks along the border there is four-strand barbed wire, mostly designed to contain cattle, and anti-vehicle barriers that do not impede crossing by foot (as Oscar proved).

Efforts to build extensive border barriers go back to the 1990s, a far different time. The first official border fence designed specifically to keep people out of our country was erected south of San Diego, near Tijuana.[2] By 2006, well after 9/11, Congress passed the Secure Fence Act, which was supposed to authorize reinforced fencing for not fewer than seven hundred miles of the border notably "in locations where fencing is deemed most practical and effective."[3]

That act prompted a lot of activity, but it often resulted in uneven and haphazard barriers. Border Patrol often grabbed whatever government surplus it could find to put up fencing, including simple sheets of corrugated metal. Some barriers were repurposed "landing mat" panels (literally panels of metal used in Vietnam that were designed to join together to make landing strips for helicopters and aircraft). Along the Rio Grande, proposed fencing created many issues for private landowners whose ranches went right up to the river's edge. Some barriers eventually constructed cut some ranchers' land in two. In other spots the federal government fortified existing flood levee walls to make them more difficult to climb and to funnel traffic to areas easier to patrol. There were protests and lawsuits.[4]

Walls that become dams

Barriers have an important role to play in border security, but the realities of terrain and geography, physics, national sovereignty, and common sense mean that barriers must be designed not only on the basis of what can keep people out, but also on what works within the context of a given landscape. And the variety of landscapes along the U.S.–Mexico border stretching from the Pacific Ocean in California to the Gulf of Mexico is incredible.

The challenges tend to fall into several categories: natural features such as mountain ranges, rock formations, washes, and canyons; a crossing point's access to transportation corridors like roads or hiking paths; hydrologic factors like seasonal flooding; and primarily on the Rio Grande, which separates Mexico and the United States, challenging river border ecosystems and riverbank shapes that create fingers of land and unusual access points.

Near cities like San Diego or Nogales today, thanks to Operation Gatekeeper, there are elaborate fence and wall systems, including double and triple fences, some with concertina wire and separated by several yards of empty ground. That makes sense in populated areas near a border where individuals can blend into a crowd of people both while waiting to cross and soon after crossing. However, as you get farther away from populated areas and POEs, these systems would be prohibitively expensive and difficult to engineer. In rural areas, barriers typically do not prevent crossing, but they deter climbing and expose individuals who are in the act of climbing, which buys patrol agents time to respond.

Barriers tend to be permanent and rigid, but border crossers, particularly drug smugglers, are flexible. They use different tools and techniques in each location and shift tactics in response to changes in Border Patrol deployments. In areas with solid fences, smugglers often keep ladders on the Mexican side of the border, and therefore after climbing over the top they just jump or climb down when going north; when they return south, they look for the lowest convenient fence area and either just climb it, or they may signal to a friend on the Mexican side to toss a rope over. If Border Patrol catches on to this and increases its presence, they move somewhere else.

A permanent and rigid wall, on the other hand, can become a big liability in terms of hydrologic events. A dam, in other words. Each year, Arizona experiences periodic, intense monsoon rains. Mission Oaks has creeks crisscrossing it that can explode into flash floods, and it sits at a lower elevation than the Huachucas, which focus runoff into the valley. CR is situated in a much drier, more rolling landscape, but it, too, has washes that can carry high-velocity flood-waters during monsoon season.

None of these seasonal water systems magically disperse when they hit the national boundary. The washes and riverbeds occurring on the land direct the flood waters with great force, and they require that any barrier have floodgates or grating systems. Without that en-gineering, a fence or barrier will be destroyed in a flood, or create a giant pond. The majority of our ranch fencing on Mission Oaks in ar-eas affected by water flow have special swing gates, allowing water to push them open. This keeps cattle in but it does not keep peo-ple out. It also requires constant maintenance, and if we fall behind or are unaware of debris collected against the fence, the fencing is damaged. At MOR we have had steel tube fencing set in concrete footings pulled out of the ground in a flood situation.

At CR, the existing border fence has large gate systems that the Border Patrol is expected to open during monsoon season. There, flood water flows from our side of the fence to Mexico, and also flows north onto our property from Mexico. These gates create openings that migrants and smugglers can use to try to cross the border, as these gates typically remain open from June through August.

Our foundation's ranch near Rio Grande City, Texas, is another example of where flood plains and water issues are at odds with a "wall" structure. For one thing, we are among a number of farmers who pump water for irrigation from the Rio Grande. All farmers who do that would be seriously affected by a barrier.

There is tactical complexity when you create a no-man's-land between a wall and the Rio Grande. The river side of the wall is still U.S. soil. How and where do you deploy Border Patrol? If you have agents remain on the non-river side of the wall, you essentially are surrendering U.S. territory. It could create a gathering area where smugglers and cartel operatives can move and hide among migrants and refugees who need only touch U.S. soil to request asylum. On the other hand, if agents operate on the river side of the wall in anything other than large numbers, they may risk being caught in a dangerous position if violence erupts and the wall is at their backs.

We must consider agent safety. Border Patrol agents on the ground tell me they do not like the idea of a solid wall barrier because it would obscure their view of what's coming at them. Whether it's a large group of economic or refugee migrants assembling to climb and make an entry attempt, or cartel operatives with weapons, realize that these patrol agents often are alone in vehicles in the middle of the night. It's just common sense that you don't want to create a giant bunker for an "enemy" of unknown size and with unknown firepower to hide behind.

The third important issue is that for high cost and dubious security value a high, solid wall would create serious, long-lasting damage to border landscapes and ecosystems. Warner Glenn explains: "People will get over a wall, but it will ruin the wildlife corridors."

Warner is known in conservation circles for his rare sighting of a jaguar in Arizona in 1996.[5] Jaguars were feared extinct in the United States, and it was believed the animal had migrated up from Mexico. Warner saw another one in 2006. Jaguars are not the only species that migrates through the region and whose resources and habitat would be negatively impacted by a wall. What's more, says Warner, just building the new roads it would take to bring in the equipment and materials to erect a structure would do serious environmental damage to the area. And it would invite more illegal vehicular traffic and habitat destruction. Warner showed me a road along his ranch, where a stretch of Normandy fencing and another of metal posts helps discourage vehicles but not most wildlife. He thinks that is adequate.

Relentless pressures

It's important to remember that we don't have invasion forces attacking us, we have the relentless, persistent pressures of small, nimble groups exploiting our vulnerabilities. Cartels don't have to worry about union rules or commit to multiyear appropriations cycles or manage big contractors. They hedge their bets so they can shift to alternate smuggling routes when one becomes compromised. They use lower-level personnel as scouts or guards who are completely expendable to them. As a law enforcement friend of mine in Arizona once put it, "The most flexible, cunning predator in the world is a criminal human being."

Case in point: In the small town of Naco not far from our foundation ranch, in 2015, Bisbee, Arizona, police, ICE investigators, and BP uncovered a sophisticated tunnel dug about fifteen feet underground that extended from under a nondescript shed-like building next to a trailer home.[6] After getting a tip, police pulled over a large box truck that had been parked in the lot where the tunnel existed. It contained two tons of marijuana worth $3 million. They obtained a search warrant for the property. They discovered the tunnel under a false floor that was activated by a hydraulic lift system. It continued nine hundred feet south under the border into Mexico. It featured underground wooden supports, air vents, and a lighting system.

Two more tunnels were discovered in 2017 in the Naco area, and dozens more along the length of the border;[7] I'm told Border Patrol believes many more exist. It's incredible to me that you could dig these elaborate and functional tunnels without being detected.

Build a wall, in other words, and the cartels will turn to a whole alphabet's worth of Plan Bs and Cs. In western Arizona, law enforcement is battling the use of T-shirt cannons, those handheld devices used at sporting events that send T-shirts soaring thirty or forty yards into the stands. Near crop fields or even empty lots in towns along the border, drug smugglers wait for the all clear from spotters, then stuff drugs in soup cans, wrap them in fabric, and shoot the drugs over a border barrier, and then contacts on the U.S. side run out and collect them.

As part of the environmental and wildlife surveys we conduct on our ranches, we collect twenty-four-hour video, and our database of smugglers crossing our property shows that they grow ever more sophisticated. They utilize camouflage clothing and slipper-like shoes with carpet fabric designed to obscure footprints. We have even seen military sniper-style ghillie suits, or heavy full-body camouflage created from strings and shreds of fabric imprinted with vegetation patterns.

In recent years, the cartels have begun putting a GPS tracking device in individual bales of marijuana—particularly when they have buried highly profitable drugs such as cocaine or heroin inside the bundle. The tracker offers two advantages to the cartels: It discourages a mule from trying to run away and steal a load of drugs, and it also serves as a back-up plan if the entire group is discovered. The mules can drop or hide the drugs, then take off running in another direction. If they are caught, they may say they're just migrants trying to cross the border for work or to join family. On one video, we have evidence of an armed cartel drug recovery unit driving quad runners across our property in broad daylight headed to pick up packs of drugs a group left behind after they were apprehended by Border Patrol. Another smuggling option that utilizes the trackers is flying ultralight aircraft over unpatrolled border areas (and any wall or fence); in a matter of a few minutes, the pilot can drop a drug load and return to Mexico. Recovery units on the U.S. side come find the drugs later.

Not long after we bought CR, we were informed that the federal government was going to build a communication and surveillance tower on one of our hilltops. They asserted the federal government's right to eminent domain; in other words, this was a notification, not a request to the previous owner. They built an elaborate concrete road and a tall tower equipped with cameras. We don't have access to the information from that technology. However, we know cartel scouts occasionally climb up the hill the tower is constructed on and sit directly beneath it and radio smugglers about which way the camera is pointed. The government spent millions building this tower, and the cartels found a simple way to circumvent technology using a kid with binoculars and a radio. (I believe, by the way, that these towers and this technology are vital to a comprehensive system—I just mention this to point out that the smugglers adjust to everything we do, and we have to be just as flexible to shut them down.)

Changing the game

In Yuma, border security stakeholders have figured out how to work together. Yuma County sits in the corner of southwestern Arizona and is bordered on the west by California and the south by 110.5 miles of international border with Mexico.[8] It has a population of about two hundred thousand people year-round, but just over the border are almost five times that many people in Mexicali,

Mexico. Yuma County has a significant variety of terrains, including sand desert, mountain ranges of up to four thousand feet, and the Colorado River, which supplies irrigation water to thousands of acres of prime farmland.

One of the qualities about Yuma's Sheriff Wilmot that always impresses me is that he keeps an open mind to the big picture and the need for a balanced approach and solid partnerships. He is quick to give his partners credit when he talks about success, and I have to say Yuma's experience in fortifying its border security over the last decade has been impressive.

In 2005, Yuma County was experiencing a huge wave of illegal immigration, with roughly 139,000 illegal entries logged by BP. Sheriff Wilmot said at the time BP admitted that they were only catching one out of three UDAs attempting to cross the border in Yuma Sector. There were significant spikes in serious crimes such as robberies, rapes, and homicides, and organized drug and human trafficking organizations were operating in his county.

By 2008, Yuma had reduced its border apprehensions by over 90 percent and has had years with fewer than six thousand apprehensions, although crossings of economic migrants and refugees have surged again and annual numbers are closer to fourteen thousand. As we've discussed, apprehensions are an incomplete measure, but Sheriff Wilmot says crime dropped significantly. Vehicle and equipment thefts all but disappeared. When apprehension numbers rose Sheriff Wilmot says that was connected to large groups of people, including a big contingent of Haitian refugees, for example, crossing into Arizona and immediately asking for asylum, rather than more criminally inclined individuals Yuma experienced streaming in the first part of the century.

How did Yuma achieve this success? It was no single factor, Sheriff Wilmot believes, but there was a concerted effort among law enforcement and federal agencies to listen to community concerns and address the very specific demands of the geography and land use of the area.

For example, prior to 2006, the area I have described along the federal bombing range had only the remnants of old barbed-wire fences, which were easily breached. Criminals drove over from Mexico with drugs and people in the vehicles. After dropping off drugs with contacts on the U.S. side, they would sometimes then also drop off thieves who would steal U.S. vehicles and drive them back over to Mexico. It is such a remote and wide-open area that large numbers of people on foot also came across as well, day and night.

All that traffic was not only facilitating drug and human smuggling; there was a unique issue: Reports of any traffic or activity on the bombing range meant the Department of Defense would have to suspend the training activities they conduct here, which sometimes involve personnel flown in from all over the world. "You had millions and millions of dollars' worth of aircraft and personnel here to train that had to stop what they were doing every time a group was detected on the range," says Sheriff Wilmot.

Since the barrier I visited was built vehicle traffic has stopped entirely here, and foot traffic is greatly reduced. That is an important win for border security in this area. It would be virtually impossible to make this area foot-traffic-proof with a barrier. The border literally cuts right through mountains all along the area. The only way for the existing fence to be continued on flat terrain would be if you angled the fence well away from the mountains inward from the border.

But Border Patrol did not give up on stopping foot traffic. There are sensors in the ground to pick up movement. The agents who patrol this area drag tires chained together to create a smooth surface so when UDAs do attempt to climb and jump down from the wall, or they climb the rock faces and then keep moving north into the U.S., the agents can track their footprints in the sand. It's low tech, but effective. More agents deployed near the rocky areas would mean faster response time and would likely reduce whatever traffic is crossing here now even more. That is one way to fight persistent pressure—with persistent presence.

We drove about thirty-five minutes from this spot on the bombing range but still within Yuma County, and there the geography and activity are completely different. Unlike the bombing range's dry, fine sand and absence of people or structures, this second area I visited follows along the course of the Colorado River, also a border with Mexico, and is a rich agricultural zone with acres of crops—lettuce, alfalfa, cotton, wheat, lemons, and dates. According to the Yuma Chamber of Commerce: "Yuma County is responsible for 90 percent of all leafy vegetables grown in the United States, November through March. So, while New Yorkers are bundling up to go get dinner, Yuma farmers are in the sun producing, harvesting and processing the lettuce that goes in their salads, on their burgers and in their tacos."[9]

Sandbag bridges

We drove along a road built on top of a levee in an area that had been a source of concern to Yuma. Especially in summer, the Colorado River flow is reduced and the river gets very low, almost dry, here. Mexican and Central American immigrants by the thousands were wading or walking across and some went into the nearby town of Gadsden. The sheriff said large numbers of UDAs were hiding in backyards, stealing items, and congregating at a local park. Also, thugs from the Mexican side would just toss sandbags into the low river area to create a bridge. Then they would cross into Yuma County and steal farm equipment, such as tractors and trucks, and drive them back across this sandbag bridge into Mexico. The problem got so bad that Sheriff Wilmot says local insurance companies stopped writing policies for farm equipment. Two Native American reservations in this area lease land to the farmers, and they were feeling the pressure both from the concern of farmers about the risk of working these land parcels and from criminal groups who were congregating on both sides and making river areas unsafe.

The community sat down and took on the problem together. Sheriff Wilmot says law enforcement, including local police, Border Patrol, and other federal agencies, like the Bureau of Reclamation, came up with solutions suited to this specific environment, whose natural features change almost acre by acre.

A solid wall along the river would not make sense. "A flood situation would take it out," the sheriff explains. But to address those equipment thefts, Yuma worked with the federal government and installed low but very sturdy anti-vehicle barriers along the path of the river. Those stop vehicles, but don't impede water at all. The Bureau of Reclamation helped security by clearing significant amounts of brush and nonnative vegetation along the riverbanks, which discouraged criminal groups from hiding along there and allowed the community to use the river for recreation again, as it had many years prior.

"It helped on the Mexican side as well, because some of these criminals were victimizing the people who lived over there as they crossed back and forth," Wilmot says. In fact, he says the Mexican authorities were a huge help to his deputies in tracking down the farm equipment thefts; in return, Yuma County sends resources over to help Mexico support local law enforcement, such as divers to retrieve victims of floods or drownings. "We've had a good relationship," he says.

Driving along the levee road, we pass several Border Patrol vehicles. At one spot, a high metal mesh fence begins—well inland of the actual border—and runs for several miles. This is a barrier designed to keep illegal border crossers from running into the neighborhoods in Gadsden. The fence funnels foot traffic to areas where Border Patrol is better able to see and apprehend people crossing.

A final element that Sheriff Wilmot thinks was critical for improving security in Yuma was a 2006 federal program called Operation Streamline, which pursued 100 percent prosecution of all crimes committed by illegal border crossers.[10] He was very frustrated during the Obama administration when he said the U.S. Attorney's Office in Yuma was declining to prosecute a lot of the backpack drug smugglers, although his complaints eventually meant another federal prosecutor was assigned to Yuma.

By emphasizing partnerships and cooperation between agencies, infrastructure barriers specifically designed for a given location, and prosecuting lawbreakers, Yuma has a significantly more secure border.

Cooperation is key

Sheriff Wilmot would be the first to tell you he does not consider Yuma's border security issues solved. Yuma experiences surges from specific groups seeking asylum or access to the U.S. through his county. He is constantly on alert for new threats from tunnels, T-shirt cannons, and even catapults some drug smugglers have rigged up that can fling bales of marijuana for a hundred yards or more. Recently, the cartels have begun using powerful drones to cross the border under the cover of darkness and drop high-value drug loads outfitted with GPS trackers. Operatives on the U.S. side wait for Border Patrol to leave an area, and then rush out and collect the drugs.

But Yuma has shown that while border security is a never-ending challenge, it's one best taken on by partnerships of stakeholders who know the border and the mile-by-mile conditions even better than those trying to cross the line.

Part II

COUNTRIES OF ORIGIN

Whether you are Republican or Democrat, living near the southwest border, in the Midwest, or in coastal New England, I hope I have made the case that we all need to take border security more seriously. And if we have the will to do that, we cannot focus only on our side of the border. There are global forces and human conditions in other countries impacting our security today. There are criminal organizations infiltrating the United States, but there also are people living in areas of intense poverty equivalent to conflict zones who are seeking safety and basic economic security. The instability in their countries is destabilizing our country. I know this in part because our foundation has invested $350 million in livelihood development and citizen security initiatives in Latin America over a period of almost two decades.

Just as there are myths about how we can become secure, there are myths about the real threats. I want you to see some of what I've seen and meet individuals I have interacted with in Mexico and Central America. If you are a teenage boy in a village in El Salvador or Honduras and you see your future as one of two places—"prison or the cemetery"—what will deter you from joining a gang and surviving however you can? If you are a mother who loves her children and finds them threatened by that same boy, you will take extreme risks to protect them. When we find new opportunities for people in these violence-ridden areas to live in peace, we will be more secure here at home.

Chapter 10

RED SHOES IN HONDURAS

Leaving one's home country is not a decision made lightly; often, it is prompted by extreme poverty and violence.

As we drove up, just for a moment I thought the young man in the red T-shirt was Oscar himself standing on the edge of the dirt road.

We'd driven just over two hours north of Tegucigalpa, Honduras, into a mountainous area. Signs of poverty were everywhere. We passed lean-to homes made from corrugated metal sheets and retaining walls built from stacked automobile tires sunk in mud. We saw livestock and dogs so skinny every rib was visible. In Arizona, Oscar had told me that his family was poor, and they did not have enough to eat. Looking around the town where he had been living, that was easy to believe.

I'd traveled a long way for this meeting. I knew there was only a fifty-fifty chance that Oscar would be there. In the weeks since I first met him on our ranch and spoke with him as he sat in detention, I became determined to see where Oscar had come from. I had many questions: Would his story check out? Was he really running from poverty and violence at home? Was he involved with a gang or cartel? Had his father really died trying to find him in Mexico?

Before he left Arizona, Oscar connected us to his Facebook page, and we looked at it in some detail. The posts mostly showed the life of a friendly, outgoing young man having fun with friends and showing off a haircut or a tattoo. But some of the posts were concerning. Was he just clowning in a video we found that he made in Mexico—or flashing gang signs? Was another video where he made reference to the Gulf cartel a clue to his real life, or was he putting on some kind of show?

There was another reason I wanted to see Oscar's home and meet his family. Like many Americans these days, I hear a wide variety of opinions in the media and from people I talk to about migrants and refugees. Many are based on stereotypes and, to be honest, ignorance. Some are expressed using extreme and offensive language.

I've already talked about my objections to those who advocate for open borders, or who attack local law enforcement for helping federal law enforcement. If some of these individuals personally were victimized by the crimes of people who should not be in the country, or lost a child to overdosing on drugs provided by the cartels, I expect that their views might change.

On the other side of the debate, however, another sentiment concerns me. Many people, even including law enforcement along the border, say they don't understand why so many people are coming to the United States. They don't believe that people fleeing Central America deserve asylum, and they suspect most of having criminal intentions. I've even heard people describe asylum seekers as individuals who "refuse to respect" our borders, as if attempting to reach American soil is an insult. As if they're just players in a vast conspiracy of con men and women who would be just fine at home if they put effort into working hard in their own countries.

Most Americans have no idea what true poverty is like in the developing world, or what it is like to be surrounded by violence and be unable to turn to local police. Our foundation has spent nearly two decades investing in efforts to help small farmers improve their crop yields and increase the level of their families' health and income. I've also visited over twenty refugee camps from Darfur to Yemen to Latvia. To leave everything you own, everything you love, everything you know in order to seek asylum is a radical, risky decision. I don't believe people do it for any other reason than survival. Finding out more about Oscar might help me tell a larger story—that most refugees, in fact, would not be "fine" at home if they just worked harder.

The bones of hunger

I mentioned our foundation's support of the Pima County Medical Examiner and the nonprofit Colibri Center for Human Rights. Colibri works to match remains found in remote areas with missing persons' reports from families who know their loved ones were making a border crossing attempt.[1] It's difficult and tedious work. It often involves interviews with families who are worried about coming forward. Colibri tries to collect and record every detail that could provide an identification, from a fragment of a clothing label on skeletal remains, or a rosary or lucky charm near a body, to photos and dental descriptions a family might provide.

We support Colibri's work for a number of reasons, including because it offers some unique and valuable perspectives on the people crossing our borders. The stories of what made people attempt these perilous crossings, what their assumptions were, and sometimes what they were promised by *coyotes* who left them behind are important. In some cases, the family members of migrants begged them not to go. In some cases, lonely teenagers who've been separated from a parent for years have attempted journeys for which they were not prepared, and they paid the ultimate price.

Anthropologist Dr. Robin Reineke, co-founder and executive director of Colibri, shared something with me not long ago that I think is an important insight to the background of people like Oscar. In analyzing the skeletons of migrants who perished crossing the harsh deserts of the southwest, forensic scientists have determined that about 65 percent of the individuals' bones indicate that the person likely experienced significant malnutrition from childhood.[2] This has nothing to do with the individual's weight or access to food as an adult, but rather evidence in their bones that shows the lasting impact of insufficient vitamins and minerals and protein in their diets at developmental stages. "The dead reveal how serious life is for those who are surviving," Dr. Reineke says.

This hit home with me. Oscar and many other immigrants over the years have said to me that they were motivated to come to the United States in large part because they didn't have enough to eat. Mothers like Elisa, the woman from Guatemala I discussed in chapter 5 who works in a Los Angeles sweatshop, have told me they've made a painful decision to leave young children behind so they could come to the United States and send money back to family members to better feed their children.

"Having enough to eat" and "putting food on the table" are abstract clichés to many Americans, another way of saying, "They don't have enough money to be able to buy what they want." I sometimes hear the comment "They have a cell phone, but they claim they don't have enough to eat."

This skepticism is off base. Hunger is not abstract in a poor country; a large number of people from Latin America and the Caribbean are persistently hungry and fundamentally malnourished. The United Nations estimates about 37 million people are affected by hunger in the region.[3] In my many visits, I have observed families living on the street and even within garbage dumps, searching and begging for food every day. Their suffering is clear.

But there also are families who may have land, a home, even a vehicle, and almost certainly a cell phone who run out of money for food on a routine basis (as there are in the United States, by the way). There are small farmers whose only source of food is what they grow. When there is a drought or a flood or an insect infestation, they may first turn to friends and neighbors in hopes that they will share, but eventually they must pack up and leave and try to find somewhere they can survive.

Unlike in the United States, where we think of buying the latest smartphone as a luxury purchase, wireless networks often are one of the few infrastructures that are reliable in developing countries. Cell phones have become essential. People don't have landlines, and some don't even have a home, but communication can be a matter of life and death. Buying prepaid phone minutes to connect to family and friends or an employer is a high priority. In Sonia Nazario's Pulitzer Prize–winning book *Enrique's Journey*, she vividly describes the Honduran teenager Enrique's weeks spent in a squatters' camp full of criminals and drug addicts in Nuevo Laredo, Mexico, across the river from Texas. He is so desperate to earn money to buy a phone card so he can call his mother in the United States and try to reunite with her that he eats only one meal a day at a church shelter and he spends night after night in a parking lot with a bucket and two rags, offering to wash cars for as little as a dollar.[4]

I've been to the three countries of the Northern Triangle many times, and hunger and malnutrition are widespread. In my last book, *40 Chances*, I wrote about María, an eleven-year-old girl from Totonicapán, Guatemala; I met her when she was hanging ears of corn from the ceiling of her home. Hanging corn protects it from rodents and keeps it from developing mold. But what looked like a lot of food is deceiving. Corn and beans are satisfying, but they represent a nutritionally incomplete diet. María was physically much smaller than a typical American eleven-year-old. At the time of my visit in 2007, one in sixteen children in the area died of malnutrition before they reached age five, and there were high rates of blindness. That's because they lacked micronutrients like iodine and iron and other vitamins from fruits and vegetables.[5]

On a trip to El Salvador in 2012, we flew above the coastal mountains, where farmers are so desperate for land to grow food they plant on steep hillsides and tie ropes around their waists and lower themselves down to tend to and harvest their crops. As was obvious from the chocolate milk–like, mushroom-shaped discoloration in the mouths of rivers where they emptied into the Pacific Ocean, this kind of farming erodes the soil. The muddy rivers were transporting it out to sea, and eventually those mountainsides will not produce food.

One of the most disturbing situations I have ever seen took place a few hours from where Oscar's family lives. A large landfill sits outside Tegucigalpa, and when I visited in 2005, dozens of children lived on the perimeter, some in small groups sleeping in cardboard boxes. They were completely on their own. I watched them pick over rotting garbage looking for scraps to eat. I had to stuff Kleenex up my nose because the smell of methane and other toxic fumes was so strong my eyes were burning and my throat hurt. And here were these little kids, glassy-eyed, competing for anything edible they could find.

There, I photographed a thirteen-year-old girl named Carla, who looked much younger but whose survival also depended in part on selling her body to truck drivers for a few dollars, I was told. She and her friends spent some of the money on food and some on glue to sniff to block out the misery of their surroundings.

You don't forget images like these.

At the time of those visits, I was focused on trying to figure out how to make meaningful grants in agriculture to improve food security in these regions. I was aware that predators walked among the poor—like the garbage truck drivers who exploited the starving children at the landfill. But I had a more limited understanding of the social threats to the poor from criminal gangs and corruption among law enforcement. Since my early visits two decades ago, those factors have become orders of magnitude worse in Honduras, Guatemala, and El Salvador.

I had a feeling Oscar had told the truth about his motivation to come to the United States from Honduras. To see if my instincts were right, I wanted to investigate his story.

The Death Train

One important element of Oscar's story was his reference to his father dying while riding freight trains. I figured some of my personal contacts in the railroad industry could help me check that out, and I made some calls.

Death is an ever-present threat for people who hop on and off freight trains. Many times I have photographed people riding these Mexican trains, sometimes called the Death Train or *la Bestia* (the Beast). I also have photographed individuals in respite centers who have lost a foot or leg when they fell getting on or off a moving train and the wheels sliced off their limb.

In 2016 I met Alejandro*, a young man from Honduras living in Tucson who tried three times to get to the U.S. border by train after fleeing the frequent beatings of his violent stepfather. He learned to bring a rope with him on the freight trains, and he would climb to the top so he could tie himself to a pipe or rail in case he fell asleep. It was a troubling image for me, because I had visited a respite center in southern Mexico, where I was told there had been a train accident and migrants who had tied themselves on were killed when the train derailed.

I met the *Enrique's Journey* author Nazario in Decatur in 2017. A brave journalist, she spent months traveling on the same trains her subject Enrique had used to travel north from Honduras. She had more protection than many migrants have: An official Mexican government unit called Grupo Beta, whose officers attempt to protect migrants and arrest human smugglers throughout Mexico, provided security to her in the most dangerous areas (Grupo Beta units are no longer armed, but at the time they were and at one point they fired their weapons in the air on the top of a train when a known gangster approached her). She also carried a letter from the former president of Mexico Vicente Fox that vouched for her project and urged officials not to arrest or detain her on this journey.

And yet Sonia still suffered assaults and close calls, such as when a tree branch nearly swept her off a train. She still has nightmares and post-traumatic stress from riding the train and seeing migrants fall and get pushed off. When you fall, she explained to me, "There is a sucking effect that pulls people under the wheels of the train."

I thought it might be difficult to confirm the death of Oscar's father. But we knew his name and roughly when he died. Not long after I reached out to my contacts, they sent back confirmation that in September 2016, a Honduran man with the same name as Oscar (the Oscar I met was Oscar Jr.) was killed on train tracks near Veracruz, Mexico. The evidence was both conclusive and graphic, including a bloody driver's license found on his body, his death certificate, a report that the local funeral home had turned his body over to the Honduran Consul General, and a photograph of two police officers at the scene of the accident standing over the body of a man lying on the tracks in a tangle of clothing. So far, Oscar's story was checking out.

When Oscar returned to Honduras after being deported by ICE, our foundation had arranged for one of our NGO partners to meet him in San Pedro Sula. The contact made sure he had some food and fresh clothes, and he helped Oscar get to his family's village north of Tegucigalpa. I was planning a trip to Central America for another project, and I reached out to the NGO contact. He said there was some tension in the family about Oscar's return, but he agreed to help me try to meet with Oscar and his family.

We communicated with Oscar through his brother, Jaime*, who had a phone. We had several weeks of stop-and-start exchanges. Oscar agreed to meet with us. But then the family lost track of him for a few weeks. We thought he may have made another run at going to the United States. Jaime said that he and his aunts and cousins were willing to speak with me even if Oscar wasn't available. Then, a few days before my visit, Oscar resurfaced.

As we pulled up to the family's home, the NGO staffer waiting for us looked disappointed. "Oscar did not show up, and his family does not know where he is," he said, as I got out of the vehicle. "But this is Jaime, and he's happy to speak with you."

I shook hands with the young man in the red T-shirt. The family resemblance to Oscar was obvious. He was a leaner, slightly taller version of Oscar, with a more serious expression and shorter hair. We made our way down a sloping, rocky path into the courtyard area between what functioned as a compound of several buildings. The walls were mud with dirt floors and metal roofs. A woman was tending a hot cooking fire in one small, open-air building. A teenage girl washed clothes in a sink with water gravity-fed from a pipe that drained out a hole in the bottom and ran down the hill. A few chickens pecked around the sloping dirt and rocks. The NGO team had brought a table and chairs, as the family didn't have a central place to gather.

One dreamer, one realist

Jaime, age eighteen, and three of Oscar's aunts on his father's side sat down with us. They were pleasant, but reserved. We'd heard that Oscar's situation had caused pain in his family and that the aunts blamed him for the death of his father, their brother.

We talked for about an hour. Jaime could not have been more polite or gracious. I appreciated that, because I realized how strange my visit must have seemed. Out of the blue, the same American who turned his brother in to U.S. Border Patrol, in many ways denying his dream, had come to visit him 1,900 miles south in Honduras.

Jaime told us Oscar had been talking about going to the United States since he was about fourteen. He and Oscar used to live with their grandmother in Tegucigalpa, he said, but it became dangerous for them because of gang activity and violence. That was where Oscar had encountered threats from gangs who wanted protection money and wanted the brothers to join the gang. Their grandmother sent them to the area where we were meeting to live with their father's sisters, who already were providing for many children on little income. At least there was no gang activity.

The gangs extort money from small business owners and sometimes farmers, but clearly there was not much money to be had around here. There is a lime quarry nearby, and some local people earn money loading powdered lime into sacks. It's a nasty job that is hard on the lungs. Jaime showed us heavy calluses on his hands; he works as a day laborer digging trenches and also loading timber and lumber on trucks at a sawmill. We asked about food. He and his aunts laughed at the question of whether they managed to have three meals a day. "Sure," said Jaime, with a slight hint of sarcasm. "And the same food at each meal." Beans, tortillas, and an occasional egg. It was clear they often missed meals.

As I kept returning to questions about Oscar, the aunts grew visibly uncomfortable. I got the impression that Jaime loves his brother and was relieved to have him home. Twice before, Oscar had attempted to go north to the United States. Both times, he'd been caught in Mexico and turned back. Jaime said he had started out with Oscar on the trip that landed Oscar on our ranch at Mission Oaks a few months prior, but after they crossed into Mexico they became separated and Jaime turned around. Oscar pressed on.

Jaime confirmed that his father had traveled north to Mexico last September to find Oscar, and that he had been killed on the tracks. The women both had tears in their eyes when we talked about Oscar and Jaime's father.

A picture of Oscar began to develop for me of a likable but impetuous young guy. Jaime projects a different personality—calm and steady. He seems to accept his role as a responsible male figure in this extended family. I give him credit for being direct, at one point asking me: "You keep asking about Oscar and wanting to help Oscar," he said. "What does Oscar have that I don't have? Why don't you want to help me?" I smiled. "Well, let's talk about that."

Jaime only completed sixth grade before he had to quit school and find work to help support the family. He said he would like to return to school, and he said there was a school nearby where they hold classes on the weekends so he can continue to work. I said I would see if we could help make that happen.

As I looked around, I could see that the family compound had electricity. Jaime explained that they buy water from the local village, although it is too salty to drink. They use that for washing clothes and bathing. Their drinking water they haul up a hill from a well.

They are poor but proud people. Two of his aunts pointed out their daughters. One is studying to be a nurse, getting excellent grades. Within a few weeks of our meeting, we worked through our

NGO contact to make sure that Jaime and one of his cousins, who also had stopped attending school, had the support to enroll again.

Gang sign?

By far the most dramatic moment of our visit came when I did something I had not even planned to do. Although I knew it might be upsetting and risky, I wanted to ask the family about Oscar's connections to gangs and drugs. I thought it was unlikely that Oscar was crossing the border near our ranch because he was a marijuana mule. But that did not rule out other drug-related jobs, including operating as a scout, or carrying smaller, lighter amounts of higher value drugs like heroin.

I asked Jaime straight-out, "Do you think Oscar was involved with the gangs or the cartels?" When our interpreter translated my question, I saw both aunts shake their heads. So did Jaime. "No," he said. "I think that the only time he got involved with gangs was before he left [Tegucigalpa] because he liked to smoke marijuana. He bought marijuana from them and then they wanted him to join. But he wasn't in the gang."

I believed Jaime. He didn't have to tell me anything about the marijuana, and if he was trying to be deceptive and whitewash Oscar's behavior, he probably would not have mentioned that. Instead, I think he just told the truth. Because of that, I went a step further: "What about the cartels? Do you think when he was in Mexico he became involved with the cartels and worked for them?"

"No," he said, frowning and shaking his head. "I do not think he did that."

"I have a video where he talks about the cartels," I said. On Facebook, our team had found a video of Oscar speaking into the camera. The sound wasn't always clear, but our interpreter had picked out a reference to Oscar saying the Gulf cartel had offered him money to work for them. Then he had made some elaborate gestures we thought might have to do with a gang sign.

I had my iPad with me. I told Jaime, "I don't know if you want to see this. It's difficult to interpret, but he possibly suggests that he is involved with the Gulf cartel." Using my iPad to show photos or videos to someone to help me explain something is second nature to me. But here at this small table under the trees, talking about Oscar, I suddenly realized this could go very badly. There had been a young man who lurked around the edges of our conversation, staring at us. The older daughters kept walking up to the road and talking with others who were gathering. If there were gang members around, there was no telling where this could lead. Or, if the video was the first evidence the family saw that Oscar had crossed the line who knew what it might mean for Oscar's relationship with them.

Jaime looked me in the eye: "I want to see the video."

I handed him the iPad. He hit the Play button and the volume was turned up. Oscar's voice came from the speaker, talking in Spanish. His aunt at the far end of the table became upset and more tears began to run down her cheek the minute she heard Oscar's voice. Jaime was laser-focused on the video, expressionless. *What have I done*, I thought?

Then all of a sudden Jaime looked up. He smiled. The relief on his face was obvious. "Now I see what he was saying," Jaime said, smiling bigger.

The interpreter leaned in as Jaime pointed to the video and explained what he meant in Spanish, which she translated for me. "Do you see what he did with his hand here," he said, showing her Oscar waving his pointer finger back and forth. "What he said here is that the Gulf cartel offered him seven thousand pesos to work for them operating a radio as a scout, but he says "No, no, no, I'm not going to do that. I have a family in Honduras I love, and I want to get back to them."

I later talked with the interpreter who came with us; she confirmed that Jaime's translation of the video was consistent with what she saw, and that he was shaking his finger to indicate "no" in her opinion, not flashing a gang sign.

We made plans to stay in touch, and Jaime showed me around the family's compound before I left. He took me into his small room made out of rough wood panels, which had only a bed and a small wooden dresser. I had brought along a photo of Oscar that day on our Mission Oaks Ranch. In the photo, Oscar was sitting on a low wall next to me, wrapped in a blanket, wearing sweat-soaked, dirty clothes and those bright red high-topped sneakers. His eyes are tightly closed, his mouth stretched as if he was in pain. I gave the photo printout to Jaime, who kept looking at it as we spoke, sometimes reaching down and tapping the image of his brother.

As Jaime showed me his room, I remarked on how clean and neat it was. Then I told him in a joking voice that the interpreter conveyed, "When Oscar's here, do you make him sleep on the floor, or does he get the bed because he is the big brother?"

He laughed and said, "We share the bed." Then he held up a finger. "Oh, I have something," he said. He went to the dresser in the corner and reached under it. He pulled out one of Oscar's bright red shoes. They'd taken quite a journey. "From the photo!" Jaime said, and he smiled bigger than he had since I'd arrived.

Chapter 11

STOLEN HARVESTS

Police pressure on gangs in Central American cities is pushing some to rural areas where they are terrorizing smallholder farmers.

It's amazing how a smile can burn itself into your memory. In 2012, I took a trip to El Salvador to meet with subsistence farmers. I'll never forget driving down a rural dirt road two hours outside of San Salvador and seeing a small group waiting for me in front of a farm. One woman had such a beaming smile I could see it from fifty yards away. When I got out of the car she rushed over to me and started talking so fast in Spanish our interpreter had to ask her to slow down. She was excited to show me her corn crop, which was mature and ready for picking. As an Illinois corn farmer, I knew we were going to be friends. I also couldn't wait to see that field.

Her name was Carmen*, and she and her husband, Tomas*, had benefited from a global agricultural development program our foundation had invested $25 million in helping the World Food Programme (WFP) launch in 2007. El Salvador was one of the countries where it was rolled out, and it had made a huge difference in Carmen and Tomas's lives. Carmen's family had lived and farmed in the region for generations, but the output of the farm had not been keeping up with the growth of their family, and they were barely producing enough to eat.

But thanks to techniques Carmen learned that both improve yields and conserve soil, they now were producing plenty for their family and also surplus to sell. That helped them send their three children to school. What's more, she had had such excellent results—doubling her yields of corn, for example—she had become a leader in the local farming community and she taught others some of these techniques. It was great to see someone benefit from a program I hoped would help thousands of farmers, not just in El Salvador but in other Central American countries as well.

Food is power

You don't have to spend much time in the developing world to realize that food is power. There are many consequences of food insecurity beyond the daily, physical pain and long-term health consequences of hunger and malnutrition. When subsistence farmers cannot grow enough food to support their families, they sometimes migrate to cities where they have trouble finding work, and their situations may become even more desperate. There, they may become the victims of criminals who also are hungry. Or, their children, who see no future for themselves on the farm, may be lured to join extremist and criminal groups as much or more for survival as for their ideologies or criminal activities. The cities suffer as well, becoming overpopulated and incapable of meeting the water and sanitation needs of everyone. Slums can develop from this food insecurity and migration dynamic.

This is a lesson I've learned all over the world, particularly in Africa and parts of Central America. It's one reason our foundation has invested in supporting smallholder farmers—to improve food production in general and to build stronger rural communities by helping farmers support themselves and stay on their land. The link between food insecurity in developing countries and U.S. national security is complex, but it is real. Every country has unique issues, but my friend Carmen's experiences in El Salvador offer some particularly important insights.

More than a decade ago, I became aware of the widespread food insecurity in El Salvador, and since then I have visited the country many times. I love its people. Salvadorans are friendly, hardworking, and resilient. They need to be resilient because their country has experienced extreme challenges for many decades.

Roughly the size of the state of Massachusetts, El Salvador is the smallest and most densely populated country in Central America. Its location on the Pacific coast makes it vulnerable to earthquakes and extreme weather events. Hurricane Mitch in 1998 left 240 people dead and 59,000 homeless, and it killed ten thousand cattle.[1] It also wiped out major portions of bean, corn, and sugar cane crops, which exacerbated widespread food insecurity. Many storms since then have wreaked similar havoc on homes, roads, livestock, and crops. The percentage of Salvadorans living in poverty in 2015 was estimated at 34.9 percent.[2]

Backfire

El Salvador also experienced a civil war from 1979 to 1992 characterized by massive population displacement, death squad assassinations, and widespread poverty. More than seventy-five thousand people died.[3] The politics of the conflict were complicated, but one result of the war was that hundreds of thousands of Salvadorans fled to the United States, many to the Los Angeles area, during the 1980s. In LA, the newly arrived Salvadorans were targets for existing gangs, and so they formed their own gangs. The most powerful were Mara Salvatrucha, commonly called MS-13 (according to some accounts the "13" stands for thirteen seconds of beatings members need to experience to join) and 18th Street or Barrio 18. These two gangs, made up of large numbers of children of refugees, fought not only the existing LA street gangs but also each other. The gang presence spread to other U.S. cities where large numbers of Salvadorans had settled, including New York and communities around Washington, DC.[4]

As gang violence increased in Los Angeles and other cities, in the 1990s large numbers of young gang members originally from El Salvador and other countries who committed crimes were deported back to Central America. In El Salvador, that huge influx of criminals came at a time when the Salvadoran government was still trying to sort out how to integrate former armed combatants into its postwar society. The deported MS-13 and 18th Street gang members arrived and saw an opportunity to reconstitute themselves in San Salvador and other cities. The deportations were designed to ease gang violence in the United States—but led to a steady escalation of violence in El Salvador. And as the *Los Angeles Times* put it, the plan "backfired" on the United States: Some gang members made their way back to the United States again, setting up a revolving door of criminals growing more organized and lethal in both countries.[5] Also, as violence escalated in El Salvador it triggered more refugees from that violence arriving at U.S. borders.

Salvadoran gangs specialize in murder, extortion, and robbery. They divide and fight over turf like old-school mafia families, and they punish enemies and bribe and threaten police. By 2015, with more than 100 murders annually per 100,000 citizens, El Salvador was one of the most dangerous countries in the world that was not technically at war. The rate has since dropped back to about 81 murders/100,000 people, but compare that to about 4.5/100,000 in the United States.[6]

Early in our foundation's history, we approached food security like many other NGOs did, project by project. Particularly in a crisis situation where floods or a drought or conflict has diminished food resources, we provided support to organizations delivering relief materials like emergency food or bags of seed or fertilizer.

But over time I realized that one-off agricultural projects and aid shipments were isolated relief measures, but they don't help communities achieve food security. They don't change the underlying dynamics, which usually were strained before the emergency developed. Sometimes aid even makes a situation worse, as criminals find a way to profit from it.

Over time, I gravitated to the idea of supporting investments in changing the underlying conditions for farmers, including teaching better soil and water management techniques. Those can improve farmers' resilience to extreme weather and improve their crop yields. I also encouraged our partners in El Salvador and in other developing countries to build some level of business training, such as how to work together in co-ops to buy equipment and negotiate better prices for crops. It's also important to help farmers connect to markets. WFP purchased some of Carmen's excess production directly, and the program helped her sell beans to the Salvadoran Ministry of Education for its school feeding program.

When I visited Carmen and Tomas in their fields in 2012, they had good reason to be proud. I borrowed a shovel and dug up a corn plant and picked through the roots, which were dense and held the soil well. Then I stripped the husk off an ear of corn from the stalk and I broke the ear in half. The kernels were good-sized and the ear had eighteen rows—just like on my farms in Illinois. There was no sign of insect damage. I complimented Carmen on her good work.

Strained expressions

Four years later, in 2016, I saw Carmen again when I visited El Salvador and WFP brought a number of farmers, including Carmen and Tomas, to a meeting in San Salvador. When I saw her, she smiled, but it was not that beaming, happy smile I remembered. She and Tomas looked stressed and tired.

Since I had last had an update from WFP El Salvador had faced a number of challenges, including a multiyear drought that had depressed productivity on farms throughout the country. Some of the farming organizations had taken on too much debt, and WFP had other management challenges as the program expanded.

I was not surprised. Scaling up a project in a developing country is rarely a smooth process, and the weather is always a wildcard. But one item on the brief I received before the meeting stood out: "Violence heavily disrupted operations in the last year. One (farmer co-op) was forced to close due to extortion threats made by gang members to executive board members." WFP was also forced to suspend support to a group of farmers due to gang threats, and a farmer had been killed after not complying with a gang order that he stop all agricultural activity.

Gangs threatening, even killing, rural farmers? I knew El Salvador's cities had some of the most brutal gang violence in the world, but I had thought the violence was confined to urban areas. In El Salvador, gangs are notorious for extorting money from businesses large and small, ranging from tiny roadside stands selling tortillas to grocery stores to gas stations. These businesses handle cash and face constant pressure from gangs who demand a weekly or monthly payment called *renta* and threaten to beat or kill those who refuse to pay. I was familiar with this activity in part because we have supported some gang prevention initiatives in El Salvador. But farmers mostly ate what they grew and were not generating a lot of extra cash.

Pushed from the cities

In the four years since we had visited Carmen, the police pressure on gangs in the cities intensified so much that some gang members decided to move out into rural areas to extort what little resources smallholder farmers had. And one problem was that after the WFP project taught farmers like Carmen how to take out loans to invest in equipment, seeds, and fertilizers to be more productive, gang members wanted a share of the resources.

After the meeting, we stayed to talk with Carmen, Tomas, and the other farmers. No wonder their expressions were strained. All the farmers had had the experience of gang members showing up at harvest and demanding "jobs." That meant that the gang members told the farmers what they expected to be paid when the harvest was completed, and they would come by the field and hang around and keep tabs on progress. One farmer told us that after he and several members of his co-op delivered their corn harvest and placed it in a shared grain bin, the gangs emptied it one night. Grain that would have been the basic food and income for several families for months was gone.

Carmen and her husband had been targeted and terrorized. She said she got a call one day from a man her co-op had hired as a security guard. He said a gang member had just dropped off a cell phone that he had been instructed to give Carmen. If the guard did not deliver the phone to her, he said, the gang member warned the guard he would be killed. If Carmen did not answer that phone, he continued, she would be killed. When the call finally came, the gang member said he knew the co-op must be receiving money from somewhere, and they wanted a share of it. He mentioned the name of all the farmers and their children, to drive home that there would be violence if the co-op did not cooperate.

Not long after that, Carmen, who had been the leader of the

169

co-op, closed it down. But that didn't stop the harassment. She and her husband own an additional plot of farmland some distance from the land where their home is located. She and her neighbors began to travel together to those fields in groups, jammed into an old Suzuki car, because the gang set up roadblocks. They had to pass through one area controlled by MS-13, and another by the rival 18th Street gang. Gang members on each trip would demand anywhere from $1 to $5 for the car to keep driving. That was a lot of money for these struggling farmers to surrender.

Telltale haircuts

Of all the stories Carmen told us, some of the most memorable for me involved her son Antonio*, who was thirteen at the time. As the gangs spread to rural areas, they were repeating the patterns in cities where they would target boys and give them sodas and other small gifts to entice them to join gangs. And if that didn't work, they would threaten to kill them. The gangs are territorial and react with hair-trigger violence to any perceived aggression or slight by rival gang members.

Small acts could get a child injured or killed. Carmen said local children are taught not to use the numbers 13 or 18 in casual conversation for fear that a rival gang member will hear it. Carmen and Tomas told Antonio to say he was fourteen, not thirteen, if someone asked his age. They made sure an adult walked him to and home from school every day. "Our children cannot go to any park whatsoever and we don't allow them to talk to anyone," said Tomas. "Before two years ago it was voluntary recruitment. Now, it is compulsory or they kill you."

Carmen said Tomas purchased an electric hair clipper to cut Antonio's hair at home. Gang members preferred certain hairstyles, and they extorted money from barbers. Tomas feared a local barber might

170

cut Antonio's hair to mark the boy as having an association with one gang—and that could get him attacked or killed by the other.

This meeting was very discouraging, and I wanted to follow up on how MS-13 and 18th Street had moved into rural areas. Less than a year later, on the same trip where we visited Oscar's family, we again went to El Salvador and to Carmen's farm. She was as gracious and warm as I remembered, and she and Tomas invited us inside their home. Her three children joined us around the family's dinner table, and she cooked a special chicken soup that filled the house with wonderful smells. Regardless of the dangers around them, her kids are bright and engaging, and she has good reason to be proud of them.

They had been impacted by the drought, although the farm was still producing. But Carmen's eyes filled with tears as she spoke of the violence and threats. It was another example that food is power—and criminals will take your power away. Only four years since we had had such a pleasant meeting, it turned out providing resources to help poor, hungry farmers grow more food had in some ways backfired.

I wish I could say this is the first time something like this has happened. These are the stakes of development; you take one step forward and three steps back. You go beyond naïve ideas that showing up with bags of seed or fertilizer can make a meaningful difference and you try to support a comprehensive, long-term initiative. But when individuals who also are competing to survive don't perceive that resources benefit them, they still find a way to take what they want.

They'd prefer to stay

As we sat at her kitchen table, another thing Carmen said was that everyone in her village who could leave and try to go to the United

States was doing so, especially families with young men who'd been targeted by gangs. These were not greedy, selfish, scheming criminals looking to exploit American generosity. These were families who had farmed these regions for generations. They did not want to leave. But after surviving years of poverty and civil war and various environmental challenges, the arrival of gangs had finally broken their backs. The process of trying to apply for legal visas or refugee status was something well beyond their abilities or resources, and it could take years. The violence in their community was now a daily, unrelenting, unpredictable threat.

For the safety of their children, Carmen and her husband had considered leaving as well. But they do not want to break the law and they feel the journey is too dangerous. They are a close, devoted family and they have an extended family in the area. Carmen said either they will all go when they all have a chance of doing so legally and safely (which is no time soon), or they will stay together in their village and get up every day and work to keep their children safe.

Time after time, when I have spoken to both poor farmers in rural communities in the developing world and people who are on the run and have left their homes in search of safety and a better life, they tell me they love their country and wish they could stay. In the case of Central America, some poor farmers first migrate to cities in hopes that they can make enough money to someday go back to their farms. These days, many of them find that to be impossible, and so they take the next step and head north. Others go straight from their farms to try to escape violence and make a new life in the United States.

To me, Carmen and her family represent the polar opposite of the idea that migrants fleeing violence and poverty have no respect for the borders and laws of the United States. Carmen, Tomas, and their neighbors are weighing decisions that could mean life or death for their children. Many Salvadorans also have existing ties in the United States—there are an estimated 2 million Salvadorans living in the United States compared to a home population of 6.2 million.[7] I believe it is because of their great admiration for the United States that they see our country as a safe haven and freedom in these dark times in their homelands. This is where our challenges collide: How do we maintain rule of law without discarding our compassion for those seeking help?

It will take a more coordinated approach to using our foreign aid resources, private philanthropy, and NGOs. We must work with the governments of the Northern Triangle countries not only to foster the rule of law but also to value and support livelihood development that provides people in both cities and rural areas viable options and a reason to stay and invest in the future of their own countries.

Chapter 12

TWO-LEGGED PREDATORS

Violence in the Northern Triangle countries today is extreme, but for those who feel threatened and decide they must leave, options are limited.

After a struggle Juanita Morales*, age twenty-two, finally won the tug-of-war and had her three-year-old son Carlitos* back in her arms. She staggered backward in the shallows of the Rio Grande, retreating to the Mexican bank near Reynosa. A man piloting a rubber raft already overcrowded with migrants had just tried to pull Carlitos from her and jam the boy onto the raft.

Carlitos could not swim, and Juanita knew he would drown in the fast-moving current if he fell in the water. She said the man operating the raft, who she was sure was high on drugs, was furious. He yelled that he was going to leave them both to be eaten by wolves. Wet, shivering, terrified, and gripping Carlitos, Juanita watched the boat head for the U.S. side of the border. "I could hear howling," she says.

I suspect the howling was probably either coyotes or dogs. But regardless which four-legged carnivores were nearby, it seems fair to say Juanita had been surrounded by dangerous two-legged predators for some time.

In the summer of 2015, Juanita promised a *coyote* $6,000 to take her and Carlitos through Guatemala, then Mexico, and then to the United States, where she hoped to reunite with Carlitos's father, Pedro*, on the East Coast.

As she sat on the riverbank, Juanita had few options left. The original *coyote* guide who had steered them past cartel operatives demanding bribes in Mexico was long gone. He had turned her group over to the boat operators. She says she prayed, and an hour later she was convinced God listened and "touched their hearts." The raft returned and the man told her to get in with Carlitos so they both could cross after all.

Once they were ashore on the U.S. side, the boat paddler directed her to follow a road into a town, where he said they could find a phone to call their families. Juanita began walking, but the first vehicle she and Carlitos encountered belonged to Border Patrol, and she was promptly taken into custody and sent to an ICE detention facility near McAllen, Texas.

Juanita was fingerprinted, and ICE interviewed her and initiated removal proceedings. But ICE facilities were overcrowded, and since she had a small child, ICE put an ankle monitoring bracelet on Juanita and authorized her travel to stay temporarily with her sister, a legal U.S. resident, in the Washington, DC, area. She was given a "notice to appear" at a court hearing near her sister's home. She called Pedro, who wired her $420 for a bus ticket to Virginia, and an ICE transport vehicle dropped her off at the McAllen bus station. But it turned out Juanita had not entirely run out of miracles, thanks to a humble, compassionate nun named Sister Norma Pimentel, who is the executive director of Catholic Charities of the Rio Grande Valley.

Returning their dignity

In 2014, an unprecedented surge of unaccompanied minors and families with young children flooded into south Texas along the Rio Grande. Sister Norma had always maintained good relationships with Border Patrol, and when she visited the migrants at the Rio Grande Valley Sector Station, she could see that "These people were in poor condition. They were dirty, the children were dehydrated, sometimes sick."

Sister Norma asked the pastor of Sacred Heart Catholic Church in McAllen if she could temporarily use the parish hall as a respite center. He agreed, and she recruited volunteers to help her collect the migrants and young children at the bus station and bring them to Sacred Heart to clean up and rest for the next phase of their journey. "This is humanitarian care. We let them take a shower, get clean clothes, have a warm meal, see a doctor. We are trying to give back to them a sense of dignity."

"Temporary" turned into months and now years. I met Juanita in 2015 at Sacred Heart, about forty-eight hours after she was apprehended by BP. She was part of a large group of migrants who arrived at the parish hall when I was there to visit Sister Norma. The tradition at the center is for volunteers to welcome the migrants who arrive from the bus station with smiles and applause. At first they look bewildered, but "You see them transform back into human beings," says Sister Norma. The center collects donations of clothing, diapers, baby formula, food for the migrants' bus journeys, basic medicines. There is a tent outside with cots for those who may have a few hours to rest before they have to be back at the bus station.

The McAllen community has embraced this effort, Sister Norma says, and during the crisis people also traveled from all over the country to lend a hand. But from the beginning Sacred Heart made clear that the center is for temporary respite, not a permanent home. Sister Norma insists the staff and volunteers focus on humanitarian needs, not politics.

When I met Juanita at Sacred Heart, she had just put Carlitos down for a nap. We sat at a table in a small room in the back of the center. She looked tired, but she was gracious in answering my questions about what had made a twenty-two-year-old woman follow such a risky and dangerous path with a three-year-old child in her arms. This is a question I have asked many times over the years. I always remember a woman in a train yard in Mexico who also had a young child with her, but explained to me: "The risk is less than doing nothing." According to Juanita, her immediate motivation was not money, not a job, not a "promise of a better life." It was staying alive.

She explained that she and Carlitos's father, Pedro, had attracted the attention of MS-13, which controls her hometown in El Salvador. Pedro is from a nearby *colonia* (or community), which is controlled by the rival 18th Street gang. When Pedro started dating Juanita in 2011, MS-13 tried to recruit him. When he refused, they accused him of being a spy for 18th Street. Meanwhile, 18th Street also tried to recruit him and he refused, attracting more threats. By 2014, MS-13 members would come to Juanita's home several times a week when Pedro was there, threatening them, and demanding the family turn him over. He decided leaving the area was his only way to stay alive, and so he headed north.

MS-13 kills every day

The plan was for Pedro to go the United States and then work and save money, in hopes that he could pay for Juanita and Carlitos to follow. But soon after Pedro left, gang members told Juanita they knew Pedro must be sending her money. They threatened to kill her if she didn't hand over *renta*. The final straw came in June 2015 when she was walking home from a park with Carlitos and a masked man jumped her from behind, grabbed Carlitos, and put a gun to the three-year-old's temple and a knife to Juanita's back. He threatened to kill both of them unless she promised to pay him two hundred dollars. "The man said he was going to kill Carlitos in front of me and then kill me because I had not paid *renta*," she says. "I grabbed Carlitos and started running. The masked man followed us. There was a police car on the same street, so, luckily, the masked man turned around and ran away. I didn't go to the police, and the police did not see what happened."

She called Pedro in Virginia and they made a plan for her and Carlitos to leave the next morning. Pedro borrowed and wired money that she combined with money from her mother. "In my hometown, MS-13 kills people every day. I believe that if I return to El Salvador, Carlitos and I will be killed by the gang members who threatened us before and who are threatening my mother now," Juanita told me.

It's hard to hide in El Salvador. The country is very small, and smartphones make it seem even smaller. Gangs text photos of people they are targeting to contacts in cities where people may flee. "Going anywhere in El Salvador is not an option for me," says Juanita. "No matter where you go in El Salvador, gangs threaten and kill young women who are on their own."

During our visit in McAllen, Juanita had her paperwork for ICE in her hands. The documents have their case numbers and instructions to appear in court, and the staff at Sacred Heart tries to help migrants understand what they must do next. The help is pretty basic. Sometimes the staff gives migrants a simple sign to carry: "Please help me, I cannot speak English."

When I heard Juanita was headed for Virginia, where Pedro was living and working, I realized we might be able to get her some help. A number of years ago I served on the board of Kids in Need of Defense (KIND), which is a Washington, DC–based organization that coordinates free legal support to immigrant children who arrive in the United States alone.

I reached out to KIND's president, Wendy Young. KIND does not typically represent families because the need for help for unaccompanied minors is so large. But Wendy agreed to help Juanita find representation, and I passed along to Wendy the numbers Juanita provided ICE as her contact numbers. Wendy explained something we've already discussed—that first-time immigration violators detained by ICE normally are charged with a civil, not a criminal, offense, and therefore they have no right to counsel. The result is crowded, chaotic, complicated court procedures that can leave detainees, many of whom have minimal education to begin with, bewildered. Says Wendy, "It's like traffic court, but with life-and-death consequences."

Juanita had not asked for asylum when she was apprehended, but she was still eligible for what is called "defensive asylum," which is a defense against removal after one has been caught entering the country illegally and is in active removal proceedings.[1] The other form of asylum request is "affirmative" asylum, which is what a person asks for upon reaching U.S. soil. I remember watching spy movies when I was growing up where the myth was that if someone could just get inside a U.S. embassy anywhere in the world, they could request asylum and be protected. In reality, almost no one without legal representation is granted asylum.

When she finally arrived in Virginia, Juanita reunited with Pedro. Juanita began doing weekly check-ins with ICE, and she connected with a lawyer KIND found for her; after four months ICE removed her ankle bracelet. She finally got a hearing before an immigration judge on April 4, 2016, when her lawyers filed a petition for defensive asylum. She waited for many hours and then appeared before the judge for just five minutes, and he set a February 17, 2017, court date for a hearing on the merits of her case. In this world, that is fast. Some petitioners can wait two to three years for a court date.

Just under a year from her arrest in McAllen, our team visited Juanita and her pro bono attorneys at an elite law firm in Washington, DC. Juanita's transformation into a calm, upbeat mother was dramatic, and we gained more insight on the complexities and risks of these cases.

Targeted

Historically, asylum developed to shelter people who were fleeing well-defined state actors—governments persecuting citizens. In Central America today, most of the people I would call refugees have been targeted by criminal organizations.[2] Juanita's attorneys explained to us that they planned to use the argument that Juanita has been targeted due to her membership in a "protected class" or a group characterized by a common religion, sexual preference, or other identifier an individual cannot escape and that marks a person for persecution. Because she is a member of a family that has been targeted by gangs in her homeland, her attorney plans to argue that Juanita will be in grave danger if she returns home. A few years ago, this defense would be a stretch; today it is reality.

As Pedro sat bouncing his young son on his lap, he calmly answered Juanita's lawyer's questions about his own experiences over the past year. To call them dramatic is an understatement. For starters, when he had to leave quickly in fear for his life, the *coyote* charged him $6,000 but he only had $2,000, so he gave the *coyote* the deed to his brother's house and promised to pay off the $4,000 in a year. On his first try, Pedro was arrested in Mexico, shortly after he crossed over the border with Guatemala. He spent five days in a

180

jail and was sent back to El Salvador, where he said he waited in a motel for a month before trying again.

On the second attempt he crossed the U.S. border in Texas with a group of about two dozen people. They crossed the river at night, but within five minutes of climbing the bank, ICE arrived, and the group scattered. Pedro was with several men who hid and were not caught. But when they accepted what they thought was friendly help by a man in Texas, he turned them over to armed kidnappers who began calling Juanita and threatening to kill him if she did not send money. Eventually, they let him go when his brother managed to send some money, and he traveled to Virginia.

Never identify the *coyote*

Juanita offered more details from her journey from El Salvador. She said it took about ten days by bus and car for Juanita and Carlitos to make it just south of the U.S. border on the Rio Grande near Reynosa. She traveled with a large group, and twice they were stopped and asked for bribes by the Mexican police. Both times, she says cartel members known to the *coyotes* brought the bribe money. The group was told never to identify the *coyote*, who posed as one of them when they were stopped. They eventually went to a staging house and waited there. They could see Border Patrol on the far banks of the Rio Grande, so they were delayed there for more than a day before Juanita and Carlitos finally crossed the river.

Juanita's immediate motivation was to flee the gangs, but she admits she dreamed of coming to the United States her entire life. She grew up in intense poverty, the youngest of ten children. Two died, but the rest all live in the United States now. The older members of her family had lived through the civil war in El Salvador and often scrimped to try to send her brothers and sisters north, one at a time, even selling land. She was often hungry as a child.

Juanita has only a seventh-grade education and understandably seems naïve at times. She says she grew up thinking the United States was some kind of paradise where if you worked hard you could have a good life and where "people never get sick. Everybody has a perfect life."

Pedro, on the other hand, says he would have happily stayed in El Salvador if he hadn't been targeted by gangs. The problem is there are so few jobs. "People in El Salvador say one thing about the U.S.—you can make a lot of money. But they don't talk about expenses. Here I'm working but there are times we can't pay for everything. I've been walking everywhere; I finally have a car I'm paying for in installments. I never had a car in El Salvador; it wouldn't have been a possibility. I could make five dollars a day and it doesn't even buy the food you need." Today, Pedro can never imagine going back.

Daunting odds

Juanita's attorney admits he usually spends his days on white-collar criminal cases. This case has involved unusual efforts such as trying to figure out how to get statements supporting the threats from Juanita's mother and a friend back home. Her mother, she says, has been threatened by the gangs since Juanita left. Juanita has a friend she talks to occasionally who would be a good witness but who is terrified to say anything; after Juanita left, she says her friend told her she made up a story for the gangs that they had had a big fight and never talk anymore.

"The odds are pretty daunting," continued the attorney, who did not want his name used for fear of complicating Juanita's next court appearance. "There has been a massive wave of thousands of people and the case law is all over the place. Courts are overwhelmed." Wendy Young points out that even the treatment between jurisdictions is dramatically different; in Atlanta, for example, only 1 percent of asylum petitions are being granted, while in San Francisco, the rate is 80 percent. "The courts operate very independently," she says.

There is another risk in Juanita's case: The attorney represents Juanita and by extension Carlitos, but not Pedro. The more details about Pedro and his experiences and threats from the gangs her lawyer can offer the court, the stronger her case for asylum will be. But Pedro, remember, was never apprehended. He is a UDA, and he has not applied for asylum. By coming forward to help Juanita and Carlitos, he could conceivably end up deported himself.

Almost a year after we visited Juanita and Pedro in Virginia, we got word that their case had been postponed again, to the fall of 2018. Delays like this remind me why we call it a justice "system." If you overwhelm any one element of it, the consequences reverberate through the others. During the 2014 surge, the immigration courts had to process unprecedented numbers of children and women with children, but the fallout has meant that thousands of people are living all across the country in uncertainty. They have temporary legal status while they wait for the courts to hear their cases, but they are unsettled, unsure about their future. Communities often are not welcoming, and so they become insulated and vulnerable to predators—including gang members in the United States who begin the cycle of recruiting their children all over again. There are large Salvadoran communities in the Washington, DC, area. It's not unusual for Juanita and Pedro to see people with MS-13 tattoos at the gas station or local park.

Shifting dynamics

Our foundation now owns a ranch in south Texas along the Rio Grande; when I'm headed there I often go by Sacred Heart and check in with Sister Norma. She is a strong, compassionate, inspiring person, very focused on the needs of children. She also has a unique and frontline view of the trends and issues for the migrants who move through her center. In late 2016, we funded a research position at the center so someone can do interviews with migrants in order to better understand some of their motivations and experiences. One insight these interviews have given us is just how fast the driving forces can change in the countries of origin.

From April through June 2017, for example, Sacred Heart received 286 families, and 220 of them participated in interviews. Most interviewees were males between twenty-nine and thirty-three, and the majority came from Honduras.

- Over half of the individuals are married and are financially responsible for their family. The top three jobs held by migrants interviewed: farmers, business owners, or housewives. The top reason for migration continues to be direct persecution from gangs. Most said that they are not able to file a police report because local gangs have control over these authorities. If they do file a police report, they risk being killed.

- Asked how long they'd been planning their trip, 114 said the trip was unplanned and resulted from direct threats; 66 said the trip had been planned for between one and six months; 40 said they'd been planning to travel north for years.

- Over half of those questioned traveled in a combination of bus and car.

- The journey from their home country to the United States takes anywhere from fifteen to thirty days. Some traveled for three to six months because they had to stop and find work in Mexico in order to be able to pay for the next phase of transportation.

- Over half of them traveled without the help of a *coyote*. Some encountered Mexican drug cartels, and they were required to pay them a certain amount of money in order for them to receive a code. The code is needed in order to travel through Mexico safely; if they are stopped and can't produce the code, they are kidnapped or robbed.

- Once they cross over to the United States, the majority did not run from Border Patrol; they sought BP in order to request asylum (and in every single case among the 220 interviewees, the person was apprehended on the day of crossing). Every person was scheduled to appear at the Immigration and Customs Enforcement office within one week of being released. The individuals expressed their desire to follow the legal process and to be able to obtain asylum.

- Of those who answered the question of whether they would like to return to their home country if conditions changed for the better, 99 said yes; 8 said no.

This was only the second report created by the intake interviewer, but it was interesting to us that in the two-month period prior to this one, March–April 2017, there were some fairly dramatic differences in the groups. For one thing, in the first group there were large numbers of Salvadorans and Guatemalans, and the majority of people said they'd been planning their trips for months.

We noted the shift in the composition of the migrant groups and we looked into what was going on in Honduras during this period. One factor getting press coverage was that Honduras had stepped up arresting and then imprisoning gang leaders in high-security facilities with no cell phone service. One consequence was a surge in violence in communities where younger gang members or rival gangs try to take advantage of the power vacuum and increase violence to take control.

In August 2017, the interviewer updated us that there had been a surge of Guatemalan and Honduran bean and coffee farmers coming into south Texas, and about fifty families per day were arriving at the respite center. A man from Guatemala whom we will call Ignacio* provided disturbing details of what motivated his journey. He is from a small village in the Chiquimula Department of Guatemala, where, according to his account, members of the Zeta cartel from Mexico traveled to his community posing as tourists. But as soon as they arrived they changed into military-style gear. Ignacio said they offered him the equivalent of $20,000 in exchange for allowing them to plant drugs in the six acres of land he owns (he didn't specify what kind of drugs). Ignacio said that when he refused they threatened to kidnap his three-year-old son and harvest the child's organs for sale. They took a person from his village, beat him, and returned him alive three days later as an intimidation technique to get local landowners to comply with their requests. He said they eventually offered to build Ignacio a house in addition to the cash payment and gave him fifteen days to "decide."

It was in that interval of time that he and his family fled. His wife is Honduran, so she went to stay with her mother in Honduras, while he traveled with their son to the United States. They left Guatemala on August 9, were apprehended by BP on August 19, and were released with a notice to appear on August 22.

Ignacio's story and the reports from Sacred Heart are more evidence that the gang and cartel violence continues to escalate and threaten farmers who depend on growing food for their survival. They come to the United States because they are out of options.

Ronaldo

On one of my visits to Sacred Heart in 2016, I met a police officer from El Salvador named Ronaldo.* Unlike many of the migrant men coming through the respite center who seem tired and beaten down, Ronaldo projected confidence and fitness. He had just had a shower and changed into fresh clothes. He was outgoing and comfortable talking, even though we communicated through an interpreter.

Ronaldo said he had been on the road for about three weeks after leaving his home in a village outside San Salvador with his six-year-old daughter, Christina*, who played nearby as we talked. He'd spent about a week on the road, traveling mainly in buses, and then he crossed the Rio Grande. Right away, he surrendered to Border Patrol and asked for asylum.

He left, he said, because even for a police officer the violence in El Salvador was so extreme he feared for his life. Ronaldo said he had spent ten years on a local police force. He became a policeman in part because his father had served in the Salvadoran military, and because he was halfway through his studies to become a lawyer when Christina's mother got pregnant and he could not afford to continue his studies. Without an education (and even with it) he saw no other good job options. He attended the National Academy for Public Safety and graduated after eleven months of training. He said he had three sisters: Two are also police officers, and the youngest is in the academy now.

In El Salvador, Ronaldo worked in the San Martín area, one of the most dangerous divisions. We only talked for a short time, but I was interested in his unique perspectives on the corruption and mistrust between communities and police in El Salvador, something our foundation is working to address with the Salvadoran government.

When I asked what had prompted him to leave, he didn't hesitate: the violence. "About a year ago a close friend of mine was killed. He had a shop where there was a small window and customers would go and pay at the window." Because Ronaldo's friend did not pay sufficient extortion money to a local gang, a gang member walked up and asked to buy something. When his friend turned around to get it, Ronaldo said the gangster shot him in the back.

That was just one of a list of assaults, murders, and threats that Ronaldo talked about, but the final straw for him came from threats on the police force itself.[3] "Last year was the most violent year ever for police," he says. In April 2016, the president announced he was going to dispatch six hundred military and more police to fight the gangs. "That was the point where I got really scared," he said. "A friend heard that the gangs were saying if the government was going to dispatch military, they were going to target police."

When word of that spread in his community, everyone became frightened. Ronaldo and Christina's mother had split up several years ago and she moved to the United States. The woman who was watching Christina while Ronaldo worked heard about the threats to police and told him she no longer felt safe in his house alone with the child.

As he told the story, Ronaldo took out his phone and went to a Facebook page. The first photo he brought up shows a man lying on a patch of dirt on a dark pool of blood. He was the local "hit man" for his neighborhood, Ronaldo explained, and died in an exchange of gunfire with local police that took place near Ronaldo's home. The next social media page he showed me featured a heavyset man in a soccer jersey. The caption noted that he was a policeman who had been arrested. He had worked himself into a position with the police where he handled incoming calls and for years he had been tipping off gangs to the deployment of police officers in the area. "This is an officer I worked with," Ronaldo said.

No safe spaces

I have heard accusations about the Salvadoran police being corrupt and conspiring with gangs to extort citizens. I have no way of knowing, nor could ever know, how many of the details of Ronaldo's stories were accurate. But I was curious and asked Ronaldo about what he perceived his other options to be before he resorted to entering the U.S. illegally.

Just like Juanita had told us, Ronaldo said that moving to another area is out of the question. "There are no safe spaces in El Salvador...If you move from one place to another, the other gang gives you twenty-four hours to leave or they start killing your kids." Ronaldo's hometown is connected to the MS-13 gang, and so the first assumption is he would be too. Ronaldo says the intelligence capacity of gangs is better than that of police. "They are so diligent, so careful, and more sophisticated than police in doing intelligence. If I move to an area controlled by a rival gang, I'm a dead body."

He said many police officers are anxious to leave the country. Being a police officer, he says, is dangerous in the extreme. "There always has been death and violence in policing, but nothing compared to the last few years," he says. One gang practice to lure police into a trap is to call 911; when the police arrive, the gangs are ready with their guns.

The gangs near his home had grown so bold, he said two young guys came to him one evening and asked to borrow his pickup truck. He realized that what they wanted it for was to kidnap someone and take the person out to the woods to kill and then bury the body. He refused to loan the truck. "They have no respect for anyone. Not police, not their families. I had a neighbor with two sons and all of a sudden I see them changing how they dress, going out at night, the way they spoke. They had joined a gang. That's my next-door neighbor. I might even be off duty but if they think I see something, see them doing something wrong, I could be held accountable for that by the gang."

Ronaldo said he had reported certain gang activities near his home not to his direct superiors who he was afraid might tip off the gang, but to a level above them. He was scared, but two gang members were arrested; another, the hit man whose photo he showed me, ended up dead after a police shoot-out.

Ronaldo tried applying for a tourist visa, but he said when the U.S. embassy saw that he was a policeman, they denied it because the chance of him overstaying his visa was high. When Ronaldo finally decided to come north, it happened quickly. He contacted the *coyote*. The price to take him and his daughter to the border was $5,000. That included "special" trip considerations for the child, such as guaranteeing they'd travel in a vehicle that had air conditioning for her, and safe places to spend the night.

But he says the *coyote* was clear that the price he had quoted Ronaldo was for him to cross the border and surrender and ask for asylum. If Ronaldo wanted to evade Border Patrol and try to make it to his family in the interior of the United States, the price would be $12,000 for him, $7,000 for the child. In those scenarios "Your feet never hit the ground," he told us, meaning the plan includes more elaborate smuggling connections and a team of people working with the *coyote* on the U.S. side, including U.S. citizens who don't draw the suspicion of the police or border patrol.

They left El Salvador on June 20; they surrendered on July 7, after they crossed the Rio Grande. They surrendered to a police officer, who then called border patrol. ICE processed Ronaldo and Christina and then released them with permission to stay with family members in Texas and instructions to check in with ICE pending a court date.

When he asked for asylum, Ronaldo presented papers from the police department in El Salvador where he worked saying that he had been given a two-year leave of absence because he had received threats. "I do not want to go back if I do not get asylum," he says, but realizes he may have to. If he had to return, he might be able to get his job back, but who knows whether that would be a death sentence. "I would like to work as a police officer again. When you go into it you have a sense of love and family. For a good citizen, the police are seen as having an honorable job doing dignified and honorable work. But I think it would never be possible."

Too dangerous to gather evidence

We have stayed in touch with Ronaldo. His case attracted the attention of a pro bono clinic at a law school. We looked into trying to help him provide evidence of how dangerous his situation in San Martín had become. Our contacts in El Salvador said that when they described the neighborhood where Ronaldo had lived and worked to private investigators, they concluded it was too dangerous an assignment and declined.

Ronaldo has found life in the United States to have its own difficulties. He and his daughter were living with relatives near Houston, where he had limited access to transportation. For a time, he was working illegally as a day laborer for a landscaping company where he says he would see other laborers with gang tattoos he recognized from El Salvador. This made him wary; have they come north for a new life, or are they still involved in gang life? He eventually moved to a new state.

Ronaldo believes that to solve the violence and gang problems in El Salvador, "You need massive militarization across the country. Police officers are doing their jobs, but gangs terrorize judges and their family members." He also said that police officers are underpaid. "Every four years their salaries go up twenty-five dollars per month." Ronaldo started at $390 in 2007. He agreed that in some areas of the San Martín area, gang members provide better protection from rival gangs or other criminals than police. And he also said the police who end up working with gangs don't always do it because they are taking money or are basically dirty, but because they are threatened and fear for their lives.

It's clear that police corruption exists. But I also believe that many police officers are honest people who want to uphold the law. And yet they live in these dangerous communities, and they have families who are vulnerable to gang threats and violence. Sometimes that pressure is too much even for those who have more power than the average person, and they either are corrupted or find they must leave or risk death.

The details don't always add up

I chose the stories of Juanita and Ronaldo from several dozen conversations I've had with Central American migrants over the last few years. The meetings have taken places in many different locations and circumstances, including U.S. detention centers, respite centers run by churches in the United States and Mexico, even a repatriation facility in El Salvador where migrants who've been deported are returned.

Each person's experience has unique elements, but I've found they do convey some common themes. The aggressiveness of Central American gangs like MS-13 and 18th Street in threatening and killing children is one of those themes. The pattern of extorting money from anyone who has resources is another. When our team has researched the hometowns of people we have met who have claimed they fled violence, our review of both popular media and social media often reveals stories and photographs of murders and gang violence.

I cannot vouch for the details in these or any migrant's stories, but one reason we chose to use Juanita's and Ronaldo's accounts and not others is that we have kept in touch with both of them for some time now. We have found that the details they shared with us have remained consistent with what they told me the first time we met.

Some migrants are coached by *coyotes* or others to offer details that are more likely to support an asylum claim and obtain at least temporary release from custody. For example, we once met a woman at Sacred Heart, I'll call her Patricia*, who said she'd been traveling for more than three weeks with her small child. She said she had coincidentally just emptied her bank account to buy supplies for her tortilla business in Honduras on a day when she learned from a friend that gangs had burned her house down because she had not paid *renta*. She said instead of going home she found a *coyote* and paid him to take her north to the United States. She said she'd had no threats or assaults on the trip (which is unusual for Central American women traveling alone or with a child). Patricia was apprehended after crossing the Rio Grande, and she asked for asylum. When she passed her credible fear hearing, she asked ICE to be released temporarily to her "friend" in a major city in Texas, who she said has legal status in the United States, and ICE agreed.

However, later in our conversation, Patricia said that she had never met the friend, but that they had become acquainted on Facebook. The more they talked with Patricia, the more our foundation team began to notice inconsistencies. She said she paid several hundred dollars for the *coyote*, for example, which is much less than the several thousand most Central Americans have to pay. They also observed that she had a perfect manicure and she had fresh highlights in her hair; since she came straight to the respite center from federal detention, that might suggest she was not on the road from Honduras for three weeks.

Patricia gave us the "friend's" phone number, and in our presence called her to warn her we might call. As Patricia spoke, our team member who spoke Spanish noticed Patricia used formal address, indicating the person was in fact not a close friend. Patricia said the friend said it would be fine to call her to reach Patricia. We followed up a few days later after Patricia was due to arrive at her home. The friend answered the phone once, said Patricia was "working" and then blocked our calls from there on. We could not find any record on Facebook of the name she gave us, although she encouraged us to contact her that way.

We suspect there was a lot Patricia was not telling us. That does not mean she was a criminal, and she could very well be the victim of criminals. The Texas contact may have been supplied by a human trafficker, and Patricia may have been told to use the Facebook story to cover up a network. Or, she might be traveling to the United States to work as a prostitute or as a drug courier to pay for her freedom or to pay ransom for another family member. Our impression was she was intimidated by the "friend." But we will never know.

I would estimate that less than 10 percent of the migrants I've spoken with have prompted the concerns and skepticism that Patricia's story raised. Most seem to me to be truthful and living with extreme stress, exhaustion, and fear. They have left everything they know for a dangerous journey and an uncertain future—not something any of us would want to do. In the next chapter you'll meet some of the individuals who inspire that fear and those journeys.

Chapter 13

PRISON OR THE CEMETERY

What turns a child into a cold-blooded killer or a human trafficker? Can it be as simple as a free soda or a pair of sneakers? Can anything turn a young person headed down that path around—and into a productive, optimistic citizen?

Whenever I think about my visit to a maximum security prison called Izalco in El Salvador, one word comes to mind: surreal.

Senator Heidi Heitkamp, Cindy McCain, and I share a commitment to fighting human trafficking, and one of the drivers of trafficking in our hemisphere is Central American criminal gangs. The gangs not only kidnap and traffic vulnerable adults and children themselves, but they terrify, prey on, and threaten their own communities and drive people to flee. Many of those individuals end up trafficked in Mexico and the United States by the cartels and other criminals.

In 2015, I invited Cindy and Heidi to join me on a trip to El Salvador. In addition to field trips to agricultural areas, I set up a visit to a high-security prison. We would go inside Izalco Prison without any security and speak directly with gang leaders. That might scare some people—not these two. At the time, Cindy said that large numbers of Salvadoran children were arriving in Arizona without their families, and many had experienced assaults along the way. Among other things, Cindy wanted to understand the gang involvement and also what was motivating parents to send their children on these dangerous journeys. Heidi also believes that "In order to solve border security we need to understand the socio-economic and cultural complexities" of the countries whose people are fleeing to the United States. What's more, "We can't just put gang members on an airplane back to El Salvador and think we have solved the problem."

We drove about forty miles from San Salvador and turned onto a narrow road in a densely populated community. The road snaked up a hill, and as we approached the prison gates, we saw guards patrolling wearing identity-hiding balaclava masks and armed with automatic weapons. But among these fierce-looking characters were women and children, including little girls in party dresses here to visit with family members who were prisoners.

Inside, we faced an elaborate metal detector. I asked to see it demonstrated, and the prison staff admitted it didn't work. We had been warned that we could carry absolutely nothing into the prison, not even a pen or pencil. And yet, once inside, we visited a shop class where the inmates were working with chisels and other tools that could be used as lethal weapons. We visited classrooms where every inmate student held a sharp pencil. As we walked across the recreation yard, Heidi pointed out a drainage gutter that had shards of glass and the blade top of disposable razors in it—objects that would never have been left where inmates could access them in a U.S. prison.

We walked past a large wooden gate with peepholes. Through them we could see a several-story-tall wall of prison cells with a huge open courtyard. There were hundreds of men, packed like spectators at an outdoor concert or a political rally. It was

Chad Larner

Trail Camera

TOP: A Mexican cartel spotter just over the border observes our foundation's southern Arizona ranch called CR, 24 hours a day. Here, he adjusts his scope so he can radio smugglers to help them avoid law enforcement. MIDDLE: In Illinois, I interviewed five occupants of a vehicle that had broken down. One man said he had entered the US illegally twice, which I explained was a felony. BOTTOM: A "drug mule" hauls a double pack of marijuana likely weighing 60 pounds or more across CR.

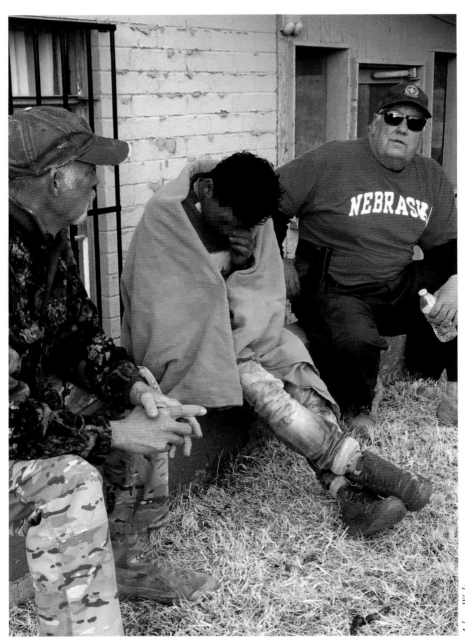

When Oscar arrived at our foundation's ranch (MOR), he was shaken and hungry.

CLOCKWISE FROM TOP LEFT: We think Oscar crossed the border along this stretch of MOR that has a barbed-wire fence and a low vehicle barrier separating the US and Mexico; I traveled to Honduras to speak with Oscar's family. Here, his brother holds one of the red shoes Oscar was wearing when Oscar and I met in Arizona; Oscar's family is poor and lives in a rural village. The family cooks outside and they wash utensils and clothing in water from a gravity-fed pipe.

Trail Camera

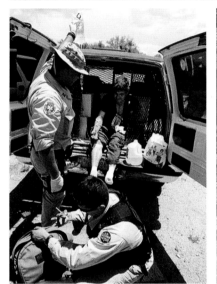

Howard W. Buffett

CLOCKWISE FROM TOP LEFT: Flowing water has carved deep crevices across MOR, and this drug smuggling group uses them to conceal their travel in daylight. The large bags and weight pulling on the straps indicate heavy loads; Drug smugglers leave trail signs, like this shoe buried upside down, on CR; I photographed this Border Patrol apprehension in a remote, hot, dry desert area of Arizona; Border Patrol's special BORSTAR agents provide emergency assistance to an "undocumented alien," or UDA, who was stranded in the Arizona desert and otherwise might have died.

I spoke with the young women in this group detained in Arizona, and they told me they barely escaped a sexual assault on their journey. Roughly 60% of migrant women say they are sexually assaulted traveling to the US.

Traffickers sometimes hang a woman's underwear or clothing from a "rape tree" as a way of bragging about a sexual assault.

CLOCKWISE FROM TOP LEFT: About 1,200 feet north of the Mexican border, these smugglers struggle through rough terrain on CR. Note the carpet-covered shoes, which obscure footprints; These smugglers already delivered their loads and now are climbing the border fence on CR to return to Mexico. Note the radio strapped to the one smuggler's hand; These signs are common on public lands in the Southwest; I was in a helicopter when we spotted these UDAs. They don't appear to be smuggling drugs, but when we flew over them, they scattered and ran back to Mexico to avoid apprehension.

Smugglers easily hide in the terrain and vegetation of the southwest. Above, can you spot four members of our ranch crew wearing camouflage? I took this photograph, then I asked them to hold up red flags to identify their positions...

It's very difficult to see the men even when you know exactly where to look.

I rode along Arizona rancher Warner Glenn's property with him to look at the border fencing.

This new section of tall fencing near Naco, AZ, will be difficult to climb and will be fitted to allow flood waters to flow through the fence.

Along the border today it's not unusual to see an abrupt change in structures. Here an imposing, tall fence changes to a low vehicle barrier that someone on foot could easily cross.

At an Arizona Border Patrol field office an agent monitors cameras positioned along the border to look for security breaches.

In Yuma, AZ, a fence can only go so far when the border is an international waterway.

CLOCKWISE FROM TOP LEFT: Border Patrol agents are trying to figure out who the *coyote* or human trafficker is among this group of UDAs. The *coyotes* often try to pass themselves off as migrants; In my capacity as a volunteer deputy commander in the Cochise County Sheriff's Office in Arizona, I support a variety of law enforcement activities. In this photo, I am releasing a detainee who was questioned as part of a drug raid; In Texas, I rode on a Border Patrol boat on the Rio Grande, where securing the border is a very different challenge than in Arizona.

CLOCKWISE FROM TOP LEFT: Arizona Border Patrol apprehended this UDA, but five others traveling with him got away; In a Texas respite center for those who have been detained and temporarily released by Border Patrol, a little girl looks at the monitoring device federal agents placed on her mother's ankle. We were told the devices sometimes frighten the children; It takes enormous resources for Border Patrol to process individuals seeking safety, work, or a reunion with family—and that reduces agents' ability to stop drug smugglers and violent criminals.

CLOCKWISE FROM TOP LEFT: Some UDAs cross the border to work, to flee violence, or, like the 13-year-old boy in the purple hat, to reunite with family. In this Altar, Mexico, shelter, migrants wait for guides to take them to the border; For decades the majority of U.S. crop workers, like these individuals in California, have been immigrants. Many are undocumented, but they are critical to our nation's food production; At our farm in Texas along the Rio Grande, life vests and inflatable inner tubes lay in our shed. These were previously used by Mexican farm workers to "swim" to work.

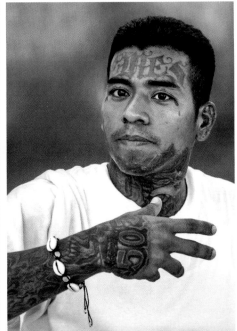

CLOCKWISE FROM TOP LEFT: Soldiers like this one guarding a Salvadoran prison must conceal their identities to prevent gang retribution; This inmate in El Salvador's Apanteos Prison says he no longer wants to be in a gang, but like many others he is a "marked man" because of his tattoos; In Salvadoran *bartolinas*, or holding jails, prisoners are packed into a subhuman environment so overcrowded that some must spend many hours in hammocks.

CLOCKWISE FROM TOP LEFT: Poverty is one driver of immigration to the US. These girls in Guatemala live in an area where most people are hungry every day; Life in rural areas has always been difficult for people like this Honduran farmer, but in recent years gangs have moved out from cities and are terrorizing rural areas, too; These crosses on the wall of "La 72" respite center in Mexico near Guatemala commemorate 72 Central American migrants who were brutally murdered by a drug cartel in 2010; Each year, thousands of Central Americans hop freight trains like this one traveling north through Mexico. Some jump off when the train slows because they are too exhausted to maintain their grip. Recently police have cracked down on these riders.

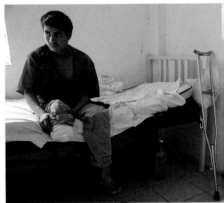

CLOCKWISE FROM TOP LEFT: I took this shot while flying in a helicopter over train yards in souther Mexico. Unless we support investments in developing countries, many people, like this group of migran with small children, believe even these incredibly risky journeys are safer than staying in their home cou tries; I met this young man in Tapachula in Chiapas, Mexico, where he was being treated at a migra center after he fell from a train and lost part of his leg. He told me he would continue trying to get to the U I watched this boy leap between cars on a moving train in a Mexican rail yard. Until we address the violen and poverty in their home countries that motivate so many to take incredible risks to reach the US, bord security will be an ongoing challenge.

like a buzzing beehive. Clothing flapped like pennants from railings and cell bars. Then, our view was blocked when the viewing holes filled with faces, most heavily tattooed, of curious men looking at us.

Izalco Prison was named for a nearby volcano, and given that the prison was built for 768 inmates, but held 2,386 prisoners when we visited, the name made sense. It definitely had the feel of a place that could explode.

Notorious

El Salvador's prisons are notorious for being overcrowded, under-resourced, and controlled as much by the inmates as by the staff. The average cost spent per prisoner is only $1,100 per year (compared to an average annual cost of $32,000 in the United States), and within the walls of Izalco live members of both of Central America's most violent and powerful gangs—MS-13 and 18th Street. On the streets of El Salvador, these rivals murder one another if given the chance. Gang members used to be separated by gang affiliation and incarcerated in different facilities in El Salvador, but the practice only made the gangs stronger. Many facilities like this one house members of both gangs, although they are separated inside the prison by their gang affiliations. Those visitors we saw out front were family of MS-13. The gangs are such bitter enemies the prison assigns their family members alternate visiting days so violence doesn't break out as they wait to enter.

Our visit was set up by Catholic Relief Services (CRS), an NGO that we have partnered with on livelihood development projects in Central America and Mexico for many years. Incarcerated gang leaders maintain considerable control over what happens outside the prison by passing messages through visitors or other channels. Therefore CRS is committed to maintaining a presence in the prisons. CRS supports government rehabilitation programs, such as Yo Cambio (I Can Change), designed to prepare prisoners for reentry into society. CRS was also working to train and develop a core group of prison peace advocates who they hoped could work with gang leadership within the prisons to reduce conflict by gangs both inside and outside. We were able to meet with MS-13 representatives in the context of the rehabilitation program.

It's hard to exaggerate gang violence in El Salvador. This country of only 6 million people has been estimated to have more than fifty thousand active gang members, but family affiliations to specific gangs multiply the potential for conflict significantly. Originally, we were supposed to visit Quezaltepeque Prison, which currently houses 1,060 prisoners even though it was built to house only 250. The week before we were supposed to arrive, however, Quezaltepeque went on lockdown. Inmates there were accused of ordering bus strikes back in their neighborhoods to protest their living conditions. When eight drivers had ignored the strike order from the gang, they were executed. A week after our visit, Quezaltepeque erupted in violence and fourteen inmates were killed.

The warden of Izalco seemed calm and upbeat. When we explained that we'd like to take notes during our visit, the warden grabbed paper and a pen off his desk and handed them over as if carrying these items was no problem whatsoever. As we walked toward our meeting, I asked how he had determined which of the members of MS-13 we would meet with today. He seemed surprised at the question and responded: "They chose."

I have visited several prisons in El Salvador, and one of the first things you notice is how respectful the inmates are in the presence of visitors. They are dressed in clean white T-shirts, pants, socks, and sneakers, even though they spend much of their time outside in dirt yards. At Izalco, inmates are moved around outside their cells chained together, ordered to follow a yellow line painted on the ground. The men have mostly shaved heads, and many lifers have elaborate tattoos that cover most of their faces, heads, and necks. Some have fierce expressions; others are glassy-eyed and blank, likely from drugs smuggled into the prison.

Unlike what happens if you tour a jail or prison in the United States, nobody yelled at us or addressed Cindy, Heidi, or me. We walked past a courtyard where inmates were weaving hammocks with a polyester cord; they did not look our way. We visited classrooms teaching basic skills, which many prisoners lack. Heidi still talks about seeing "this big grown man with tattoos on his face sitting there reading the Spanish equivalent of a second-grade Dick and Jane book." We visited a shop class where men were carving plaques and lamp bases out of wood; they showed them to us with great pride. We were told they were among the prison's most trustworthy inmates and near their release dates.

In one area there were several sewing machines pushed against the wall; the warden said inmates used to sew prison clothing but the program was stopped because they were adding secret pockets and distinctive identifying features. We heard singing and clapping; we were told there are evangelical services led by inmate "pastors."

Finally, we walked to a roughly fifteen-by-fifteen-foot space in the yard—a chain-link cage that felt like a dog kennel with several plastic chairs inside. A guard led two men in who wore handcuffs that were connected by a chain to cuffs around their ankles. They sat down and the guard stepped back outside and locked us in.

The interpreter introduced the men. On the left was Manuel*; on the right, Francisco*. They were representatives of Izalco's MS-13 population. Manuel wore glasses and had a thick, bullish build. Francisco was slender with a friendly smile. Neither had facial tattoos, although both had tattoos we could see around the neck and hems of their white T-shirts. Manuel was thirty-nine and Francisco forty. Both seemed confident and calm.

Make no mistake, both are killers. Francisco admitted he had 160 years left on his sentence. In El Salvador, one murder tends to get a thirty-year sentence. Francisco said, "We're the founders of this violence, but we'd also like to negotiate a way out of it from inside the prison. We're here to speak for our group; to eliminate ideological barriers. When you get to know us, you can see that we're not the monsters we're made out to be. We're people who've made mistakes. We'd like to find pathways without losing our identities. We want to return to society and find work." Manuel is also serving a life sentence. He added: "We can not only sow terror, but good. We try to play clean, but society and the media have made us out to be worthless."

The men clearly were intelligent and articulate. Put them in a suit and tie and behind a desk and they could have been bankers or corporate marketing executives. Everything they said was carefully considered. They were a gang version of spin doctors.

"Find pathways without losing our identities," for example, may sound like a benign, even politically correct desire to move forward with dignity. My sense was that it was more like a veiled threat. They would retain their "identities" as violent gangs if they don't get what they want—as the bus strike and subsequent executions showed. What's more, Heidi recalled later, "It was clear they were the equivalent of the wardens of the prison. Between the razor blades and the overcrowding, you wouldn't control that prison without the acceptance of the gang."

Francisco, age forty, said he had seven children. He graduated from a university with a degree in business, and he has a son in university today. He joined MS-13 around age seventeen. He also had a daughter in the gang. He said that he grew up middle class, not poor, but he was a rebellious kid "raised in war and repression."

He said that is the case with his daughter as well—she's rebellious. "She ran to a gang to get back at her mother." Francisco continued, "We made mistakes, that's who we are. At the end of the day we want a different outcome for our children. We don't want them to feel sorry for us, just not to end up here."

Our partners briefed us before the visit and said that a typical scenario that can land someone like Francisco in jail for life might be set in motion by gang activities when a member is between seventeen and twenty-one. Later, he might go on and get married and find legitimate work. He may go off to college, or settle down with a family and stop actively extorting money or committing crimes. But as time goes on, the person gets careless in avoiding the police, or is ratted out by rival gang members with a grudge and gets arrested and convicted of old crimes and murders.

Violence seemed a little closer to the surface with Manuel, age thirty-nine, but he shared a glimpse of humanity when he talked about his own path to MS-13. Leaning forward, he said his father was killed when he was very young, and his mother abandoned him when he was nine. "If I had had my family intact and I had a way of getting ahead in life, I might not have joined. In the nineties I lived in extreme poverty. I lived in a house of plastic sheeting and lit by a candle at night. I lived with my half brothers and they made me feel I wasn't part of the family. The gang guys would say 'Here, have a soda. Have some new shoes.' When I saw how they treated me versus how my family treated me, I got in deeper and then I couldn't get out. If anybody had told me how this would end…" He shook his head and added, "I have three children eighteen, fourteen, and ten. By God's mercy, none are in a gang. When God gives us the opportunity to become parents, we realize we don't want the same for our children."

It was hard to believe the sincerity of men who had unleashed so much violence. Cindy recalls, "I don't doubt that they came from difficult circumstances, but this was a shtick. It made me mad and even more determined to stop these guys."

The answers to all our questions tended to end up with complaints about police and the government. Manuel said, "The police are rounding up boys and beating them for five or six days at a time. The boys decide, 'Maybe I should join a gang.' Repression drives them into the gang." Manuel tried to sound like a youth leader getting kids together for a pickup baseball team: "I'm active, he's curious, we're friends. In his mind he comes to the decision that he wants to be part of us." As we hear repeated several times, MS-13's official line is that they don't recruit, they just welcome kids who express interest. They said their rivals in 18th Street are more violent and instigate trouble, and they actively recruit members through threats.

We asked Francisco and Manuel if it is ever possible to leave the gang, or become inactive. Manuel said yes. "We have a test. We have seventy-five members who are tattooed but they became Christians in prison. At another prison four hundred prisoners chose life as Christians. If you say 'I want to dedicate my life to God and to living a good life' you can do that." But Francisco added that the gang tolerates no hypocrisy: "If you demonstrate that you're going to be in good faith, not drinking and smoking dope all day, you can become inactive. If you don't…" He didn't finish that thought.

They dodged specifics about the crimes they had committed. As for Francisco, who has served time in five different prisons in total, "Some crimes I did, some I did not." Manuel: "I have a thirty-year sentence for a homicide I did not commit. A guy said he saw me go by in a line-up and I got accused of a crime at work. I worked for a telecommunications company…"

A telecommunications company? Like I said, it was surreal. Francisco added, "We've been part of the problem, now we want to be part of the solution." And yet he added: "If they attack we will defend ourselves. If they want war they will have war. We're talking about the other gang, and we're talking about the government." As our time wound down and the men rose to leave, Francisco dialed up the charm again, and said, grinning, "I just want a hamburger." (Family members used to be able to bring in local fast food, but no more.)

The calculated, veiled threats, the calm reflections of two murderers, the regular guy who just wants a burger...I felt almost like some marketing expert had helped them rehearse the message: We are the gang with morals and values. As Heidi said later, "They were trying to convince us they are victims. I'm not buying it. They rape and murder their way around the country, but I think they believe they are victims. It tells you how hard it is going to be to change the culture around this."

It's critical that we and other peace-seeking countries offer the government of El Salvador support in creating positive, legal options outside of gangs for young people. If we don't, gangs will continue to attract members by claiming they are filling the void created by an indifferent, hostile government. But ultimately their pitch is a threat: Fight with us—or die alone.

Young gang members

On the same day as the visit to Izalco, a foundation team member and I met with a group of young gang members in the poor, rural community of Los Angeles, which is tucked into an area in San Martín, about twenty-five miles from the capital. This is near where the policeman Ronaldo had been posted. As we arrived, chickens pecked around the dirt streets, and children played in weedy patches. Skinny, feral dogs and the occasional goat wandered along the roadside. Many homes were simple wood or mud construction with metal roofs. We passed a school with a giant portrait of the late archbishop Óscar Romero and a quote from him painted on one side.

A local NGO is trying to engage young people at risk to join gangs as well as those already involved with gangs. The idea is to provide safe places where they can gain skills and employment so they find other options to crime and violence. We entered a concrete block community center where a wall mural celebrates peace and family. However, the dozen or so young men who had assembled and sat in a row of folding chairs made clear they celebrate something quite different—over the hour I spoke with them they made a calm, calculating defense of the solidarity they feel from gang membership in MS-13.

At first look, they had the variety of sometimes grinning, sometimes blank-faced, slouching, leg-jangling array of postures you see in any group of high school–aged boys. They ranged in age from fifteen to twenty-two. They wore sports jerseys, clean T-shirts, jeans. I didn't see any tattoos. They were polite and respectful.

One seventeen-year-old wearing a pressed white collared shirt was jabbed by friends for dressing "gang style." A boy explained that is a style that attracts local police like flies and results in stops and, they claim, frequent beatings when they are detained, their shirts pulled up to see if their bodies contain gang tattoos. The boy in the white shirt ignored the teasing; he never changed his expression.

Each of the young men wore sneakers in immaculate condition—again, startling in a town with dusty dirt roads. Apparently, this is a point of pride among local gangs in El Salvador. And several wore jerseys and hats with the logo of Los Angeles (the one in the United States) pro sports teams on them. I later was told American sports gear and sneakers are like currency in gang culture here; they are highly prized, and worth fighting, even killing, for.

At one end of the row was Jorge*, age twenty-one. He wore his LA Clippers flat-brimmed ball cap skewed to the side. He wore a white, sleeveless T-shirt and baggy jeans and what looked like a wedding ring. When each of the other boys said his name and age, he didn't bother at first, saying, "Everybody here knows me," but eventually offered a first name. Apparently, Jorge is the primary leader of this MS "local structure," as they call it.

Next to Jorge was his lieutenant, Roberto*, age twenty-two, also in an LA Clippers hat. He wore a bright green T-shirt whose slogan celebrated a fraternity rush at an American college. These two admitted they dropped out of school years ago. Leading this gang clearly is their career now. They were reserved at first, but later relaxed. They clearly liked the attention and being asked questions from someone not connected to police or government.

In the middle of the group was Ricardo*, age seventeen, in a blue soccer jersey. It was clear he saw himself as next-generation management. He demonstrated a glibness that is disturbing given the real business of gangs here. "We're united. We're mellow. When we get behind something, we see it through," he explained. Ricardo went to school through ninth grade but dropped out. He said, "We'd like to learn something, a trade, a way to fill our time."

Ricardo talked about the support and community of the gang, and that it gave back to the community by protecting it. "We do this for our survival," he said. He claimed MS does not start trouble in this community; it protects the community. If a rival gang member comes onto the turf, Ricardo says he and his comrades will stop and ask what is going on, but not resort immediately to violence. He claimed that 18th Street goes straight to violence.

I was curious if these young men ever think beyond their circumstances. What would they like to do with their lives? Ricardo said he liked to paint when he was in school, and added that he enjoyed participating in a local project painting murals over gang graffiti. Graffiti is a point of conflict in these communities. The gangs paint their symbols and slogans on their walls, or they go into each other's territory and tag. The local community is afraid to touch any of it or change them. The mural painting activity organized by a local nonprofit group has become a popular solution. Ricardo seemed genuinely frustrated when he said he couldn't join the other boys to finish a mural because the police were nearby.

The feeling in the room was an odd mix of arrogance and despair. Nobody wants to show weakness, but nobody argues that the gang life is fun or ideal. Several times I asked the leadership about their futures, about their dreams. Where do you see yourself in five years, I asked Jorge. He replied, "Prison—or the cemetery." Nobody laughed, nobody flinched. They contended that their biggest problem is a corrupt police force that hassles them and beats them up. Every boy raised his hand when I asked who had been beaten up by the police.

I asked whether it would make sense to set up meetings with the police to try to work out a better atmosphere. They all shook their heads, suggesting I had no idea what I was asking or what they are up against. "Their mission is to arrest and stop us. They are corrupt. Their authority comes from extreme abuse," said Ricardo.

I asked about school. Only the fifteen-year-old seemed to be in school, and he didn't seem too thrilled about it. Will he stay? Jorge claimed, "We're going to support him and get him through school."

Gang life, Jorge continued, "is a way we survive. It's the way we get ahead every day. We have more opportunities to be ourselves inside the gang. If you go someplace without this affiliation you may not make it. But when you have this affiliation, you know who backs you up." Ricardo added, "We have our own way of living together and supporting each other."

What about your younger brothers, we asked. Do you want them in MS-13? Again the same party line we heard in Izalco. Jorge said,

"No," and other members also shook their heads. "It's not something you want to see your child get into or a way to live. We're going to end up in the hospital and eventually in the cemetery. You have to stay inside" so the police don't see you, Jorge explained. "Our parents get mad at us," Ricardo said. "We tell our mothers, you do what you do, we do what we do."

Regarding recruitment, Jorge claimed, "Other groups take drastic measures to get people to join," but, he insisted, not MS-13.

Roberto listed complaints that he says help explain why these boys have joined MS-13: There are no jobs...the police are corrupt...the president is the worst. "What good is it to try to improve our community when everything is falling apart?"

Finally, time was up. They said goodbye, adding that we were welcome to return any time.

I think about this visit often. A few months after it occurred, I was in a respite center in Mexico talking with a young man from El Salvador named Miguel* about the journey that had landed him and his brother in Mexico City. Miguel and his brother were in high school, he said, when gang members started making overtures to them. They were friendly, and they gave the brothers new sneakers and bought them food. The boys had come from an abusive family and welcomed the attention. But after they accepted the gifts for about six months, the gang members asked them to sell drugs at their school. They refused, and a gang member urged them to think it over—or they would be killed.

After these threats, Miguel and his brother decided they better leave El Salvador. Someone must have tipped them off, because they had just begun their journey when members of the gang came looking for them. They began to run. Miguel heard shots and ran as fast as he could. He didn't dare look back even as he worried his brother might have been shot. Fortunately, they both outran the gang and made it out of El Salvador and then began hopping on and off freight trains, eventually landing in Mexico City. But their futures were now uncertain, and they were hoping not to be deported back to El Salvador. That's quite a price to pay for "free" sneakers.

The gangs understand marketing. They may arrive offering soda or sneakers, but what they're selling is a form of support and protection some of these kids don't have. I don't think most young gang members joined MS-13 because they wanted to be violent criminals. I think they are desperate to be part of something that feels like a family. They already know gang life is wrong, and they know it will not end well. But they see no other options. Unless we can figure out how to give them better opportunities, they will live for the moment and the illusion that gang life will make them feel like men united with a common purpose instead of boys afraid for their lives.

Bartolinas de Zacamil

Although my visit to the Salvadoran prison was intense, few things that I have seen in my life prepared me for the 2017 visit I made to what is called a *bartolina*, or a local holding jail, in San Salvador. I have experienced many more tragic and dangerous situations—in fact, at the *bartolina* I never felt concerned for my safety or threatened in any way. What I felt was shock at a system that packed human beings together in such inhumane conditions. It was a cage of humans so overcrowded that inmates had to hang from the walls and ceilings in hammocks.

Local jails in El Salvador are supposed to act as holding facilities for no more than seventy-two hours. This is the law. But the government's efforts to crack down on gangs and violence in recent years have resulted in *bartolinas* bursting with inmates, and the justice system is incapable of processing the cases. For one thing, plea bargains—one of the best tools we have in the United States for efficiently clearing cases—are rarely used by Salvadoran prosecutors, and prosecutors and the police have typically done a poor job of collecting evidence that stands up in court. El Salvador doesn't have adequate forensic technology and labs; prosecutors' case management systems involve an awkward mix of paper boxes and digital records; files often are lost. According to law enforcement leaders, 20 percent of the people in the jails have finished serving their sentences, but there aren't enough judges to review the paperwork and order their release.

The nation's own Supreme Court found the conditions in seven prisons to be unconstitutional because of overcrowding, and yet nothing is being done because officials say the criminal justice system lacks the resources to properly address it. According to one report I read, inmates in a typical *bartolina* like the one I visited have less than four square feet of personal space. That is slightly smaller than a standard doormat.[1]

Reports of outbreaks of diseases, including tuberculosis, are common. The guards themselves seemed embarrassed. The head of the National Civil Police told me the evening before our visit that he knew it was unacceptable. "*Bartolinas* are a grave problem all over our country," he said. Juveniles are mixed in with adult murderers, and sometimes women with men. The attorney general of El Salvador told me, "Our penitentiary system violates the rights of the detainees."

I visited and photographed a facility for men that I would describe as two high chain-link cages on a concrete floor. Inside, thanks to cheap nylon rope hammocks, men were living in three levels. There were at least eighty men in facilities that had enough floor space to handle perhaps ten to fifteen. Men were literally hanging from the walls and ceilings. They appeared to take turns sitting or lying on the floor; otherwise, they hung from the hammocks. Looking through the chain-link front of the cage was almost disorienting; there would be a foot next to a face or a horizontal face next to a vertical face. It seemed shocking there wasn't a nonstop violent revolt occurring. And parts of the roof were not covered, which provided light and gave some relief from the heat, but also allowed rain to soak them.

Around the corner from the men's enclosure two dozen or more women prisoners were living in a large, dark room. When the guards opened the door, the women blinked as their eyes adjusted. The women were mostly on the floor, sprawled all over each other. Their bucket toilets were scattered around. They seemed dazed and disoriented. A single shower was supposed to serve the needs of all the men and women.

Outside, family members holding clear plastic bags line up every day to deliver food for inmates. Often *bartolinas* do not have the resources to feed all the prisoners they hold. I could only imagine what kind of mayhem must break out when the youngest and weakest prisoners get a care package of food from family on a day when the stronger and more aggressive inmates do not.

Our foundation has initiated a significant, multiyear project to work with the government of El Salvador to support reforms in its justice system. I have met some impressive public servants who want to correct these challenges. The reason we are supporting changes in the justice system is that today in El Salvador, impunity is one of the key drivers of violence. Fewer than 10 percent of all crimes result in conviction. This creates a vicious cycle where Salvadorans do not report crimes to police because they think that the police will not be able to perform an effective or timely investigation, or because they fear the police have been co-opted by gangs.

These concerns are not unfounded. For one thing, the system lacks a true investigative capacity; police tend to round up suspected criminals and leave them in detention in *bartolinas* for months, eventually releasing them for lack of evidence. And as we learned from Ronaldo, the Salvadoran police officer, the police live in communities where gangs threaten them and their families.

Some say, these are criminals, some of them vicious killers. Why worry about conditions in a jail when innocent poor people are going hungry? For me, the answer is that these unacceptable conditions in El Salvador's jails and prisons do not deter anyone from committing crimes against innocent people, or deter a boy from joining a gang. To the man, woman, or child who has seen or heard about these conditions, there is no reason to believe the police or government is any more just or humane than the gangs are.

The essence of the rule of law is that it must be applied consistently and that no one, and no organization or agency, is above it. Without acceptance of that fundamental principle in a society, justice is unreliable, and you cannot bring violence under control.

As you are about to read, El Salvador is not alone in coping with that reality.

Chapter 14

SILENCING THE CANARY

The erosion of the rule of law in Mexico is one of the most significant threats to U.S. national security that exist today.

The ranch that our foundation owns near Naco, Arizona, which we call CR, runs along several miles of the U.S.–Mexico border. When I drive to the main buildings of CR, I park and get out of the vehicle, and then I always look across the nearby border fence toward Mexico, and then up. Over the fence there is a hill about seven hundred feet above ground elevation that is about one mile into Mexico. It's within the boundaries of a privately owned cattle ranch. At the very top is the shack where a spotter for the drug cartels lives and works 24/7. He walks around in plain sight. Every few days men bring food, water, women, batteries, the next shift spotter, and who knows what else up to the shack. U.S. Border Patrol has told me that from the U.S. side they see his binoculars or scope flash during the day, and they assume he uses night vision goggles after dark. His job is to direct drug smuggling teams sneaking over the border on which way to go to avoid BP.

If we know he's there and Border Patrol knows he's there…then Mexican law enforcement officials also know he's there. And yet he's been there since we bought the ranch in 2014.

So I have come to think of that spotter as the "canary in the coal mine," or better put, the reverse of the canary. As long as he's there, as long as that canary is singing to his smuggling teams through his two-way radio with no fear of being arrested or punished, I know the drug cartel is in control of this area of northern Mexico. It's pretty simple. The day he and hundreds of other spotters who operate in plain sight are gone is the day our border will be much more secure.

Will this happen soon? No. The rule of law has collapsed in this area and in much of Mexico. Our canary and those like him operate with impunity. An estimated 175,000 people have been killed since 2006 when Mexico supposedly launched its own "war on drugs";[1] desperate migrants from Central America moving through Mexico are being kidnapped, tortured, extorted, and targeted for other forms of abuse; the leadership of Mexico is drowning in corruption paid for by cartels; and the drug cartels recently again have accelerated their killing sprees in Mexico as they battle for control of key smuggling corridors and regions.

May 2017 was the deadliest month for murders in Mexico since the country began tracking that statistic in 1997.[2] Some attribute this to different cartels jockeying for control in the wake of the capture of drug lord Joaquín "El Chapo" Guzmán in 2016 in Los Mochis, Sinaloa.[3] Guzmán escaped from supposedly maximum security prisons in Mexico twice before he was captured and his government extradited him to the United States.[4] That tells you what's going on with the rule of law in Mexico—its federal government would prefer to deport the nation's most notorious criminal rather than be embarrassed yet again by his escape from one of the country's own prisons.

Brief optimism

Mexico's struggles are frustrating for me to watch for a number of reasons, some of them very personal. Almost three decades ago I began traveling to Mexico on a regular basis when I was an executive with Archer Daniels Midland, the large Illinois-based global agricultural processing company. I traveled throughout Mexico evaluating and buying corn and flour processing plants for ADM. At the time, there was a lot of optimism both inside Mexico and among those interested in helping Mexico develop its economy.

I felt welcome everywhere I went, and I made many good friends. I did not travel with a security detail, and I rarely worried about my safety. I would meet with local businessmen and government leaders in open-air restaurants. Once in Hermosillo, which is near Mexico's huge wheat-growing region in the state of Sonora, I remember a local business leader being proud of the Naranjeros de Hermosillo (the Orange Men) baseball team, and I went to watch a game with him under the local stadium's lights.

In the early 1990s, U.S. companies were making significant investments in Mexico in many sectors—agriculture, food processing, energy, telecommunications, manufacturing—and that was creating jobs.[5] The leadership of companies and the country felt that investment was a sign of respect, and they welcomed it. For the first time, people whose families had lived in poverty for generations in urban areas were beginning to move into a middle class. There were more new cars on the roads, and people began to afford items we take for granted, like television sets.

The North American Free Trade Agreement (NAFTA) was signed in 1992 and implemented in 1994. It was designed to eliminate barriers to trade and investment. By 1996, the government of Mexico was pleased that total trade between the NAFTA partners increased to record levels, registering a total of $441 billion, an increase of 46 percent over 1993, and there were significant increases in trade between Mexico and the United States and Mexico and Canada.

Mexico still had significant challenges. In 1994 a recalibration of the peso threw the economy into a tailspin, and GDP growth did not resume until 1997.[6] There was political turmoil surrounding NAFTA, and in the long run it hurt people in rural areas where poor farmers were left to compete with ever-increasing imports from U.S. farmers. Low-skilled, uneducated farmworkers had limited job options, and many crossed into the United States illegally in order to work in agriculture and other jobs in the United States that paid more.

Bribes

Drug trafficking was a major problem in Mexico then as well— as was related corruption. Ironically, I'm certain NAFTA indirectly led to more drugs smuggled into the United States thanks to increased trade, which meant more commercial vehicle traffic back and forth to Mexico, with more opportunities for smuggling. In 1996, the Mexican Congress passed a law designed to crack down on the drug cartels. In 1997, President Ernesto Zedillo was disappointed and embarrassed when the army general he appointed to serve as Mexico's anti-narcotics czar, General José de Jesús Gutiérrez Rebollo, was arrested and jailed for taking bribes.[7] While in office Gutiérrez even moved into an apartment in Mexico City that was owned by Mexico's most notorious cocaine trafficker, which was what led to his arrest.

After I left ADM in 1995, I became president of international operations for the GSI Group, an Illinois company that made grain storage facilities and other agricultural equipment. I continued to visit customers in Mexico on GSI's behalf for the rest of the decade. I also served as a board member for Coca-Cola Enterprises, the largest Coca-Cola bottler in the world at that time. In that capacity I would meet with regional bottlers in Mexico, which represented an important market for Coke. I remain friends with many of those bottlers today.

In 2000, I flew to Mexico City, where President Zedillo bestowed on me the Order of the Aztec Eagle. That is the highest honor the government of Mexico awards to a foreigner,[8] and I was proud to stand on the podium with former Texas governor Ann Richards; Senator Lloyd Bentsen; former U.S. trade representative Carla Hills; and Robert Mosbacher, the former U.S. secretary of commerce. All of us had worked to support Mexico's economic development. That was a proud day for me, and I think giving that award was symbolic of Zedillo's commitment to keep Mexico's economy growing.[9]

As years went by, I spent less time in Mexico. Our foundation's work in Africa expanded, and I began living on our foundation research farm in South Africa as much as six months per year. However, we funded agricultural development projects for Mexican farmers, and we supported several efforts designed to support legal paths for Mexican agricultural workers to support U.S. agriculture.

In 2012, I took a trip to Mexico that was eye-opening in several respects. I traveled to the Yaqui Valley in the state of Sonora, where the International Maize and Wheat Improvement Center (in Spanish the acronym is CIMMYT) is located.[10,11]

For a number of years our foundation directly supported CIMMYT research on our farm in Africa, where they developed seed varieties for corn that improved yields for thousands of food-insecure farmers throughout Africa. On this visit, we flew into the city of Obregón and drove out to CIMMYT's research facility and fields.

Pirate's highway

I had realized from speaking with my friends in Mexico that I could no longer travel to this part of Mexico without a high level of security. There were increasing numbers of stories about kidnappings and armed assaults in the region. The road from the airport in Obregón to where CYMMIT and the wheat and corn fields are located was particularly dangerous. The roads farmers and field workers traveled were safe during the day, but became a pirate's highway at night, when cars would be stopped at illegal roadblocks and armed criminals would extort money from those who wanted to pass. The trip went fine, but it was disappointing that a place where I had such fond memories had become a kind of war zone.

In Hermosillo, the capital of Sonora, where I had once done a lot of business and where I enjoyed that baseball game, our security team advised that we should conduct our meetings in our hotel and provide transportation to local farmers and others to attend. I met with farmers who were worried about a number of issues, including water rights and land ownership. But my most dramatic meeting was with a Franciscan priest who was born in the United States but had spent many years as a pastor in remote rural communities in the mountain area of Sinaloa.

The priest explained to me that the drug cartels were forcing subsistence farmers who had supported their families growing corn and wheat to replace their food crops with marijuana. In some cases they were then "paying" the farmers for doing that in weapons and alcohol instead of cash. Families were now starving and children were beginning to idolize local narco bosses the way my friends and I dreamed of being cowboys and sheriffs when I was growing up. He showed me pictures of children playing with toy trucks in which they'd put little mock marijuana bundles in the beds. If farmers disobeyed or refused the demands of the local narcos, they were killed on the spot.

Hearing about the increase in violence among people already struggling to grow sufficient food to survive was depressing. I'm sorry to say these situations have become measurably worse in just the last five years. I tried to find a way to visit the priest in Sinaloa, but one of the most capable security firms I work with convinced me they could not ensure our safety because criminals, primarily the drug cartels, were in complete control of the area.

Basically, the cartels make no secret of the fact that they run Mexico, and even some resort areas are experiencing cartel violence.[12] Even in places that were once high-end tourist destinations, like Acapulco, the cartels have moved in. In 2017, *The Economist* published statistics showing the city of Acapulco had the second-highest murder rate *in the world*.[13] It trailed San Salvador and was followed by San Pedro Sula, Honduras.[14] Think about that for a minute: El Salvador and Honduras are relatively small, poor countries. Mexico is the world's fifteenth-largest economy, and it is the United States' third-largest trading partner.[15] It has tremendous oil and natural gas resources. And one of its prominent cities is so controlled by drug cartels it is one of the most dangerous places *in the world*. These are our neighbors.

Because of my work with law enforcement in Arizona, I often see regional reports about crime trends in Mexico. The drug shipments seized at POEs in trucks and vehicles are often measured in tons— and so are the incredible caches of weapons and ammunition going back and forth across the border. But the photographs of murders testify to the staggering levels of violence.

"This will be you"

Mexican drug cartels now routinely kill enemies, informants, police, journalists, and literally anyone who gets in their way.[16] And the standard practice is to kidnap and torture these people first, then leave a "narcobanner" or a hand-lettered sign on the body or bodies with messages: WE ARE CLEANING UP THIS COMMUNITY AND WE ARE IN CONTROL. WE DON'T KID AROUND. WE MEAN WHAT WE SAY. IF YOU IGNORE OUR DEMANDS...THIS WILL BE YOU. And then they're signed by the cartel trying to retain control of or take over the area.[17]

It's not that the Mexican government ignores these acts, but as Sylvia Longmire succinctly put it in her 2011 book *Cartel*, "Finding good cops in Mexico is a serious challenge." Sylvia chronicled the long list of challenges Mexican law enforcement has had. She notes that the Mexican government has tried to reorganize the country's law enforcement structure five times since 1982, yet corruption runs deep.[18] At the time of her writing, she cited reports saying four hundred municipalities didn't even have police, and almost two thousand municipalities had police departments with fewer than one hundred employees. In 2011, 62 percent of officers made less than $315 per month, and 68 percent didn't have a high school education. Those factors offer a perfect target for cartels with lots of money to bribe cops who do not have a lot of other options.

Many see the Mexican military as the only entity with the resources and standards to go after and respond to cartels. I have been told by U.S. military leaders that, while there have been some proven cases of corruption, as a group the Mexican military is committed and courageous. U.S. military leaders are particularly impressed with the Mexican marines—the organization that captured El Chapo in Los Mochis.

Yet some peg the cartels' intensifying violence to former president Felipe Calderón's efforts to deploy the military to disrupt the cartels in 2006.[19] Two years later that effort was aided by $2.5 billion worth of resources, including planes, helicopters, K-9s, and training from the United States as part of the 2008 Merida Initiative, designed to strengthen the rule of law and help Mexico crack down on smuggling at its ports of entry, and share information with U.S. law enforcement.[20] Tens of thousands of Mexican military personnel were sent into cartel strongholds.

There were some positive impacts of that collaboration, experts say, notably the Mexican government's crackdown on illegal migrants at the Guatemalan border headed for the United States. On the other hand, it's also true that those efforts triggered massive bloodshed and deaths as the cartels fought back.

"Don't they care?"

I first met President Zedillo after his election in 1995. Since he awarded me the Aztec Eagle in 2000, I have seen and spoken to him many times in my visits to Mexico and at other events. He is an economist and now runs a research institute at Yale. I have always respected him and found him thoughtful and willing to address challenges in a straightforward way. In 2016, as I was researching this book, we met over dinner.

As we talked about the situation in Mexico and how it had changed since the 1990s, our conversation became very somber. He agreed with my assessment that most of Mexico—he estimated as much as 70 percent of the states—is now controlled by the drug cartels.

At the time of our dinner, Donald Trump had just won the U.S. presidency, and his inflammatory rhetoric about Mexico bothered us both. Our biggest concerns were Trump's belligerent posture toward the Mexican government and insults to the people of Mexico. Zedillo brought up something I had not thought about in a long time. When Zedillo was in office, he tried to drive a subtle but important shift in the culture of Mexico. His administration's focus on the economy, and the investments from the U.S. and rising employment levels, deemphasized a topic that had been a bitter pill to Mexicans for a long time. Zedillo explained, "Mexicans universally feel that the country was dispossessed of half our territory by the United States. To them this remains a tragedy of incredible proportions."

He's referring to consequences of the Mexican-American War. In the mid-19th century the United States invaded Mexico. After the fighting was done, the Treaty of Guadalupe-Hidalgo and later the Gadsden Purchase ceded what are now California, Nevada, Arizona, New Mexico, Wyoming, Texas, Utah, and Western Colorado—525,000 square miles in all and, at the time, almost half the territory of Mexico—to the United States. That is a lot of land. The Mexican people felt intensely wronged by the outcome of that war, and those feelings have complicated our relationship to the present day. Mexico felt so betrayed and abused by the U.S. government that even during its most difficult periods, it has resisted having U.S. military or law enforcement presence in Mexico, and has resisted other forms of cooperation with the United States that countries such as Colombia have welcomed.[21]

In the 1990s, however, a group of politicians, including Zedillo, began encouraging the Mexican people to look forward and focus on economic development. I think it's fair to say that process unleashed some of the optimism that we both recalled from that period. But Zedillo said that the rise of the cartels exploiting America's huge appetite for illegal drugs and now the anti-Mexico rhetoric from Donald Trump had turned the clock back decades. "We're seeing the rise again of calls for socialism, nationalism, and anti-American political candidates," he observed.

President Zedillo has a dry sense of humor. I laughed at one point he made about how cavalier Americans can be when they say things like "Why can't Mexico figure out how to shut down the drug trafficking through its country? Do they just not care?" He told a story of being at a meeting once when an American official asked him a similar question. He replied, "You know that is a very good question, but it seems to be a problem we share. How is it that drugs cross your southern border and then they get all the way to Chicago or New York? Why can't you figure out how to shut that down?"

Although he presided over an aggressive government-backed war on drugs in the 1990s, today Zedillo calls such efforts a proven failure. He blames the criminalization of drugs and the long-fought "war" for creating the lucrative black market that has motivated the cartels to try to gain and hold on to power with such vicious violence.

As always, our discussion was respectful, even on points where we disagree. As an economist, he has become an advocate for de-criminalizing drugs on a global basis to lower their value and thus the cartel's power. As a law enforcement advocate, I believe that massive decriminalization of all drugs would take too big a toll on innocent people over too long a period, and I also believe it would trigger many negative unintended consequences.

But we were in full agreement in one of the most important points: "Mexico is having serious problems with the rule of law," he said.

"A loose tongue"

In July 2017, about seven months after my meeting with Zedillo, I read a story in the *Wall Street Journal* and recalled Zedillo's comment. The headline read: 11,155 DEAD: MEXICO'S VIOLENT DRUG WAR IS ROARING BACK.[22] The story begins with an account of the murder of a journalist named Miroslava Breach, a newspaper reporter who had written a number of stories connecting the cartels with politicians they had bribed. She was waiting outside her home for her fourteen-year-old son to get in the car so she could drive him to school. Gunmen drove up and fired eight shots into her vehicle, killing her instantly. They left a note at the scene saying she was killed "for having a loose tongue." The story also chronicled how the murder rate of Mexico had jumped 31 percent from the previous year.

Corruption, which has long existed in Mexican politics, now is so woven into the fabric of governance it sometimes seems insurmountable. The story claimed nearly a dozen state governors are under investigation for corruption, serving time, or in active prosecutions now, and another three have fled the country to avoid prosecution. In March 2017, a top prosecutor in one state was arrested at the U.S. border on drug trafficking charges.

The story continued: "In an interview, [the new governor of Chihuahua, Javier Corral] said that before he took office the state prosecutor's office had been 'totally dismantled' and thousands of open criminal investigations filed away and forgotten, including crimes of murder, rape and kidnapping." Apparently the newly elected Corral accused the previous state administration under the PRI (a political party) of making deals with drug gangs. After Corral, a former journalist, was voted into office in October 2016, the previous governor of Chihuahua fled to Texas right before a warrant for his arrest was issued that claimed he embezzled hundreds of millions of dollars from the state. This gives you an idea of the scale of the money available to those willing to ignore the law in Mexico.

The story also suggested other troubling dynamics at work. PRI, the party of the current president, Enrique Peña Nieto, has been accused of creating alliances with cartels where it allows them some leeway to smuggle in exchange for keeping killings low. But in some areas of Mexico, citizens fed up with corruption and ineffectiveness have voted PRI candidates out of office in the last year. Some believe the uptick in killings is one result of those previous alliances breaking down, according to the *WSJ*.

One new factor is that anticorruption activist groups in Mexico have become more vocal. In April 2017, the *New York Times* quoted the executive president of Mexicans Against Corruption and Impunity, María Amparo Casar, whose organization has done research showing that of forty-two governors suspected of corruption since 2000, only seventeen were investigated and three jailed. The level of impunity for so long triggered brazen behavior because "They know it will be the people below" who take the fall for their illegal acts, Casar told the *Times.*[23]

Is Colombia a model?

One question I continue to research: Is there a model for how a country has successfully battled and recovered from extreme criminal elements once they become so deeply entrenched? Some point to Colombia as a model of a nation that was dominated by the criminal element during the years of Pablo Escobar and the Medellín cocaine cartel. The leadership of Colombia vowed to break the cocaine cartels' grip and it sought help. Plan Colombia was a fifteen-year initiative beginning in 2000, in which the United States sent aid and military support to Colombia, trained Colombian forces, and provided helicopters, weapons, and other technology to help the government secure its territory from violent insurgents and disrupt the activity of criminal cartels. There is debate about the long-term success of the plan. Many experts have noted that Colombia continues to produce huge amounts of cocaine and is the largest source of cocaine used in the United States. But it did ultimately break apart the cartels that had wreaked havoc inside the country for many years.[24]

Retired general Simeon Trombitas commanded the U.S. Military Group in Bogotá, Colombia, from 2003 to 2005, at which time the United States was executing Plan Colombia, and he later commanded other important missions in Mexico, South and Central America, and the Caribbean. The general explained that the successes of Plan Colombia were due to the fact that "The Colombians bought into it. They had a history of being a democracy, and the people were very proud of that. The people did not want to turn their country over to the cartels." General Trombitas said the revolutionary group FARC and the Colombian cartels were always seen as a separate entity fighting for control of the government. However, "the Mexican drug cartels ... are like businesses. They want to buy and sell product and they will buy and sell government officials to get what they want, but they don't want to take over running the country."

Like Zedillo, Trombitas reinforced that an overriding but underappreciated cultural element in Mexico is the deep historical resentment of the Mexican government, military, and population toward the United States. "Their world view is not linear, it is circular and they come back always to the idea that the U.S. stole their territory. They are very protective of their sovereignty."

Trombitas points out that in Mexico, corruption was far more established along party lines and institutions. The PRI party ruled for seventy-one years, until 2000, and the Council on Foreign Relations, among others, has detailed the cartels' infiltration of the entrenched party to protect drug trafficking.[25] Prior to the demise of the power of the Medellín and Cali cartels in Colombia, Mexicans were not the originators of the drugs, but they were the transporters. The unintended consequence of bringing down the Colombian cartels was that the Mexican cartels took over more of the cocaine distribution business not only through Mexico but in the main market in the United States. They also became producers and distributors of methamphetamines and heroin.[26]

Trombitas also noted that in Mexico in recent years there has been a cultural embrace of the cartels and their outlaw image, including even *telenovelas* where cartel members are portrayed as

225

heroes, and song ballads called *narcocorridos*, popular songs that glorify cartel traffickers and their lifestyle.[27] That may be starting to change, based on the rise of anticorruption activists and communities that are voting corrupt politicians out of office, but there is no question that Mexico's tolerance of impunity for so long has been catastrophic. "Mexico's legal system is so weak, the prosecution rate is 5 percent. How do you fix problems when you have a 95 percent chance of escaping prosecution or punishment when you commit a crime?" asks the general.

I thought immediately of my talk with the priest in 2012 and the photos of the boys playing narco trucks. In their games, the narcos are the heroes and the bad guys are the police. The children aspire to wear clothes and items with marijuana leaves on them. These are more insidious consequences of erosion of the rule of law. Violence, crime, and battling the authorities become normal, even idealized.

I think about that when I hear that more Mexicans now leave the United States to return home than head north. The primary explanation for this trend is a sharp decline in Mexicans interested in migrating. After the U.S. recession of 2008 it became harder to find work in the United States;[28] meanwhile the Mexican economy began generating jobs so fewer people have to leave Mexico to support themselves. Also, the birthrate in Mexico has dropped steadily (in the 1960s Mexican women had an average of seven children; today, they have an average of two), so there aren't as many young people without options.[29] But I talk to so many Central Americans fleeing violence, and I think back to those farmworkers in south Texas who have lived in the United States for years now and who say they never want to return to Mexico. They live on low incomes and have many challenges and struggles, but clearly they have a sense of safety here that they do not want to surrender. I wonder, *Have the Mexican people become so used to living with corruption and violence that it is accepted as normal?*

I also think back to the businessman in Hermosillo who was proud of his city's baseball team. That's the kind of cultural activity that creates positive role models for kids. These days, I have heard about murders at baseball games in Mexico, and border area teams whose attendance has dropped because of fears of violence. Security forces with automatic weapons patrol some stadiums. I could not have imagined during that evening under the Hermosillo lights so many years ago, that the kids I saw cheering for home run hitters would switch to wanting to be cartel hit men. I suspect the "canary" sitting on that hill by our ranch is one of those kids who could have been inspired to lead a very different kind of life if provided the opportunity.

One thing I know for sure: Insulting, bullying, or belittling Mexico will never help us improve border security. To help Mexico change for the better, we need to change as well. We need to treat the Mexican government as a partner and help it stabilize the country, drive out the criminal element, and achieve better security for us both. Like it or not, we are neighbors, and we need to think about how to help our struggling neighbor regain its sovereignty and direction—for their sake and ours.

Chapter 15

RED SHOES ON THE ROAD AGAIN

Once Central American migrants and refugees decide their only hope for a better future is to live in the United States, many will keep trying until they succeed . . . despite the dangers on both sides of the border.

I was disappointed but not surprised that we could not connect with Oscar during our visit to Honduras in May 2017. I was glad I traveled there, nonetheless. As he told us in Arizona, life for his family in their remote village was difficult. Work was scarce, and the family was surviving on very little. Oscar and Jaime's aunts are proud, hardworking women who love their families and want to see their children get an education and improve their prospects. The family was a little wary of us, and that made sense to me, too. It was hard to tell exactly what their feelings about Oscar were. Wherever you travel in the world, whatever the circumstances, families are complicated, and dynamics can change overnight.

After I met his family, I was rooting for all of them. I was hopeful Oscar could settle in a safe place and find a legal, productive way to build a better life for himself in Honduras. We still had Oscar's Facebook page, and my team kept trying to make contact. A few weeks after our visit with his family, a message from him arrived: "Hola! Que tal?"

One of our foundation associates who lives in Mexico exchanged a number of messages and a phone call with Oscar. It turned out that he had in fact left Honduras. He said there was very little work and so he decided to go north again. I have heard many times that when young men decide they want to go to the United States they will just keep trying until they succeed. We've heard estimates that the majority of those who attempt to cross the border will eventually make it. Yet Oscar had seemed to be so traumatized by his experience in Arizona it was hard to imagine him turning around and coming back for another try. We wanted to ask him about that.

He said he was living in Tequisquiapan, a tourist-style town in the Querétaro state about 120 miles north of Mexico City. He didn't elaborate on his trip there beyond saying that he'd traveled there by train. He said he met a nice woman who fed him and took him in to stay with her family. She needed some help delivering baked goods around the town.

He also sent our Mexico City contact live video of the area where he was working and it showed cobblestone streets and a clean, orderly neighborhood. He had occasional access to Facebook and was in touch with his brother, Jaime, and had heard about our visit to see his family. He seemed happy that we had offered to provide support to Jaime and his cousin to attend school.

"I had to come here because there I suffer a lot. People and maybe you think that I left because I'm a vagrant, a criminal. No, I left because there, there's a lot of suffering and I want to help my brothers, my family," Oscar said. Our contact asked him who he was worried would think he was a criminal.

"My family. Or maybe Mr. Howard. Maybe he thinks: 'This kid has already gone again to screw up his life and come into my country illegally'."

She said: "We just want to know how you're doing, that's all."

Oscar replied: "I always leave but it's because I want to help my family. I have to rely on myself and leave and look for something good. And here I am again, and I thank God that I'm here in Mexico again...I want to have something, feel like I've gotten somewhere, one day have my little house. That's my goal."

"Your time will come"

Oscar admitted that getting to the United States was still his goal. "All of my friends from the border, they are there, all of them, in a place called Maryland. All of my friends are there. They already have their own cars, send money to their family, and they message me on Facebook and tell me 'Any day now your time will come, man.'"

After it was relayed to me later, several elements of this conversation bothered me. I wanted to talk to him myself. I just wanted to understand his experience. I realized it could be a problem because he might think I was pursuing or investigating him on behalf of law enforcement or the government.

But also, I was intrigued by Oscar's "friends from the border" comment. I suspect some of their enthusiasm was a hard sell to motivate him to come, but his friends apparently painted quite a picture of life in the United States, and he had convinced himself it was "God's plan" that he join them. I also thought about Juanita's comment about growing up thinking that the United States was a paradise where "everyone" is happy and has so much money. She had relatives who'd been in the United States literally for a decade or more; had they really told her that? Or had she not understood what they meant? Had she heard only what she wanted to hear?

This kind of talk is unfortunate because it is unrealistic, and I think it motivates people to do dangerous things. Imagine what these exaggerated descriptions of America must sound like to someone like young Carla in Honduras. Surely, living almost any place in the United States beats living on top of piles of garbage in a violent country. On the other hand, I also think many thousands of people come north with fantastic, unrealistic expectations, sometimes fueled by family or friends who miss them or are too proud to admit that the circumstances of their lives are not what they expected.

The journeys are extremely dangerous. Amnesty International has estimated that upwards of 60 percent of migrant women and girls are sexually assaulted on their journeys.[1] I have spoken with young women who've experienced this abuse. In 2005 I was riding along with Border Patrol when I spoke with a teenage girl from Mexico who had just been part of a large group of migrants who had been apprehended. She was terrified and exhausted. She said that when the group neared the border, masked men with guns, who were probably known to their guide, came and threatened to rape the girls. She escaped that fate, but said other women did not. Staging towns like Altar are known for selling birth control, which mothers of girls will buy for themselves and their daughters before they set off for the border.[2]

I have had many conversations with migrants who say they "put their trust in God" and then took incredibly risky journeys on trains or led by cartel *coyotes*. I once posed the question to a Catholic bishop in Texas: How does the church deal with this kind of faith, when surely the priests in these villages understand the dangers that lie ahead? Trying to counsel migrants who are convinced they are following "God's plan" is a real challenge, the bishop admitted. "We're going to have to be a lot better about coordinating our response as a church. But you also don't want to intervene in their conscience. Some of these people are so poor, their faith is literally all they have. You do not want to take that away."

I asked our team to set up another conference call if possible so I could speak personally with Oscar. A week or so went by and word came back: Oscar was on the move again. He had moved to another city in Mexico—Ixmiquilpan, a town in Hidalgo about one hundred miles north of Mexico City—and again he said that while he was begging for help he met a woman who agreed to let him do some work for her in her greenhouse. We learned that he was saving up money to try to rent his own room in the town.

We sent our Mexico City colleague to the village to connect with Oscar, and we successfully scheduled a conference call. Oscar was in good spirits. He said the work in the nursery was nowhere near as difficult and tiring as the jobs he'd tried to work in Honduras.

We joked about his red shoes, the ones he was wearing at Mission Oaks and that we saw in Honduras. He said that when he was in Sonora, Mexico, before he attempted to cross the border the first time, he was walking around in flip-flops and begging on the street when he met a woman who asked him how he thought he was going to manage a desert crossing in those. He said the flip-flops were his only shoes, and so she took him to a store and bought him the red ones. He never saw her again. He loved the shoes, but he left them behind for his brother Jaime because Jaime liked them, too.

Trick questions

I told Oscar I had seen the Facebook video he posted where he referred to the cartels offering him money. In it, he wears a bright green T-shirt and a ball cap turned backward. He looks tired. He said he shot the video in San Juan del Rio in Central Mexico. I explained that at first we thought that it meant he was working for the cartels, but Jaime had said no, we misinterpreted it and that Oscar was instead saying that he turned them down.

"Why did you make that video?" I asked.

Oscar patiently explained through our interpreter: "I was walking alone on the side of a road. A black truck pulled over and there were two guys in the front seat. The one in the passenger seat said, 'Hey, do you want to join the Gulf cartel?'

"I knew this was very dangerous. I answered: 'I say this with much respect and I thank you but I am trying to get to the United States so I can help my family. I am leaving Mexico to go find work so I can send money home.'"

He said the cartel member in the passenger seat talked to the driver briefly and then he said: "We are Zetas. You can work for us. We will give you a radio and we will give you seven thousand pesos to help us." Oscar said he realized there was a good chance that the first question was a test—a way to see if he was looking for or disposed to join the Gulf cartel, a sworn enemy of the Zetas. If he had said yes to it, they might have killed him on the spot. But what if this offer was now the test? What if they really were Gulf cartel, and now they were tricking him to see if he actually was looking for Zetas? Again, he said he told them that he was just passing through because he felt a big obligation to help his family back in Honduras and he would not be staying in Mexico. He repeated that he meant no disrespect.

Oscar said the two men discussed what he said for a moment, and then Oscar says the one in the passenger seat took out his phone and took Oscar's photo. Then, they drove off.

Oscar said he figured that he better get out of the area as fast as possible, because he was now a marked man. He also figured the truck might turn around and come back and kidnap or kill him right away. Or these guys might text his photo ahead and signal to others to look for him.

He went and found a friend he had made on his journey to the town. He asked to use his phone to make a video and post it on Facebook. He told our contact that the reason he made the video and mentioned the cartels was so that if he disappeared or turned up dead, his family would realize that the Gulf or Zeta cartel had probably killed him.

Oscar had good reason to be worried. The cartels kidnap and kill hundreds of people a year, and many people go missing. There also have been horrific mass murders. I learned about one of them in a 2015 visit I made to a migrant shelter in southern Mexico called La 72. The shelter was started by a Franciscan priest, and is named for the victims of what has come to be called the 2010 San Fernando massacre, in which seventy-two undocumented migrants from Central America were murdered by the Zeta drug cartel on a ranch in San Fernando, Tamaulipas, Mexico. The fifty-eight men and fourteen women were each shot in the back of the head and piled up inside a ranch the Zetas controlled; one migrant faked his death and later escaped. He told authorities, and they raided the ranch and found the bodies.[3]

Strangers on a train

Next, Oscar elaborated on his actual journey to Mission Oaks. In our previous conversations, Oscar had spoken only of his own walk through the desert and his own efforts to avoid the armed drug mules he encountered near our ranch. That had always been confusing to me. Regardless of how they travel, by bus or train or van or private car, Central Americans moving north through Mexico tend not to be isolated. At any given time there are large numbers of people on the move, and they tend to jump on and jump off trains at certain locations. They are anxious and often scared, and they try to form at least temporary alliances. They take turns keeping watch while members of their group sleep. They pick up intelligence about who to look out for, how and where to cross, what they will need, what they should say.

The idea that Oscar had walked for a week on his own had never seemed likely to me, but I have often found that translated conversations lead to misunderstandings. If we spoke the same language I might have heard details that prompted me to probe for more context or clarification.

In any event, on our phone call this time, we asked him to help us understand more of the actual details of his journey on foot. Why didn't you hire a *coyote*, I asked. Did you just not have the money, or did you think you did not need one?

Oscar explained that he, in fact, was not alone on his seven-day hike before he hit Mission Oaks. On the train from Caborca, in the Sonora region of Mexico, to Santa Ana near the U.S. border, Oscar said he became friendly with two other Hondurans, as well as two Mexican men who also planned to cross into the United States. At first, he said, the Mexican men were friendly and the five of them made a pact that they would travel together. The Mexicans said they knew the way to cross. The group bought supplies and food in Santa Ana, about sixty miles south of the border, and they started hiking. But as they continued to move north, Oscar said the Hondurans became uncomfortable with the Mexicans. They realized they had a lot of tattoos, and began to think they were criminals. He stopped short of saying they were cartel members, but he did say, "I did not want to turn my back on them." The Mexicans did not demand any money from the Hondurans, he said.

As he approached the border near MOR, Oscar had told us he was resting in a wash when the armed group of mules passed by. Now, he admitted that the two Hondurans and two Mexicans were there with him. When the armed man at the tail end of the smuggling group saw them and started yelling and firing his weapon,

Oscar said the other four men ran off. He realized his odds of surviving were probably better if he went in a different direction.

Assuming what Oscar told us is factual, we will never know the intentions of the Mexican men traveling with Oscar. I made some inquiries with Border Patrol, but they do not release details about whether, when, or where individuals or groups have been apprehended.

If I had to guess, I suspect the Mexican men traveling with Oscar were involved with a cartel, and I suspect the Hondurans' growing discomfort with them was well founded. I would not be surprised if their plan was to try to extort money from the Honduran men's families. And if they couldn't pay—who knows what might have happened. If it happened as Oscar said, no wonder he was exhausted and somewhat disoriented when he arrived at MOR.

The final new wrinkle in Oscar's account occurred after our phone call. Our colleague from Mexico City continued to visit with him after our call. She said Oscar was in a good mood, happy to have had a good meal. Oscar talked about the work he was doing in Mexico, and about his hopes to be able to send money back to the family. Oscar was talking about the work ethic and manners that his dad instilled in him, and then he said somewhat out of the blue how much he missed his father and how awful it had been to see him die.

When I first met Oscar at Mission Oaks, he said through an interpreter we called that he had lost his father after the father came to Mexico to "find him." He said the same thing when I spoke to him at Florence, and both times he became so upset he did not offer more details. Now, I learned why.

Apparently Oscar's father did find him—and then they both kept going north. One of the major hubs for migrants traveling by train is Veracruz on Mexico's eastern coastline. Oscar said he and his father were both sitting on top of the same train car. Oscar was talking with a group of young men his age while his father was sitting a few feet away with some older, heavily tattooed Mexican men. All of a sudden, Oscar said an argument broke out in that group. As Oscar watched, he said the Mexican men grabbed his father and threw him off the side of the train, close to the wheels.

The train kept moving. Oscar said he couldn't say or do anything because the men surely would do the same to him. I can't imagine what it would be like to witness your father's murder and then make yourself appear unconcerned—or risk losing your own life.

Part III

WHAT NEEDS TO CHANGE

We've talked about the connections between the decline of the rule of law in our hemisphere, border security, and the slow-motion terrorism that is killing tens of thousands of Americans each year. We've talked about the human and financial toll this takes. I'm concerned that it's also taking a toll on our basic values. The *New York Times* has done an exposé on supposed drug treatment facilities in Florida that are deliberately sabotaging the recovery of patients because they profit from insurance payments when addicts relapse.[1] The consequence of these scams for some addicts has been death. Recently, I've also seen reports about communities with high numbers of emergency overdose calls: In at least one city in Ohio, local leaders have talked about refusing to give Narcan or even refusing to roll emergency responders after repeated 911 calls involving a person who previously has overdosed.[2]

If the point of terrorism is to undermine a society's basic fabric, terrorists must be counting these situations as victories. In your vision of America, should individuals have to forfeit the chance to live because they are in the grip of an addictive disease? Some say, "It's their choice." Following that logic, will we stop treating heart attacks or strokes if a person smokes? Will we not send an ambulance if a driver with multiple speeding tickets is injured in an accident?

We won't win this war by punishing or even prosecuting addicts. We have to stop narco-terrorism at a much earlier stage. It requires both strengthening our own border defenses and supporting the countries whose current struggles are fueling the cartels' power and filling their bank accounts.

As Cindy McCain pointed out in the preface, our "enemy" here is not an ethnic group or the citizens of a given nation; it is sophisticated, ruthless, networked, transnational criminal organizations. Based on my experiences, my investigations, and many dozens of interviews and conversations, I have distilled my recommendations to strengthen border security to five, which I will spell out in this section. They are not equal in scope, but I believe each is essential. We need what military people sometimes call a multifaceted or "whole-of-government" approach. Neglecting any one of these dynamics will undermine the larger mission.

Chapter 16

REBOOT COMMAND OF THE BORDER

We cannot achieve border security without giving the command of our frontline forces the strategic control, mission flexibility, and high-quality human resources needed to get the job done. That may demand significant changes within the Department of Homeland Security.

In a business context my father once said, "Should you find yourself in a chronically leaking boat, energy devoted to changing vessels is likely to be more productive than energy devoted to patching leaks."

For fifteen years Americans have been asked to put their faith in the government's ability to protect U.S. soil in a vessel called the Department of Homeland Security, or DHS. DHS is a group of agencies assembled in the aftermath of a crisis—an unprecedented attack on the U.S. mainland by foreign terrorists. The agencies were told to prioritize making sure nothing like 9/11 ever happened again.

It is true that we have not had another 9/11-style terrorist attack. But foreign threats have delivered widespread, insidious harm to us on an even larger scale.

Remember the 2015 comments of General John Kelly of the U.S. Marine Corps, who was then commander of the U.S. Southern Command? He pointed out that the 9/11 hijackers killed three thousand people, but narco-terrorists had contributed to the deaths of nearly half a million Americans who had overdosed on drugs since then. He also told the Senate Armed Services Committee in 2015: "We continue to underestimate the threat of transnational organized crime at significant and direct risk to our national security and that of our partner nations. Unless confronted by an immediate, visible, or uncomfortable crisis, our nation's tendency is to take the security of the Western Hemisphere for granted. I believe this is a mistake."

Although President Trump tapped General Kelly to head DHS, Kelly was only in the job six months before Trump appointed him White House Chief of Staff. In early December 2017, Kirstjen Nielsen was confirmed by the Senate as the new secretary of Homeland Security. She is a cybersecurity expert and former TSA official. My hope is that she realizes the agency is due for significant reorganization. It's time to rethink and reboot DHS.

Specifically, we must focus on our border security command structure and make sure we have well-managed, appropriately staffed agencies with the flexibility, resources, and support they need to protect us. Our domestic drug problem and the growing strength of the Mexican cartels are ample evidence that our border has been "leaking" significantly. We can't just try to plug holes in the current configuration. I propose two significant organizational changes, and then I will give you the background on how I came to these conclusions. The history matters, and I will admit it is complicated.

First, we must give the command of Border Patrol the flexibility to deploy its resources to meet the threats coming at us. We need properly vetted and well-trained agents who can deploy quickly to specific locations for necessary mission durations to protect the

United States from criminal trespassers. We must create a hybrid security force similar to how the U.S. Coast Guard operates with a dual purpose both to enforce laws and defend the U.S. homeland from potential enemies.

To achieve that, we should consider separating current BP personnel into two categories. As we discussed in chapter 8, BP's union contracts have constrained its command. Although unions are effective and important advocates for frontline personnel in many law enforcement situations, securing our border with a friendly country that nonetheless harbors an aggressive and destructive criminal element that is harming us is such a unique mission that I believe we need to implement a unique change.

This is not about being for or against unions. I appreciate that the NBPC has tried to make sure that the difficult and complex realities along the border do not victimize the same people trying to keep us safe. But security must be our top priority.

For functions that do not require an agent carrying a weapon or making arrests, such as intelligence analysis, data support, processing of large groups of asylum seekers, and some (not all) of the activities at inland checkpoints, I believe union representation is appropriate. These are critical jobs, but the vast majority of the time, they do not demand the skills of armed agents who must utilize tactics requiring high-level training and proficiency in engaging a threat.

However, the armed agents patrolling our borders should belong to a category of "excepted service" similar to the Federal Bureau of Investigation (FBI), Central Intelligence Agency (CIA), and the U.S. Secret Service. These and another three dozen or so agencies are excepted from the U.S. government's "competitive service" process. They have their own hiring and evaluation systems and security clearance processes, and several are legally prohibited from collective bargaining agreements.

Today, collective bargaining agreements limit our ability to respond to the shifting tactics and surges of drug smugglers and other criminals infiltrating our border. Technically, CBP is America's largest law enforcement agency, but we have to embrace the fundamental basis of the mission: Patrolling our borders effectively today, when drug and human smugglers may be armed with automatic weapons and sophisticated communication networks, demands a combination of law enforcement, intelligence gathering, and foreign adversary engagement skills and tactics beyond basic law enforcement.

Unions may be common in some law enforcement, but the demands within cities and counties are different than they are on the border. Police forces tend to operate in well-defined, limited territory. They confront familiar criminal patterns and scheduling and job parameters can be negotiated based on predictable needs. They also can count on having officers immediately available to provide back-up. Border Patrol agents, on the other hand, cover vast, often diverse geographic territory and face unpredictable threats that fall across a wide range of risk profiles. When Border Patrol implements a new plan or deploys new technology, almost overnight crossing pressure may shift miles away. Smugglers will shift their tactics from climbing a fence near an urban area to crossing the border on remote, rocky terrain where horseback-mounted teams might be needed. Or a response to political shifts and opportunities may trigger a surge of migrants.

That happened in 2014 in Texas. Violence was escalating in Mexico and Central America, and for a brief period there appeared to be growing political support for broad immigration reform. There also were perceptions that unaccompanied minors who turned themselves in after crossing the border would be released to family members.[1] Tens of thousands of unaccompanied minors began crossing the Rio Grande, swamping BP's resources, and it took months to shore up that sector by shifting agents away from other areas that in some cases had high smuggling activity. The Associated Press did an analysis that year showing that on one single day, June 14, 2,500 agents were on duty in the San Diego sector and that sector arrested ninety-seven immigrants illegally crossing the border. Meanwhile, 3,200 agents in the Rio Grande Valley made 1,422 arrests (and who knows how many people crossed our border undetected?).[2]

Border security goals are compromised when collective bargaining agreements dictate the conditions under which officers can be transferred, promoted, and, to a certain degree, deployed. Under collective bargaining agreements, agents can file appeals to transfer, and other rules can prevent a strategically important operating facility from being staffed—as has happened for more than six years near our Mission Oaks Ranch in Arizona. Would we give an undercover CIA operative the option to accept or decline the next phase of a mission based on whether he felt he'd been given adequate warning of a change? Should an FBI leader who needs agents to "follow the money" to a different state in a laundering investigation have to delay deployment to make sure the order aligns with collective bargaining rules?

I don't think so.

With a special designation designed to support more highly trained agents should come sufficient pay increases to attract a larger pool of quality applicants with relevant experience. This is one of our nation's most important law enforcement assignments, and given the problems of the past, new, outstanding, properly vetted agents are worth that investment. As I write this, government auditors have documented that Border Patrol is losing agents at a rate faster than it is able to hire new ones. The GAO has reported the agency has 1,870 fewer agents than the 21,370 agents it is authorized to have right now.[3] To achieve the Trump administration's hope of adding 5,000 additional agents to patrol our borders, I believe DHS will need to consider an overhaul of BP's pay incentives, culture, and command.

Command change

Second, not only do we need to change the way our frontline border forces are structured, we need to rethink the command structure of the border mission itself. The immediate emergency that created CBP and ICE and separated the enforcement and investigation functions has passed. With the wisdom of fifteen years of experience, it's time to organize not only those two agencies but all the federal actors on the border, including the Drug Enforcement Administration, the U.S. Coast Guard, the Federal Bureau of Investigation (FBI), the Department of the Interior, and Bureau of Alcohol, Tobacco, Firearms and Explosives (ATF), in a more cohesive, complementary way. A former senior CBP leader explains: "We act in a very fragmented fashion. All the agencies who operate in and around the border today protect a zone…the trouble is all the entities are centric to their own interests—DEA, for example, only worries about narcotics, but not about the incursions and impacts and overall threats of what they're learning. The cartels are no longer narco-centric; they are more of a mafia, and they are moving weapons, ammunition, narcotics. [They are engaging in] sex trafficking, and even chickens are smuggled to avoid taxes. But the entities are rewarded and recognized in a matter related to their [individual] charters."

In other words, our current strategy is like assigning a different agency to attack each spoke of a wheel and rewarding them for whittling their spoke down, instead of figuring out how to prevent the wheel from rolling. Added the former CBP official: "We should be incentivizing agencies to make it more difficult for the drug cartels to operate, and to show how their work is impacting quality of life, a safer border, reduction of social costs. Instead we measure our impact by tons of drugs collected." I agree. I often say, we can begin to claim we are securing the border when we see a measurable decline in drug overdoses and drug-related violence across the United States.

"We need to dovetail, align, and coordinate the interests of all these different agencies," says the former CBP official, who favors a strengthened CBP for that role. I agree with the need for an overseer, but I am not convinced that we can achieve the impact we need by just giving CBP that authority. The agency has not had a strong tradition of cooperating with other agencies, for one thing. A clean-slate approach with leadership that is experienced with more flexible force deployment will help push the effort forward without the baggage of the past.

Based on the conversations I've had, I would raise other options involving command change. One is to give the U.S. Coast Guard overall command of our border security mission. The Coast Guard has shown flexibility and an ability to interact successfully with the general public in vastly different settings. They routinely carry out law enforcement functions, such as monitoring recreational boating, as well as operating in concert with other military branches in intense conflict situations such as interdicting drugs at sea from armed and hostile vessels. This is the kind of command flexibility needed in a complex theater like the border regions of the United States, where security will be improved by both a more traditional chain of command for this level of threat and a more cooperative and collaborative posture with the community and local law enforcement. The Coast Guard already patrols our coastal borders and has the right to operate along the length of the Rio Grande in Texas, a key border area. I'm not talking about turning Border Patrol agents into Coast Guard personnel. But I think having the

Coast Guard oversee Border Patrol and all other border agency activities will create a more balanced and flexible command vehicle that will provide a comprehensive and coordinated government response.

Alternatively, and more long term, we should use our fifteen years of post-9/11 experience to rethink DHS and its mission. In addition to the tough conclusions of the Coburn report in 2015, many different analysts have noted that the grouping of agencies in DHS has not created the powerful synergies it was designed to achieve. "Americans are not safer because the head of DHS is simultaneously responsible for airport security and governmental efforts to counter potential flu epidemics," Cato Institute analyst David Rittgers wrote in 2011. Rittgers proposed breaking apart DHS entirely, returning many of the component agencies to their original parent agencies and creating a "Border Security Administration" that would combine customs, immigration, and border patrol under one command.[4]

I think that is an interesting idea, and the increasing complexity of border threats should elevate the importance of such a command to a seat on the National Security Council. Today, data security, financial network exploitation, abuse of the U.S. mail, and post-disaster vulnerabilities also represent threats to border security, and they are complex challenges where coordination with the Department of Defense and intelligence agencies is vital. It would also be important for the kind of entity Rittgers envisioned to ensure close and integrated cooperation with the U.S. Coast Guard, which should continue to guard our coastal and inland waterway borders.

At minimum, Congress must own a problem at DHS that it created. One of the key recommendations of *The 9/11 Commission Report*, released in 2004, was that Congress needed to "create a single, principal point of oversight and review for homeland security."[5]

It also recommended that permanent, standing committees, one in the House and one in the Senate, should have a "nonpartisan staff." However, experts convened to mark the tenth anniversary of that report noted that Congress had failed to reform DHS's tangled oversight bureaucracy. The number of committees claiming oversight authority had actually *increased*, and that was making DHS far less efficient than it could be.[6]

I realize that I'm presenting ideas that the unions will likely dismiss outright. Government policy wonks will trot out a dozen reasons why reorganizing or reassigning command can't be accomplished without an act of Congress. U.S. Coast Guard leaders may not have any interest in overseeing activity on inland borders. Congressional committee chairs will point fingers at counterparts who don't want to give up any power.

But if there is one thing you have learned from this book by now, I hope it is that we need to get serious about border security and have these conversations before the drug overdose numbers approach six figures and the cartels even further destabilize Mexico and our southern border. These changes cannot alone deliver border security, but revitalizing our command structure is critical to shutting down criminal networks.

Background

Many of today's most difficult challenges have their roots in the unintended consequences of actions taken years ago.

Faced with a horrific, multiple-target assault on 9/11, the Bush administration pursued a military response but also a stepped up focus on the security of the "homeland." Reports had surfaced of warnings and intelligence that were not appropriately shared or valued prior to the attacks.[7] The 9/11 hijackers had entered our country using normal transportation channels, which was concerning enough, but in 2001 *thousands of people were attempting to enter the U.S. illegally every single day* (there were 1.6 million apprehensions on the southwest border in 2000).[8] We were vulnerable.

The administration put a team together to evaluate the gaps 9/11 had exposed and the federal agencies that could and should play a role in defending Americans from future terrorist attacks. The original plan was an "Office" of Homeland Security under control of the White House, designed to coordinate domestic terrorism efforts and make sure key information was shared. But Congress wanted a full department over which it would have oversight. The White House proposed a plan that Congress eventually approved.

According to a Bush administration insider who was on hand when a small team went to work on this, the configuration of the Department of Homeland Security resulted from "drag and drop editing." The team was described to me as having military and political experts, but minimal law enforcement expertise.

The team selected twenty-two entities from their existing homes in government and moved them into the new DHS organization chart.[9] The new top priority for roughly 180,000 federal employees was: Protect the U.S. homeland from terrorism, and communicate with each other as you do it.[10] According to the Congressional Research Service, DHS represented the most substantial reorganization of federal government agencies since the National Security Act of 1947, which put our military departments under a secretary of defense and created the National Security Council (NSC) and Central Intelligence Agency.[11]

DHS did not create any new agencies from scratch—although it did reconfigure components of several existing border security-related groups to make new ones. It combined part of the U.S. Customs Service, the Animal and Plant Health Inspection Service, and U.S. Immigration and Naturalization Service (specifically U.S. Border Patrol and immigration inspectors) into what is now called

Customs and Border Protection. CBP is the nation's largest law enforcement agency, with more than forty-five thousand sworn agents. Its personnel patrol the border, staff inland checkpoints, and carry out customs duties at ports of entry, such as collecting tariffs.[12]

The DHS designers also combined the specific investigative and intelligence resources of the U.S. Customs Service; the criminal investigation, detention, and deportation resources of the Immigration and Naturalization Service; and the Federal Protective Service (which protects government buildings and facilities). The new entity became the Immigration and Customs Enforcement agency (or ICE). The Federal Protective Service was later transferred from ICE to the National Protection and Programs Directorate. ICE, with about twenty thousand employees, is the nation's second-largest criminal investigative agency after the FBI.[13]

Complicated? Bureaucratic? Somewhat arbitrary? Yes. And it was hard to make all these actors work together. DHS became a collection of entities with very different histories, sizes, systems, and missions, all brought to a table and told to work together on terrorism, which, notably, had not been the top priority of even one of the twenty-two agencies.

First, think about how different the assembled entities were. The U.S. Coast Guard, for example, is one of the nation's oldest federal organizations and dates back to 1790, when George Washington authorized ten vessels to enforce federal trade and tariff laws. The Coast Guard is an extraordinary branch of the military; through the years it has played important roles in everything from enforcing shipping regulations on rivers, to drug interdiction at sea, to teaching water safety and navigation to recreational boaters, to frontline military duty in conflict zones. But its primary mission was never fighting terrorism.[14]

At the other end of the spectrum, there was the Plum Island

Animal Disease Center, a single facility in Long Island, New York, which spent most of its life since 1954 researching foot and mouth disease in cattle. Plum Island and its several hundred employees were added to several other groups looking at biological and chemical threats, and together they created DHS's Science and Technology Directorate.[15] Another seat went to the young Transportation Security Administration (TSA), which was created by Congress in November 2001. The Federal Emergency Management Agency (FEMA) was included in DHS; so was the Secret Service.

Ironically, the one federal agency with explicit responsibility for investigating terrorism on U.S. soil—the Federal Bureau of Investigation—was not included in the new DHS line-up (neither was the CIA or the Pentagon).

The expectation that you could assemble agencies like this and that they would immediately share data and cooperate smoothly was flawed. I am told that challenges ranged from mismatches among the various agencies' email systems, phone systems, security designations, and databases, to management issues with security clearances and collective bargaining agreements, to trying to consolidate all the DHS agencies on a single campus, which remains years behind schedule.

I'm not trying to Monday-morning quarterback the Bush administration—this was an intense, stressful time with many different potential threats. But many outside analysts, including the GAO on many occasions, have raised concerns about DHS year after year. One reason these issues are difficult to address and fix is that because of the origins of the agencies, an estimated ninety or more different Congressional committees and subcommittees have at least partial oversight responsibilities.[16]

For the Department of Defense (DOD), for example, there is a committee in each side of Congress with primary oversight, each called the Armed Services/Intelligence Committee. Over time its members develop expertise and tenure that is vital to good governing and oversight, and DOD passes authorization bills every year. When it comes to DHS, individual agencies brought their oversight committees with them; for example, the House Judiciary Committee oversees immigration, but the U.S. Coast Guard and FEMA fall under the Transportation and Infrastructure Committee. The fractured congressional oversight means that committees address DHS issues in a piecemeal way and no committee has full authority for solving problems, and so they don't get solved. Former Homeland Security secretary Michael Chertoff explained in a 2013 Aspen Institute report: "It's a little bit like childhood soccer games. Everybody runs after the ball, and they wind up colliding into each other."[17]

What would success look like?

In part 1, I mentioned that one significant challenge is that stakeholders have not accepted one definition of what border security means. I like border analyst and author Sylvia Longmire's definition: "Border security is the act of denying our enemies the means to enter the United States to do us harm. This is achieved by identifying and prioritizing border crossers based on the level of threat they pose to our national security, and focusing our resources on either preventing their initial entry or apprehending them before they can commit criminal or violent acts on US soil...Our borders will be considered secure when US citizens can reasonably expect that our enemies cannot penetrate them without resorting to extraordinary means for which there are no existing countermeasures."[18]

It's a powerful concept. The hard part is, you have now met ranchers, sheriffs, victims of crimes, politicians, Border Patrol agents and management, and humanitarian advocates, all of whom would view that definition through the lens of their own legitimate priorities and concerns. Sheriff Benny Martinez would take no issue with keeping enemies out and apprehending them before they commit crimes. But he rightfully asks, What about the security of Brooks County and the uncompensated, negative fall-out of having a BP checkpoint there? An ICE chief may feel rooting out corruption within BP is a critical way to deny our enemies the chance to do us harm, but at budget time those lobbying for more vehicles or technology get the funding he would have spent hiring internal affairs investigators.

In theory, the place where priorities should be sorted for a federal program is through the appropriations and authorization process. The Congressional "reauthorization" process is supposed to keep tabs on the performance of a department or agency, review and make decisions about budgetary trade-offs, update or redefine its mission when its funding runs out, and make further funding contingent on acceptable performance.

After writing the legislation creating DHS, the Bush White House sent it to Congress and it sailed through appropriations. But DHS was never "reauthorized," and insiders say this is a major issue.[19] Through 2017, there were so many committees involved, Congress could not agree to pass an authorization bill that spells out how DHS is supposed to prioritize risks and activities, how its components should work together, and whether initiatives are worth continuing.

The problem is that absent authorizations, the direction of DHS tends to be shaped by executive orders from the White House. I objected to executive orders from the Obama administration that demoted the importance of Border Patrol and ICE enforcing the law, but it's also true that Congress has always had the ability to create reauthorizing legislation for DHS—but it hasn't done it. Why? I'm told committee chairs do not want to give up oversight power, and that's what would need to happen to create a more streamlined and efficient oversight process.

In 2016, for the first time since CBP was created under the auspices of DHS, Congress passed authorizing legislation called the Customs Authorizations Bill mainly focused on CBP's trade enforcement activities, such as preventing counterfeit goods from entering the country. In 2017, the House Homeland Security Committee finally passed a full DHS authorizations bill that did some streamlining, encouraged consolidating duplicative efforts, and was designed to authorize moves to address cybersecurity, a category several different agencies have fought over in the past. In lobbying for its passage, then secretary John Kelly wrote that DHS "cannot keep the United States and its citizens secure with authorities drafted in a time before smartphones and social media." But I am told the Senate is unlikely to pass a similar bill, and so the House's effort will not move forward and DHS will again be funded without an authorization.[20]

To some, the border solution boils down to building barriers and hiring more bodies. In mid-2017, President Trump requested a total of fifteen thousand additional agents for CBP and ICE.[21] The inspector general of DHS raised a red flag, noting that "Neither [U.S. Customs and Border Protection] nor [ICE] could provide complete data to support the operational need or deployment strategies for the additional 15,000 agents and officers." And, according to an August 2017 story in the *Washington Post*, "DHS officials told auditors that they are still three to four years from getting a system in place that will be able to tell them how many new personnel they need and where to deploy them."[22] Perhaps the most dramatic assertion in the story was the inspector general's conclusion that based on BP's screening requirements and the high turnover of BP agents "Homeland Security would have to vet 750,000 applicants to find 5,000 qualified personnel." I support hiring and deploying more agents, but it's essential that they are well vetted, highly qualified, and strategically deployed.

Retired admiral Thad Allen was the U.S. Coast Guard commandant from 2006 to 2010, when he retired after thirty-nine years. He watched DHS be formed and unfold in real time, and he has devoted considerable energy over the last decade and a half to trying to remedy some of its shortcomings. From the beginning of DHS, Admiral Allen notes, "We haven't had a coherent policy to put (these agencies) together. Every time we have a major event or a moral panic, we create an agency or a department to address it." Unfortunately, he adds, "There is no concept of operations for an end game."

I spoke at length with the admiral, who believes DHS needs what he and others call a sense of "unity of effort." He demonstrated this concept in the heat of commanding U.S. resources during some highly stressful emergencies, including Hurricane Katrina and the Deepwater Horizon oil platform disaster. Admiral Allen explains that the border security challenge and an incident like an oil fire actually have some similar components. Chief among them is that they are efforts with a mix of military, law enforcement, and private sector actors. Therefore, you do not have what the military call "unity of command," which means that each individual involved is responsible to and reports to one person ranked above him or her. However, he says, by bringing together all hands early and laying out the goals of the operation and some fundamental principles, a "unity of effort" is achievable. It means you have to go "off book" sometimes, but if all parties realize that a situation has unique elements that defy normal systems, you can still get cooperation and eventually, a successful mission.

Speaking of "the book"...

What we need on the border is unity of effort. Former DHS secretary Jeh Johnson launched an initiative calling for unity of effort within the agency as well,[23] but the many other activities of DHS in disaster relief, protection of U.S. buildings, battling infectious threats, and other activities unrelated to border security make that nearly impossible to achieve, in my opinion. I do think a unified overseer of all border agencies, like the USCG or a Border Security Administration, could achieve unity of effort.

As we think about rebooting DHS, we have to talk about a legal issue. There is a U.S. law important to the border challenge that dates back to 1878. It's called the Posse Comitatus Act, and it prohibits U.S. military services from enforcing domestic laws.[24] It's a vital concept in a democracy: Misuse of military forces on domestic soil is a common tactic of despots and dictators. The military should defend the country from foreign threats and never treat U.S. citizens, even when they have broken the law, as an enemy to be put down first and asked questions later. But I think that law also provides a good vehicle to look at important cultural and practical differences between military and law enforcement that are literally forced into conflict on the border. The U.S. Coast Guard is exempt from this law, as it both enforces domestic maritime law and is an armed service.

From the law enforcement perspective, police and sheriffs operate (and often live their entire lives) in communities where they have a vested interest in first, safety, and second, creating good relationships with their constituencies. Sheriffs tend to be elected, and police chiefs tend to be appointed by elected mayors. That motivates a partnership. To achieve the right balance that leads to safe communities, law enforcement leaders need to listen, and citizens need to observe laws and support public safety by reporting crimes and testifying against those who break the law. Sheriffs and police agencies enforce thousands of different kinds of laws, and in doing so they must respect every U.S. citizen's civil rights. They must know the law, and they must follow orders. And when an individual officer feels those two elements conflict, a law enforcement officer possesses rights and options ranging from filing a report to filing a workplace grievance, possibly transferring to another assignment or agency, or resigning.

Beyond those duties, U.S. law enforcement promotes safety in general. They are among the first responders to whom citizens turn when they need help as a result of an accident, natural disaster, injury, or criminal activity; they educate the public about threats ranging from Internet predators to burglars working a neighborhood.

Historically, military forces have been trained to protect or take territory and to capture or eliminate an enemy based on the mission. Military personnel follow orders following a precise chain of command. As a general rule, you follow orders or face dishonorable discharge—or even court-martial. In a military engagement there is always a need for good judgment, but in a direct and threatening engagement, extending the respect for civil rights that a police officer must consider is a secondary concern. Unlike law enforcement, a military combatant does not need probable cause to believe a law has been broken to detain or engage an unauthorized individual in a specific place.

That said, modern concepts of military missions are far more nuanced. I have spent some time in conflict zones, such as Afghanistan, where the U.S. military realized that their highest priority was to earn the trust of local people and convince them to join in a shared mission of peace and development. One of the most important players in the Afghanistan command was a civilian who assisted the military leadership in community engagement. Other civilians led missions under the direction of DOD that focused on helping farmers improve their production and education, as well as starting new businesses.

In many countries, border security is handled by the military, especially in areas of regional conflict. In some international airports, ports, and official points of land entry, the process of entering the sovereign space is observed by soldiers in full battle gear with rifles. As I have experienced countless times, they have zero interest in polite conversation and no desire to be helpful to visitors. Their attitude is, if you cross onto our territory, you will follow our rules and you will remain under our control until we determine you are no threat to us.

In the United States we treat border security as a law enforcement function. We have long expanses of land border in the north and south, most of it adjoining private land that is not a conflict zone, and we are on good terms with both our neighbor governments, which are major trading partners. What's more, there is considerable commercial and tourist travel between our countries.

According to the U.S. Department of Commerce, more than 30 million Americans traveled to Mexico in 2016, while more than 18 million Mexican citizens traveled to the United States.[25] In San Diego alone, 120,000 passenger vehicles per day cross back and forth to Tijuana, Mexico, according to the *San Diego Union Tribune*. Millions of commercial vehicles carrying billions of dollars in legal goods drive back and forth across the border every year, and if CBP were to search every vehicle thoroughly, the delays would cripple many businesses on both sides of the border.[26]

I believe it would be a mistake to militarize the border. As we've discussed at length, most intruders are not armed criminals. I don't know anybody, including Border Patrol agents or ranchers, or military leaders for that matter, who thinks a desperate mother fleeing Salvadoran gangs or a Mexican teenager forced to backpack drugs by the cartel deserves to find themselves in the literal sights of military personnel.

However, I also don't think we need to choose between a law enforcement model and a military model. The border is a special, hybrid situation. We need a well-trained, well-managed, flexible force that utilizes the best intelligence and technology to guide the use of appropriate force in a fast-changing environment. We need this force to forge a productive partnership with local communities and any related agencies. And we need them to be ready for the military-level tactics and weapons they will need to effectively deal with the violent and sophisticated criminals they do encounter.

It's why I like the idea of Coast Guard command. USCG is a military service, but it has a long history of serving a law enforcement function as well. They have developed specific procedures to transfer tactical command between military and law enforcement leadership during operations. The same people who have figured out how to engage in a friendly, professional way with recreational boaters on safety issues have proven themselves over and over to be capable of conducting elaborate sting operations and finding and apprehending boats and submarines carrying large amounts of narcotics. In fact, the Coast Guard was instrumental in turning back the cocaine explosion in Miami in the 1980s.

In July 2017, I visited the headquarters of U.S. Southern Command (SOUTHCOM) in Florida, and I spent time meeting with the officers and crew of the U.S. Coast Guard Cutter *Margaret Norvell*. I also met with the leadership of SOUTHCOM, which is a combined, unified force of the Navy, Coast Guard, Marine Corps, and several other federal agencies.[27] I was incredibly impressed with the quality of the leadership and commitment of these forces. These cutters are working every day to try to shut down the flow of drugs and other illicit trafficking. The *Margaret Norvell*'s crew of twenty-six handles a wide array of tasks, including picking up migrants who are coming from the Caribbean and trying to enter the United States illegally. Coast Guard vessels also detect and apprehend handmade, semisubmersible crafts that are constructed in the jungles of Colombia and floated out on rivers to access the Caribbean and Pacific Ocean. Then, they are propelled toward the United States with a one- or two-person crew. U.S. Coast Guard vessels have intercepted semisubmersibles holding $350 million worth of cocaine.[28]

Our meeting with SOUTHCOM leadership was deeply concerning, however. Our nation has put those defending U.S. interests in the Caribbean, South Atlantic, and Pacific Coast in a position that makes me question how serious we are about stopping the flow of drugs into our country. SOUTHCOM's leadership explained to me that their radar and other intelligence capabilities give them the ability to identify at least twenty-six vessels per day—80 percent on the Pacific Coast, and 20 percent on the Atlantic Coast—that are likely carrying contraband, primarily drugs but also people and other illegally trafficked items. However, they have the personnel and vessels to pursue only about five targets per day.

Admiral Kurt W. Tidd, the commander of SOUTHCOM, told the Senate Armed Services Committee about this gap earlier in 2017. And he noted that criminals, not to mention terrorist networks, are fully aware of our vulnerability. "I think about those smuggling routes that thread through our southern approaches and into our homeland. Despite the heroic efforts of law enforcement, these are highly efficient systems that can move just about anything and anyone into our country. And what keeps me up at night is knowing I'm not the only one thinking about these routes— extremist networks like ISIS are thinking about them, too, and how to use them."[29]

SOUTHCOM's and the USCG's willingness to be transparent about these gaps, to me, is evidence of their responsible sense of command. Prioritizing and deploying resources to real threats is what we need to emphasize on the border. But I also appreciate the

USCG command structure. They have flexibility and quick reaction capability in deploying front-line personnel. That is why there are laws preventing the military from unionizing, to ensure that they can defend the homeland instantly and effectively with the fastest possible response to command authority. And as evidenced by Admiral Allen, USCG has mature leaders who appreciate the broader management value of "unity of effort" in difficult, high-stakes situations.

It likely would take Congressional action to specifically empower USCG to take on the challenge of absorbing the current BP and managing our land borders. I believe this to be well worth considering: We must make changes. I don't believe we can move forward with the status quo. There is now a legacy of bad feelings and frustrations within communities on the border and sometimes with local law enforcement in those regions that will be difficult to overcome without an overhaul of the structure and alignment of border security agencies. There has been a lack of transparency by the command of CBP, and in the past the inspector general of DHS has called out the agency for misleading and incomplete statistics.

We need more transparency and more commitment on the part of border security leaders to design location-specific responses to fast-changing threats. With the right command structure we can push more decision making and autonomy into what Border Patrol calls AORs, or areas of responsibility, which are regions within sectors.

I have great respect for most of CBP's leaders and frontline agents. But I think it's time for us to explore significant command changes. In creating DHS fifteen years ago, we built an ocean liner–sized vessel by lashing together twenty-two boats of various shapes and sizes that we had in the dock. Now we need a security plan designed for today's and tomorrow's threats.

Chapter 17

RESPECT AND WORK WITH MEXICO

We cannot achieve border security without strengthening our relationship with Mexico and helping the government of Mexico restore the rule of law throughout the country.

A transparent and strong partnership with our neighbor Mexico needs to be a key component of our strategy going forward. Without it, we cannot achieve the security we need in a global, networked world. Transnational criminal organizations increasingly know no boundaries, but they find safe haven in countries where the rule of law is weak. The immediate challenge is that recent political rhetoric in the United States has put decades of progress in serious jeopardy.

Since the 2016 presidential campaign, there has been an increase in self-defeating and indefensible commentary about Mexico. If we don't stop what Mexico is perceiving as our insulting and belligerent posture, it will limit our potential for sustainable border security. Here are three fallacies I want to tackle head-on.

1. The idea that the majority of people crossing our borders today are Mexican criminals is wrong.

    Historically, most immigrants to the United States over our southern borders were Mexican.[1] Among the population of about 11 million people believed to be living in the United States without legal status, slightly more than half are believed to be of Mexican descent. But this is not the make-up of who is crossing our borders today.[2] About 60 percent of unauthorized residents in the United States, according to the Migration Policy Institute, have been here for at least a decade.[3] And Pew Research Center has estimated that the number of Mexicans living in the United States illegally dropped by 1 million between 2007 and 2014, to roughly 5.8 million.[4] In 2014, the number of non-Mexicans apprehended at U.S. borders began exceeding the number of Mexicans.[5]

Many factors are cited for this shift: Mexico's economy has been growing and there are more jobs in Mexico today than ever before, plus Mexico has a lower birth rate. There is a perception that border security patrols and technology have been increased, deportations have increased, and crossing the border by working with cartel guides has become increasingly dangerous.[6]

I have shared the stories of Gil Gaxiola and other Mexican national criminals who are not just border crossers but repeat border crossers. They are a significant threat to us, as are the drug trafficking organizations they work for. Keeping violent criminals out of our country should be a high priority. But as we've covered, they are a small, specific, and often professionalized subset of people attempting to cross our borders.

The majority of people crossing our southwest borders outside of POEs today are traveling through Mexico, but they come from countries other than Mexico, notably the Northern Triangle countries of El Salvador, Guatemala, and Honduras, all of which are being ravaged by gang violence.[7]

The huge numbers of migrants have helped make the cartels dominant in Mexico. Almost all the people traveling through Mexico and making border-crossing attempts these days—tens of thousands of people—pay to be guided by (or agree to work for, in exchange for passage) the Mexican drug cartels. The cartels grow stronger and stronger not only by exploiting, kidnapping, and extorting Central American migrants, but also by bribing and corrupting many levels of Mexican government and law enforcement to help their smuggling.[8]

The United States has been trying to work with Mexico's federal government and the military to enforce Mexico's own sovereignty at the Guatemalan border and at ports to turn back people without proper documentation, as well as to shut down cartel operations throughout the country. This was a goal of the Merida Initiative, and while no one thought it would produce dramatic, overnight changes in behavior, many people tell me progress has in fact been steady.[9]

In March 2016, the commander of the U.S. Northern Command (NORTHCOM), Admiral William E. Gortney of the U.S. Navy, told the Senate Armed Services Committee that his relationship with the Mexican military had made dramatic strides; in fact, he cited "unprecedented levels of coordination."[10] The admiral praised the relationships NORTHCOM has with the Secretariat of National Defense (SEDENA) and the Secretariat of the Navy (SEMAR), adding, "We work closely with the Mexican military to enhance planning, tactical skills, communication capabilities to include cybersecurity, and incorporation of human rights principles."

But he reiterated that this is a "long-term fight, and we continue to help the Mexican military build partnership capacity at their pace." Among other activities like helping train and equip Mexican military with helicopters and vehicles, he said NORTHCOM is also helping to support Mexico's ability to control and regulate their southern border with Guatemala and Belize.

Shutting down criminal networks as widely dispersed as those operating throughout Mexico today, and apprehending and turning back individuals who do not have proper documentation to travel even in Mexico, will go a long way to reducing illegal crossing pressure on our border. But we cannot possibly achieve either of those goals without Mexico's full cooperation.

Corruption has steadily nullified the rule of law in Mexico, and we must help the government and military restore it. It is through that effort that together we can focus on and stop the *minority* of Mexicans with criminal intentions crossing our borders today. Our public officials referring in broad terms to rapists and killers from Mexico and expecting Mexico to build a wall to keep people in is counterproductive.

2. **We cannot ignore the historical role Mexican laborers, both undocumented and documented, play in our agricultural economy. They are not "stealing our jobs."**

Neighbors need to trust one another, and we must stop talking out of both sides of our mouths. Candidates for public office, elected officials, and citizens have insulted a nationality whose workers have been vital to one of our economy's key sectors. Chanting "build the wall" has frightened many workers into going back to Mexico, and discouraged others from coming to the United States to work. Some say, so be it; if they were here, then that's what is supposed to happen. And if others are afraid to travel here illegally, good.

But our foundation has supported extensive research in this area, and I say with no hesitation that these are not jobs native-born U.S. workers have wanted to perform for decades. In 2012, we supported a research project with Arizona State University that looked at the H-2A program, a mechanism for U.S. farmers to legally employ a reliable workforce using foreign guest workers. In an analysis of how the H-2A program impacted Yuma County, Arizona's agricultural industry, the researchers found that growers in the area would see profits decline 42 percent if the program were eliminated; that low-income Americans had few incentives to compete for these jobs, which paid much less than maximum welfare benefits; and that social costs to the area for schools, hospitals, and municipal services of about $3.5 million were significantly offset by the $45.4 million in taxes and related revenues the workers brought to the county. The most difficult thing about the program was that it was cumbersome and complicated to legally fulfill the requirements, which included advertising the jobs to U.S. citizens and proving efforts to recruit American workers.

We have firsthand knowledge of the H-2A bureaucracy. Mainly as an exercise to understand the process, we tried for three years in a row to use the H-2A program to hire workers to handpick corn on our farm in Willcox, Arizona. The forms are complicated, and our applications were rejected twice by the state of Arizona, and then twice by the federal government— which meant the first year we attempted the process we had to withdraw because the harvest was over.

After another series of time-consuming and expensive steps, we were told we had to advertise the positions in Arizona and the three neighboring states of New Mexico, Nevada, and California, and we could move forward only if no Americans applied—which is what happened. At that point we learned we had to hire a special recruiter, at a cost of more than $5,000, to match us up with workers from Mexico who qualified for the visas. We had to pay for the workers' transportation both ways, and we had to provide both lodging and meals for the duration of their stay. We also learned that if any Americans showed up—even after the Mexican visa holders arrived and began working—we had to pay the full value of the engagement for the foreign worker, send that person back to Mexico, and then hire the American. And by the way, you have to be specific in the work you say you want the foreign worker to perform. If, for example, excessive heat ruins your harvest or an unexpected freeze kills part of the crop, you cannot just have the person pick broccoli instead of onions or perform other work on the farm. Technically the visa would then be invalid.

I've personally walked the fruit and vegetable fields in Arizona and California and it was always clear to me that farmers realized how important migrant labor is to their operations. An estimated 70 percent of crop workers in the United States were born in Mexico, and the percentage of foreign-born farmworkers in California is more like 90 percent.[11] But today many U.S. crop farmers are professing to be surprised that the cost of labor is increasing and the number of available farmworkers is decreasing to a point where they are unable to harvest their crops and have at times had to leave them in the field to rot because they don't have the workers to harvest them. In August 2017, NBC news and *Fortune* magazine reported from California's Central Valley that farmers in two counties had lost at least $13 million worth of recent fruit and vegetable harvests because they could not find the labor to pick it.[12,13]

I am not endorsing illegal immigration to support U.S. farms. Quite the opposite: I am trying to shine a light on the problem of demanding adherence to some laws and ignoring others— and of scapegoating Mexican workers in the process. We can create legal avenues to provide this labor, but it requires political will on both sides of the border. That will require respectful dialogue and analysis, not insults and threats. The essence of the rule of law is that all laws must be respected and followed by all parties. If it's no longer functional or fair, the law or visa process should be changed. But nullifying any law by ignoring it or rationalizing violating it usually leads to negative consequences.

3. Threatening tariffs or other ill-considered ploys to force Mexico to "pay" for a wall is likely to backfire.

    I am as frustrated as anybody by the cartel spotter on the hill across the border from our ranch in Arizona. But no wall would remove him. No increase in Border Patrol agents can chase him away. Removing him requires working with the Mexican government to restore the rule of law across the country and especially along the border.

    As President Zedillo observed, there is now growing talk about nationalism and socialism in Mexican political circles. Anti-American rhetoric is on the rise in Mexico.[14] This represents a major threat looming in front of us if Mexico retreats even further from viewing us as a partner and good neighbor.

    I know this sounds simplistic, but some Americans still tend to see Mexico in a very superficial way: as a potential vacation destination, as the country of origin for many of our farm laborers and "illegals," or in recent years as a country suffering extreme violence (and therefore to be avoided as a vacation destination!).

    I'm not trying to be funny. This limited appreciation for the complexities of Mexico is making the larger goal of border security much more difficult. Mexico's southern land border runs 540 miles across the entire northern expanse of Guatemala, and then 155 miles of Belize. Some security experts believe that to reduce the effectiveness of the cartel smuggling networks and stem the volume of migrants attempting to cross the U.S. border, the best place to build a sturdy barrier and reinforce it with personnel could be along the Guatemalan and Belizean borders, which are about one-third the length of the U.S. border with Mexico.

Merida Initiative funds have supported some strengthening of the Mexican military's presence there. There has been talk that if the United States reopens discussions about the NAFTA treaty, looking at reinforcing this border substantially could be on the table. These are the conversations we need to be having on an ongoing basis to find mutually beneficial outcomes, but they depend on trust.

Perhaps as a country we're used to military forays we've made to faraway places like Vietnam or Afghanistan or Iraq where we may go "over there" and get deeply involved, but we mostly don't experience on our own soil the consequences of these activities. It all seems very removed from the "homeland." Mexico, on the other hand, is not a place we can retreat from. Geography is forever. Mexico will always be our neighbor, and it will always occupy a strategic location in the region that can be used for purposes with positive or negative consequences for the United States.

Today, ships from China are delivering the chemical precursors the Mexican cartels are using to make methamphetamine.[15] Some time ago, the United States passed legislation making it more difficult for individuals in the United States to get ingredients from cold medicine and other chemicals that were driving a domestic meth market; the United States worked with Mexico to help it strengthen regulations also designed to cut off the supply of these chemicals to giant cartel labs that have sprung up to feed U.S. demand for meth. According to those who have studied these activities, the Chinese responded by working with cartels to smuggle these chemicals in surreptitiously through Mexican ports, by sending them to nearby countries like Guatemala and Venezuela, where they are offloaded and smuggled by land into Mexico. These are the points of leverage where partners can work on sharing intelligence and working the problem together; without Mexico's cooperation, the United States cannot effectively shut down this supply chain. It's also widely acknowledged that Chinese chemical companies are shipping both raw materials to make fentanyl and machinery to press fentanyl into pills to Mexico, as well as directly to the United States. These kinds of threats are best faced as partners, not as antagonists pointing fingers.

We need a respectful, ongoing relationship with Mexico. Most things in life are a two-way street; we will not solve the violence and criminal activity here at home by pretending it is someone else's problem.

Chapter 18

CREATE A PERSISTENT PRESENCE

We cannot achieve sufficient border security unless we make sure technology and other solutions serve the overriding goal of achieving "persistent presence" along the border.

One of the most powerful, sensitive, cost-effective, battle-tested, flexible crime-fighting tools the world has ever known is underutilized on the U.S–Mexico border today.

I'm talking about dogs.

The value of a dog trained to sniff drugs and chase and hold a suspect is enormous. The speed and determination of a canine to pursue a person on foot is an unrivaled asset that reduces the threat of harm to a law enforcement officer. Just the presence of a dog serves as a deterrent to an apprehended suspect becoming aggressive or trying to run. Drug smugglers wrap drugs in layers of plastic and douse narcotic packets in the most sickening perfumes and noxious chemicals, but a good dog will still find them.

But there is one thing dogs do not have that manufacturers of many other law enforcement tools ranging from weapons to sensors to armored vehicles do have: high-priced lobbyists. And that is one reason we have managed to spend billions of dollars on dysfunctional and subpar "virtual" fences and other technology along the border. The divided oversight of DHS by Congress and the different agencies that don't always cooperate leads to fragmented solutions that cost a lot of money and don't deliver the security we need, as Sylvia Longmire has documented in detail in *Border Insecurity*.

One of the best examples of that was the "virtual fence" project launched a decade ago and designed to create a network of detection technology along unfenced sections of the border. Longmire calls it "the most colossal failure in the history of US border security efforts," and one that prompted the GAO to issue a report called "Secure Border Initiative: DHS Needs to Strengthen Management and Oversight of Its Prime Contractor."

Over and over, DHS has contracted out expensive technology projects to industry and then discovered that equipment did not work well in the harsh desert environment where, for example, animals can trigger false alarms or blowing sand can interfere with radar signals. The irony is that we limit budgets for proven tools like canine units. "There is nothing in the entire technological arsenal of planet Earth with a sensory capability superior to Fido's nose," Longmire notes. "And yet, DHS insists on spending our tax dollars on more machines—and paying more than they're actually worth—instead of investing in more shepherds, labs, and human handlers."[1]

Obviously, dogs alone won't make the border safe, but neither will technology chosen based on politics. As Admiral Allen said, we need "unity of effort" on the border and that extends to the human assets and barriers, technology, and nonhuman assets. With the right leadership and command structure, the next challenge of achieving border security far superior to what we have today is to deploy well-tested technology and barriers in an integrated fashion that best suits a specific geographic region's challenges. We've already talked at some length about the issues of walls and barriers where there is no one-size-fits-all solution. And instead of huge, expensive contracts to big defense and security contractors, we need to accept the complexity and demands of each unique area we're defending.

Which leads me back to dogs.

At our foundation ranch at Mission Oaks where Oscar crossed the border in January 2017, the stretch of border that runs along our property is extremely remote. There is a rocky and poorly maintained road nearby that in some spots may drop over one or two hundred feet into one side of a gorge and climb up the other. The closest asphalt road is more than a dozen miles away over a mountain pass. The actual barrier along this section of the border is four-strand barbed wire, with Normandy fencing running in parallel. Similar fencing runs across the San Rafael Valley.

This ranch has long been used as cattle pasture. We do not want to improve access to these remote areas for two reasons: We don't want more vehicles in general driving around tearing up these working pastures and protected wildlife habitats, and we don't want to create new roads for criminals to use to pick up drugs or transport people. However, what that means is that when you have individuals attempting to enter the United States here on foot, it is a strenuous but relatively low-risk crossing usually out of the line of sight of BP and with plenty of places to hide.

Would a high, solid wall here stop the determined smugglers who frequently cross our land in these remote areas? In my opinion, no. A wall or significant barrier fence would be incredibly expensive. If DHS wants to do something that will generate a good rate of return, this isn't it. The criminal element will figure out how to defeat a wall with ladders, torches, chop saws, or tunnels. Once they cross they are seconds from terrain where they can hide. So you still need personnel to track and apprehend them. You would need many agents positioned along the border, and yet much of the time that deployment would produce no results.

However, additional ground sensors, aerostats (sturdy balloons that are tethered at high elevation and carry radar, sensors, and cameras) and then rapid helicopter deployment with canine support would be an excellent solution. A helicopter arriving within minutes of the border breach would mean you could use the dog's sense of smell to track the drugs the smugglers are carrying and to find suspects that are difficult for a human to detect. A dog and helicopter team could find and hold a suspect as BP in vehicles move to the scene to apprehend and physically transport the suspects.

This is a location-specific solution. It's expensive. But otherwise to plug this vulnerability you'd need dozens of agents parked almost within sight of one another, and it might take half their shifts just to get there and back. And if you deployed a surge force, the smugglers would just move somewhere else until the surge force was shifted to the next hot spot.

That said, this helicopter and canine solution would not be right for our CR ranch. At that ranch, there are fence styles that typically prevent vehicles from crossing and slow people down. The problem at CR, which is much closer to highways and good roads, is that many encounters turn into a footrace in difficult terrain, and the smugglers are aided by spotters directing them which way to go to avoid Border Patrol. CR is an environment where a fairly tall but transparent barrier, such as the PV1 style of angled, square tubing with a broad plate designed to prevent handholds at the top of the barrier, would be a good solution to replace the old, rusting, smaller, and easier-to-breach barriers that exist along the border now. It wouldn't prevent unauthorized persons from crossing, but it makes climbing more difficult, exposes them longer in the act of climbing, and slows infiltrators down to help with apprehension. BP often uses horses in this area with good results, but upgrading existing barriers and improved cooperation with Mexican authorities to shut down the spotters would be a pivotal change.

The leadership of the border security mission needs to make

sure it routinely assesses the demands and solutions along the entire border. Literally every mile of it—the complex wet and dry border areas near Yuma, the serpentine Rio Grande, urban areas, and remote desert and mountain ranges. And don't forget the coastal borders. This variety and complexity seem overwhelming to me sometimes, but this is the challenge. The magnitude of the threat warrants addressing it appropriately.

I have not talked in detail about ports of entry, but they are a significant vulnerability. This is where, from a policy standpoint, the trade-offs between security and commerce create difficult dilemmas. This is where corruption threatens to undermine otherwise good technologies. There is pressure from businesses and shippers on both sides of the border to create a more streamlined process because POEs today are notoriously congested. But today, the security process in part depends on agents selecting vehicles and tractor-trailers to search, somewhat at random. The majority of commercial vehicles are not searched, which is a huge vulnerability the cartels exploit.

I visited a demonstration project in Texas that involves a giant scanning system designed for tractor-trailer trucks. The inventors have built a full-sized prototype and it is impressive: A tractor would drop off a trailer onto this rail-based system and it could be scanned for people, contraband, and hidden compartments on both the Mexican and the U.S. sides of the border, and then reconnected to a tractor after passing customs on the U.S. side. It's designed both to improve security and to speed up today's slow, congested situations at POEs. The system uses robotics and x-ray technology and is designed to move a lot of vehicles very quickly, allowing for the scanning of every commercial vehicle.

Our foundation looked into supporting a model installation of this project along the border in Arizona, and I thought it had a lot of potential. I think someday this kind of solution will be very effective. However, experts I consulted said we just do not have the trust and working relationship with law enforcement on the Mexican side to warrant investing in this expensive technology yet. If the cartels infiltrated the system, they could sabotage elements of it. Technology is not immune to bribes because someone still has to monitor the screen.

There are many recommendations and important insights that I and my fellow ranchers and landowners along the border could make about the defense of our properties if we were consulted. For example, when I submitted statements to the Homeland Security Committee of the Senate in 2017, I focused in part on the hydrology issues in Arizona and the threat of flooding. I noted that any barrier designs had to take flooding issues seriously.

That might sound like a straightforward recommendation that is easy to implement. It's not. Not only do the terrain and flood zones vary dramatically and require that custom adaptations like flood gates be added to a barrier design, flood conditions require constant monitoring and rapid response. Sure enough, a few months after I submitted my statement to the Senate, in July 2017, southern Arizona and northern Sonora experienced flash floods. During this period, Border Patrol had left over half of the flood gates closed along the fencing near our CR ranch house and main buildings. Monsoon rains drove large tree logs and debris into the few gates that were open, and they plugged up. That diverted water moved with a heavy force, and the surge of water ran onto our property and did more than $200,000 in damage, and it took out nine sections of the Border Patrol's fencing.

Persistent presence

To improve border security, all border area stakeholders, government, local law enforcement, and even ranchers must embrace a concept that I was taught by a military leader that I think has incredible value when people are reviewing technology, deployment ideas, and an overall strategy. That is the notion of persistent presence.

There is no one-size-fits-all technology. I'll be the first to admit that there are so many technology options, surveillance systems, sensor strategies, towers, air resources, and other tools in use today I'm sure I don't know half of them. But I do know that many government auditors, such as the Government Accountability Office and the inspector general of the Department of Homeland Security, have criticized the incredible expense with low proof of utility for some technologies that have been adopted by DHS.

Persistent presence is not a technology; it is a strategy that ensures no part of the border goes unprotected. Without persistent presence, you cannot achieve operational control. Each technology or new idea has to be judged against the notion of whether it contributes to persistent presence.

To summarize its key concepts: First, we have to accept the idea that the enemy is intelligent, networked, and relentless. We must embody those same qualities from our defensive position in everything that we do. I have advocated for the command change in part because our leaders must have the flexibility to respond to every new threat rapidly but also without leaving gaps in areas we have historically defended.

Second, persistent presence means our job will never be done. When Border Patrol moves resources to cover our ranch, the smuggling traffic may decrease. However, after this kind of staffing up, when I talk to a rancher fifteen miles east or west of us, smuggling traffic on their land has increased. This is the heart of the issue: Border security demands persistence. We have to address every vulnerability. We have to accept as a nation that our border security issue is not just the current controversy; it must be a permanent concern and priority. We cannot double down on land border security and rob SOUTHCOM or the U.S. Coast Guard of assets they need to interdict high-value drugs at sea. We cannot focus so much on technology for POEs that we neglect the development of technology to find cross-border tunnels.

One of the newest threats from drug smuggling is fentanyl and other synthetic opioids made by criminal organizations in China. They send a significant amount to Mexico to be smuggled into the United States and they also let customers buy fentanyl directly online and ship it using the U.S. mail. Battling this threat requires thinking of our borders in the broadest terms. CBP currently has an operation in New York City where most international mail enters the country; CBP is using devices that can find fentanyl without opening a package, x-ray machines, and even special dogs. This is the huge challenge of border security: We have to be vigilant about traditional smuggling routes and methods, but also add capabilities and shut off emerging channels as the enemy adapts.

In terms of shutting down more traditional smuggling channels, I'm hopeful about new surveillance systems developed for the military that offer incredible power in establishing what is called "pattern of life." Increasingly, surveillance systems are utilizing satellites and cameras mounted on drones or special aircraft to collect visual data in detail and over time.

The value of pattern of life is conceptually simple: What does a target location look like on a normal day when there is no criminal activity? What are the changes in that scene that help identify a threat or potential threat? And then, how rapidly can we respond to that threat? In the future when the scene mirrors times in the past when you know criminal activity later occurred, you can begin to predict the indicators that criminal activity is likely to occur soon.

I have accompanied government officials, law enforcement, and policy experts on tours of the border areas near our Arizona ranches as we examine the conditions and terrain for criminal activity or for educational purposes. We often fly directly above the border in a helicopter. On the Mexico side, near the San Pedro River, there is an isolated, abandoned house only a few hundred yards from the border fence. It is known to law enforcement as a staging house for drug smugglers. That means the cartel puts a team together, loads them with drugs, and then waits for a signal from spotters to begin a smuggling run across the border. On most fly-bys we don't see any people or movement around the structure. But sometimes we will see vehicles parked outside this house. That is a disruption in the "pattern of life" at this ranch house that signals a run is likely to occur, and when I observe this or something similar I call the local Border Patrol station and let the PAIC know.

Law enforcement and military agencies long have created a "low-resolution" pattern of life picture by collecting evidence like a witness observation and security camera footage, by "cutting sign" (using tracking techniques, like following footprints and vegetation disturbance), by using intelligence from law enforcement stakeouts, and so on. The idea of modern pattern of life technology would be to replace fragmented and random human observations based on history with systems that can establish pattern of life along the entire border and rapidly pick up disturbances and prepare for activity rather than simply respond.

Aircraft-based high-resolution cameras have been used to "rewind" murders. There was a case in Juarez, Mexico, where a police officer in a vehicle was surrounded by several other cars and shot by cartel hit men. A U.S. company was testing a system using a high-altitude airplane that had taken digital photos of this area every single second over a period of several weeks, and the murder occurred within that window. The company knew the date and time the murder took place and created a timeline video based on the data starting at that moment and going backward and forward in time. The company produced a video showing the cars surrounding the vehicle and then driving away after the police officer's vehicle crashed into a parked car. The frenzied driving is a disruption in the "pattern of traffic" that makes it easy to follow the assassins' cars. They are seen speeding and weaving through the town and eventually they arrive at the home of a cartel boss. The killers later were apprehended there after law enforcement reviewed the video.[2]

The technology can also be integrated with street-level cameras to pick up license plates of vehicles and thereby track their movements. And the technology's developers say they can use it in real time to direct police patrol cars to catch up with a vehicle that no eyewitnesses saw or reported and that has left a crime scene. Along the border, it's not hard to imagine it being used to monitor a staging house or other activity on the Mexican side of the border and then alert law enforcement when a group is on the move.

There has been resistance in some cities to adopting this kind of technology, which obviously raises privacy issues. Any person at a location could become the subject of a digital timeline showing every move or trip—or visit by someone else. However, in the majority of areas we are talking about, the focus would be on remote areas with known criminal activity.

I have spoken with U.S. military leaders who believe this is the future of border security: intelligently deployed barriers and sensors and surveillance married to rapid response—ideally on both sides of the border. For my part, I am imagining a scenario where U.S. border security leadership reaches out to a Mexican law enforcement partner. Together they agree to pursue digital evidence of that scout on the hill by CR, including where he goes when he's not working. If there is the will from Mexican law enforcement, case closed, canary caged, and connections to the larger network exposed.

These are the resources that create opportunities, grounded not in the fancy technology contractors may be promoting on any given day but in the human equation of being focused, thoughtful, collaborative, and aligned with the higher mission—and establishing persistent presence.

Chapter 19

REDUCE DEMAND FOR DRUGS AND ILLEGAL LABOR

We cannot achieve sustainable border security if we ignore America's appetite for drugs, and if we tolerate both U.S. businesses and individual Americans violating the law by hiring undocumented workers.

In May 2017, I was talking with the vice chairman of Berkshire Hathaway, Charlie Munger, at the annual meeting in Omaha. Charlie is ninety-three and one of the smartest people I know. He has a great sense of humor and a deep knowledge of history. I was telling him about my interest in border security and the smuggling of drugs into the United States. Charlie brought up the role the opium trade played in building several American fortunes in the nineteenth century. "It was money from opium that helped build Harvard's endowment," he said.

Charlie's observation prompted me to look into this history, and I learned that Boston's well-known Cabot family made some of its vast fortune in opium and later made large grants to Harvard and also to MIT, according to historian and author James Bradley.[1,2] Boston's Russell & Co. merchant fleet was considered the largest American opium dealer, and the Russell family funded Yale's famous Skull and Bones society. A man named Warren Delano worked for Russell & Co.—Delano as in President Franklin Delano Roosevelt, Warren's grandson. According to Bradley, Delano was known as the "opium king of China."

It's bizarre to think of Cabots and Roosevelts as nineteenth-century Pablo Escobars and El Chapos. They did not terrorize their own communities in the United States, but they became wealthy and powerful by running for-profit, global operations that exploited demand for an illegal drug in a foreign country. They obtained opium from British governors, who oversaw its production in Turkey and India, and then sold it to China, which was flush with cash from selling tea and silk to the West but buying very little in return. According to Karl Meyer writing in the *New York Times*, American traders bribed Chinese officials to allow them to import chests of opium.[3] And the consequence was widespread addiction that swept through China. It diverted so much cash and disabled so many people, the government eventually went to war with Great Britain to try to stop the trading.

Sounds depressingly familiar.

The Mexican cartels and their networks are ruthless killers, but they did not invent profiting off the misery of others or exploiting the realities of supply and demand. There are two sources of demand that I want to talk about in this recommendation: Americans who spend billions of dollars buying and using illegal drugs, and U.S. employers who deliberately violate the law and hire undocumented workers. As a society we need to take on the challenge of reducing both of these "pull" factors that motivate smugglers and economic migrants to come to the United States unlawfully and put pressure on our border security mission.

Demand is a difficult enemy

The consequences of drug use in our society today are devastating. It seems obvious that American society should reject illegal drug use as an acceptable behavior, but we have struggled with that challenge for many years. There are some incremental efforts to lower demand today that are very important: Making treatment available to addicts to get them off drugs is one concrete policy direction. Diverting low-level drug users into treatment programs instead of jail is a good idea. With overdose rates soaring, I believe our political leaders should not be arguing for legalizing substances that reduce a person's ability to make good decisions and operate vehicles and equipment safely.

That said, I know there are those who suggest that we should divert far more of our border security budgets to lowering demand rather than cutting off the supply. But I don't accept that trade-off. We cannot retreat from the effort to keep drugs out of our country, because too many people will die. And there is historical evidence that cutting off supply reduces the use and abuse of heroin, and I consider this priority critical today.

According to those who have studied the history of opioid addiction and treatment, the number of heroin addicts in the United States plummeted from around two hundred thousand in 1924 to about twenty thousand by the end of World War II in the 1940s.[4] That was because the supply of heroin to U.S. users was interrupted by wartime activities in the South Pacific and Europe and by increased military presence in ports and along the coasts. Without supply, addicts had to detoxify their systems, and the majority did; what's more, there just weren't the drugs around to hook new users. It is a proven tactic of war to fight on the physical front as well as on the diplomatic front, on the propaganda front, and certainly along the supply chain to interrupt the supply of food, water, fuel, ammunition, and medicine. Historians have noted that with

286

continued focus on cutting heroin supply, the United States might have kept heroin use very low. Instead, heroin use again began to grow after the war.

We must both secure our borders and reduce demand, and I appreciate that that is not going to be easy. The profile of addicts has changed in recent years, including more women, more employed people, and more older Americans. Today's drug addicts use a variety of illegal narcotics like heroin, meth, and cocaine, but they're also overdosing on either inappropriately prescribed or illegally obtained prescription opioids like fentanyl or OxyContin. Senior citizens and others who can't afford pain medication for ongoing pain are turning to cheaper heroin for relief.

We also have to tackle head-on the homegrown factors that set the stage for our addiction crisis. Cities and states are suing pharmaceutical companies and distributors for downplaying the addiction risk of opioid painkillers, and for exploiting drug demand by ignoring suspicious prescribing and distribution activity and data. Regulators are pursuing unethical doctors who, like those opium merchants, profited from the demand for narcotics. Investigations by the *Washington Post* and others have also shown that the pharmaceutical industry hired many high-ranking former DEA officials during a period when it lobbied Congress to pass legislation making it harder for the DEA to crack down on suspicious shipments of pain pills.[5]

The impact of opioid addiction on our country is so serious and far-reaching, it seems to me the leaders of companies who deliberately took actions that fueled it should serve prison time. But at minimum, the companies involved should help pay to address the problem.

In 1994, Michael Moore, former Mississippi attorney general, pushed the tobacco industry to pay $246 billion to settle dozens of separate lawsuits in every state with an agreement that funds smoking cessation and prevention programs to this day.[6] Now, Moore is taking on opioid manufacturers for misleading doctors and the public about the risks of these narcotics. Moore, whose own nephew has battled opioid addiction, says these manufacturers should be forced to fund a demand-reduction campaign, and also provide money for treatment. "A prevention and education program will cost at least $100 million a year," Moore told the PBS NewsHour in 2017. "We also hope and learned a lesson from tobacco that we can get court orders that money has to go into treatment; money has to go into prevention."[7]

The hypocrisy of "recreational" drugs

I know that a demand-reduction campaign has to be far more sophisticated and targeted than "Just Say No." And it has not worked just to tell young people to avoid drugs because drugs are bad for them. I will leave it to communication experts to develop the right messages, but I do want to share a powerful insight that a young man named Mario Berlanga from Mexico has argued with great passion. It's about so-called "recreational" drug use today, and I think it is a fresh and important perspective.

Berlanga is from a mid-sized town in northern Mexico. I saw a video of a talk he gave to his fellow business school students at Stanford University, and he later wrote an op-ed column for the *New York Times* in which he made the same points.[8] He sketched a picture of life in his hometown that was distressing, to put it mildly. He said children could no longer play outside because of frequent cartel gun battles. Cartels had taken over schools and shops. His relatives had had to dive to the floor of supermarkets when gunfire broke out. "My friend Maria, mother of a fourteen-year-old son, temporarily fled her low-income neighborhood in the city of Monterrey with her family when she realized a cartel was forcing boys to join the business. Two nights after their return, armed men entered her house and killed her son in front of her in retaliation."

What impressed me most was the clarity of his message to his peers. Berlanga said, Look, many of you would not dream of buying anything but free-trade coffee, and you want only cruelty-free cosmetics. "Yet I've noticed at parties and festivals that some of these same people pop Ecstasy or snort cocaine. They think this drug use is a victimless crime. It's not. Follow the supply chain and you'll find a trail of horrific violence."

Berlanga cited statistics that 80 percent of U.S. drug users—20 million people—are not addicts, they are "recreational" users. But do they realize that 20 million people regularly getting high over the weekend is sending billions of dollars to the most vicious killers, rapists, and torturers in the world? In his *Times* column Berlanga concluded: "We can shatter the misconception that recreational drug use is a victimless crime. We must put an end to the hypocrisy that allows people to make purchases based on their concerns about the environment, workers' rights, or animals—but not about killing people in Mexico."

This isn't "Just Say No." And it isn't "Don't hurt yourself." It's "Don't get innocent people, many of them poor and struggling already, hurt or killed." Don't contribute to the decline of the rule of law in our neighbor's country by doing business with their criminal networks. His message is aimed at millennials, and I hope it gets their attention.

One message that turned the tide in terms of lowering America's smoking habit was when anti-smoking forces started focusing on secondhand smoke. It's one thing to defend your own right to smoke; it's another to claim that you have the right to put carcinogens in the air that others breathe. The same logic—that drug use harms innocent people with no control over what they're experiencing—is a message more people need to understand and accept.

Berlanga's argument helps convey the larger threat of transnational criminal organizations in our hemisphere, which all Americans need to understand. It's counterproductive to spend tax dollars to support border security while our personal discretionary funds support the very criminals harming and killing thousands of people on both sides of the border.

Labor demand

When U.S. employers create an incentive for individuals to cross the border illegally by ignoring labor laws and hiring them "under the table," they are undermining border security. I think immigration reform must be treated separately from border security, but I do think we have to acknowledge and stop rationalizing this "pull" factor. Breaking the law undermines the rule of law. It's wrong.

As a nation, we have to admit that we have essential work, particularly in agriculture, that we cannot hire sufficient numbers of Americans to perform based on the job requirements and for the amount of money these businesses feel they can pay and still make a profit. And yet we have made the guest worker process so cumbersome and bureaucratic that farmers and workers bypass it. It is just much easier to proceed informally—and illegally.

When you talk with farmers and ranchers in some areas of the nation where migrant workers represent a critical element of our agricultural economy, you hear a lot about the good old days when workers crossed back and forth across the border. I've heard "it was no issue and everybody was happy." We have had candidates for judicial appointments and other high federal offices who have been revealed to have employed undocumented workers as housekeepers or nannies or gardeners. Some say, "She was like a member of the family."

That kind of language hides the inevitable complications that result when we rationalize breaking the law. If laws governing part-time labor have become unfair or unworkable, then those who need that labor should take on remaking those laws. Otherwise, the rule of law corrodes and triggers many other problems and injustices. If a mostly illegal workforce was too afraid of being deported to ask for sanitary and safe working and living conditions, does that mean "everybody was happy"? Is a person who lives in the legal shadows actually being treated like a member of the family?

There has been a long tradition of U.S. employers ignoring immigration laws in agriculture, garment work, food service, construction, maintenance, cleaning, and childcare. Individuals from both political parties do it and rationalize why that is OK. So far, both parties have been unable and unwilling to work together to pass comprehensive immigration reform. That is true even though developing more appropriate labor and refugee crisis response policies and programs would offer both legal and more humanitarian options to the majority of those crossing our borders today. And it would help Border Patrol keep resources focused on finding and apprehending the Gil Gaxiolas and other dangerous criminals crossing the border who are a higher-priority threat.

We cannot pretend to care deeply about safety and the rule of law if U.S. businesses and individuals don't accept the degree to which they have created an incentive for illegal immigration by hiring undocumented workers. As we saw with Mexico, when job availability declined during the U.S. recession in 2008 and 2009, the number of undocumented immigrants from Mexico living in the U.S. dropped, according to Pew Research Center.[9] These days many farmers are struggling to find enough labor to harvest crops, and that is a reminder of how vital foreign-born labor has been to our food supply. We should pursue a course where *illegal* job opportunities drop and create more manageable processes for guest and temporary workers where everybody wins.

Opium traders, transnational criminal organizations, sweatshop owners…the lure of profits has motivated ambitious individuals all over the world to circumvent, ignore, or rationalize violating the law. I don't profess to know how to design an effective campaign to reduce Americans' willingness to use illegal narcotics, but I hope that Berlanga's message resonates with the younger generation. And I hope that the same people who say they're concerned about border security appreciate that today the food on their tables, the clothing they wear, and the household workers in their neighborhoods are available and affordable because some employers are violating the law. We have to stop ignoring the larger cost to our society, and others, of tolerating that mindset.

Chapter 20

SUPPORT PEACE AND SECURITY IN OUR HEMISPHERE

We will never achieve sustained border security unless the United States supports the peace and security of other countries in our hemisphere. We must help reduce the gang violence and provide positive alternatives to gang involvement for young people in El Salvador, Guatemala, and Honduras in particular.

"If you could be in the U.S.," the young man said slowly, as an interpreter translated his question for me, "Why are you here?"

We were sitting on plastic chairs in a repatriation facility in San Salvador, El Salvador, one of the world's most dangerous cities. The young man in front of me, Luis*, looked exhausted. ICE had just flown him back to El Salvador from Texas, where he had been in U.S. federal detention for months. He was wearing clean clothing provided by charitable donations at this repatriation center, including a bright orange Denver Broncos T-shirt. Luis was carrying his few possessions, including some papers, a small Bible, and a belt, in a net bag that I think might have originally been used to carry onions. And he seemed aware that he was experiencing what might be his last few minutes of safety before he left the building. Gang members and smuggling guides looking to find repatriated

293

Salvadorans ready to turn around and try to go to the U.S. again often are present outside the center.

I spoke to Luis for about thirty minutes. He was facing a grim future. Luis had left San Salvador about six months prior because he had been threatened with death. He had worked in his brother's bakery and the gangs demanded more and more *renta*, to the point where the brothers could not afford to pay. The family had relatives in the United States, and Luis had hoped to join them. "I love the U.S. because it is a country that has taken in my family," he said. "I went with a lot of dreams."

Luis paid a *coyote* guide for what is called a "three-punch" ticket, meaning if you don't succeed the first time, you get two more chances. He explained that one element of working with *coyotes* today is that when you pay, they give you a password—in his case "armadillo." Guides pass clients off in crowded areas like bus stations by telling them to go to a spot and say the password among others standing there, which also is repeated to cartel members who may try to shake down the migrant while traveling through Mexico.

Luis successfully traveled north through Guatemala and Mexico, and then he crossed the Rio Grande in Texas and tried to follow instructions to walk into the nearest town. But he was immediately apprehended. He thinks a camera on a tower spotted him, and then Border Patrol released a German shepherd to chase him when he started running. Luis asked for asylum, but he did not pass his credible fear interview; he spent four months in federal detention before he was deported.

Luis seemed like a reasonable, intelligent young man. I asked what he would do now. "I'll start from scratch and look for a job." Even though Luis talked about difficult conditions at the detention facility and the fear he had for his life by returning to El Salvador, he repeated his admiration for America several times. He said he had no plans to try again to go to the United States because detention had been so miserable. I wondered how long that would last.

At the end of our conversation I asked him if he had any questions for me. He asked the one I began this chapter with: "If you could be in the U.S., why are you here?" He was not being sarcastic; he was genuinely puzzled. There was not much I could do for Luis that day, although our foundation later connected him with a company that is working with young people in El Salvador to offer jobs that represent an honest way to make a living outside of the gangs. He performed well in his first interview, and I'm told he is on the list of potential hires when the company ramps up.

However, Luis's question has stayed with me, in part because it's not so different from what some Americans ask me. Why do I invest philanthropic dollars in Congo or Rwanda or El Salvador when I could be working on problems in the United States? For that matter, they ask, Why should the United States invest in these troubled countries?

The answer for me is pretty simple: My father gave my sister, brother, and me considerable resources to try to improve the prospects for people who are experiencing significant challenges regardless of where they live or how risky or difficult the challenges are. As a philanthropist I am drawn to help people who are suffering the most and who have been marginalized. Our foundation is active in conflict regions because the people are extremely vulnerable and resources are scarce.

Uncertain future

What I have learned in nearly two decades of development work, however, is that the majority of the world's most difficult challenges impact all of us, either directly or indirectly, either immediately or as a future threat. Look at the refugee crisis in Europe today.

In 2017, I visited several resettlement facilities in Poland, Belarus, and the Baltic countries sponsored by the Office of the United Nations High Commissioner for Refugees. There, I met a wide array of refugees from many countries that are struggling with violence and poverty. There were Syrians, Eritreans, Afghans, and Ukrainians, among others. The facilities were all clean and orderly. There was enough food and in some cases excellent programs for the children. But having fled their homelands, many refugees now find themselves stranded with an uncertain future in countries that are not necessarily pleased to have them. Local communities worry they will take jobs away from citizens and resent paying for medical care or education. Most of what I heard is similar to comments I have heard at home.

Refugee camps are at best a short-term, emergency solution to crises. In past years I have visited huge camps full of displaced people in Sudan, Yemen, Congo, Cameroon, and other locations. I recognize the need for emergency shelter for displaced people, but I am always wary about proposals to build these camps because they don't solve the problem, they kick it down the road. In Africa there are individuals who were born into refugee camps who are now twenty years old and have never known any other kind of normal life. The refugees usually cannot return to their homelands, where their property often has been taken over by the government or rebel groups or even neighbors who stayed and now feel they have the right to keep the land. The Latvian and Lithuanian communities who now host Eritrean refugees may not have paid much attention to that African country, but now its issues are having a significant impact on them.

I travel to El Salvador and Colombia and Mexico to try to help vulnerable people, but also to better understand the threats our country is facing. We cannot wall ourselves off from the rest of the Western Hemisphere. Today huge numbers of people in Central

America, people like Carmen and Tomas's neighbors in El Salvador, who are poor and have few resources, are experiencing such extreme violence and fear that staying in their country of origin does not feel like an option. They are heading north and they are coerced and threatened by Mexican cartels along the way. They make the journey because they consider it a matter of life and death.

We cannot turn away from this dynamic. We have to try to help improve conditions in their countries of origin. We must find and support the honest leaders who want to bring peace to these countries, who want to find near-term solutions for people who feel desperate, and who are willing to work especially hard with young people who must be diverted from joining and strengthening the gangs.

It is essential from a national security point of view that we work to help support the rule of law in the Northern Triangle. As Admiral Tidd said in his report to Congress, once these smuggling networks are established, the cartels and gangs can bring "anything and anyone" into our country. We will deal with large immigration waves on our borders for the foreseeable future if we don't focus on helping these countries establish safer communities and provide better opportunities for people in their homelands.

It's not about just sending aid. There is little point in trying to provide development assistance like organizing farming cooperatives or even helping farmers obtain title to their land when they are surrounded by violence. Those inclined to use violence will not hesitate to take resources from anyone who has them, whether it's food, equipment, or seeds—or even family members. Gary Haugen, who runs an organization called the International Justice Mission, is someone I've known and respected for a long time. He has a deep appreciation for the role violence plays in keeping communities poor. "You can give all manner of goods and services to the poor, but if you don't restrain the hands of the violent bullies taking it all away, you're going to be very disappointed in the long-term impact of your efforts," he says.

The same day I spoke with Luis, I had a series of meetings to investigate how our foundation could make investments to support El Salvador's rule of law and criminal justice infrastructure. Our foundation is not under the illusion that we have enough resources to restore the rule of law for the country. I don't think even the U.S. alone will ever be able to commit 100 percent of the resources needed to help these countries pull out of the situation they are in today. But as the example of the Chinese sending ships full of methamphetamine precursor chemicals to Mexico demonstrates, we cannot afford not to act. Others who might benefit from a destabilized Western Hemisphere are acting in ways that undermine our security.

We can look to Colombia, which has undergone a transformation since the days of Pablo Escobar. In partnership with the United States and others, the government restored order in its institutions, ended a fifty-year-old conflict, and over time the people are taking their country back. Foreign investment from many partners is increasing.

Signs of progress

I have had a series of meetings in El Salvador with government officials that make me optimistic that the time is right to make some strategic investments in El Salvador to strengthen the justice system. My impression is that they sincerely want to reclaim El Salvador from the grip of gangs.

An important factor in this work is listening to what the Salvadorans say they need. As I wrote in *40 Chances*, so very often in global development, organizations will arrive with a recipe designed for a different place or time that they feel is going to help solve a country or a community's problems. But as Colombia also showed, one key element of success is aligning outside assistance with what the people of the country want and making sure the people are part of the solution.

In El Salvador, government officials and others on the ground have advised us that there are several critical issues to address. One of the most important is impunity. Today, only about 5 percent of crimes are ever prosecuted. Law enforcement and government officials know El Salvador needs to improve its investigative capabilities and prosecute criminals in a timely, effective manner so there are realistic deterrents to committing crime. We are considering investments to help build a modern forensics center to improve the investigation tools and raise the skill of investigators. We also hope to assist the attorney general's office in modernizing the country's case file management system, which is an awkward mix of paper and digitized information that results in important information being lost. Prosecutors have trouble even finding records on defendants' past crimes.

A coalition including the local government, NGOs, and private businesses has been pursuing a project to physically restore neighborhoods in San Salvador that have been claimed by criminals, with the goal of creating safe spaces for kids and families. We are supporting their efforts to renovate and upgrade Parque Cuscatlán, San Salvador's "Central Park." The idea is to create physical demonstrations of optimism, change, and progress by cleaning up the park and installing walkways, lighting, outdoor performance spaces, and other inviting landscaping. There will be limited entrances and a strong police presence so people feel safe.

These are not the kinds of investments we typically make, but I learned in other areas of the world, such as Afghanistan, that sometimes you need to change things physically so that people can see the change and they begin to believe change is possible.

Importantly, all these ideas have been generated by leaders in El Salvador who understand the symbols that will give their people hope. They have impressed us with their commitment to working for peace and a better future.

The U.S. government has invested in trying to shore up the rule of law and strengthen democracy in the Northern Triangle. In 2015, following the surge of unaccompanied migrants, the Obama administration tripled past budgets designed to help strengthen governance, root out corruption, and encourage foreign investments. We need more, not less of that kind of investment. We need our government to be smarter about how it approaches some of these challenges.

I have watched President Trump give speeches where he focuses on Central American gangs, specifically MS-13. His message has been that our problems will be solved if we find and deport its members. As you now realize, there is no element of border security that can be "solved" by any one initiative. Absolutely, we should apprehend, charge, convict, and incarcerate these criminals when they break the law, and then deport the gang members who are in the United States illegally. But without our border being secure, and without giving them a good reason to stay in their countries of origin and to leave gang life, expediting their deportation will keep the revolving door of criminals coming into the United States spinning.

Start early

So, it's fair to ask, What does work? What should our priorities be? In 2016, the U.S. Agency for International Development (US-AID) commissioned research to help the agency understand what approaches to attacking extreme violence and—critically—keeping young people out of gangs could work in the Northern Triangle.

Targeting interventions at young people makes perfect sense to me, based on the conversations I've had with gang members that I've already shared. They don't see a future for themselves outside of the gang. They don't see jobs where they can support themselves. Without belonging to a gang, they fear they will be killed. These regions now have multigenerational gang families; they have become numb to violence, murder, rape, and extortion. It also makes sense based on the experience of military and diplomatic leaders who have worked in these countries, such as retired general Simeon Trombitas, who shared with us his impressions of gangs in El Salvador. "These guys are hardcore committed to the gangs. There is nothing we can do to fix that now. The only people who are going to change are the kids ten to fifteen, and that is the only group you can work with. The culture will need a generation to change that mindset."

We must attack the recruitment and the appeal of gangs early. I also have visited a prison in El Salvador where an entire physical section of the prison is devoted to inmates—hundreds of them—who would like to leave their gangs. This accommodation to house them together was fascinating to see; for one thing, these inmates, some now middle-aged, showed incredible talents for drawing, jewelry making, and other projects demanding skill and creativity. Many said they had experienced religious conversions and now reject violence. But they also realized that if they were to be released back into their communities, they would not be welcome. You do not disappear into a community when your face is literally covered in gang tattoos that you may have felt protected you as a teenaged prison inmate, but that now mark you for death.

Thomas Abt of Harvard is the author of the report commissioned by USAID. Of all the interventions evaluated by Abt, focused deterrence, which clearly defines the target population and the problematic behaviors that need to be changed, proved to be the most effective. "Focused deterrence generally features…communicating clearly, directly, and repeatedly with offending groups, informing them that they are under scrutiny, that their behavior (such as shootings) will trigger responses, and they can avoid such responses by changing their behavior…These interventions deter violent behavior by reaching out directly to offending individuals and groups, explicitly stating that violence will no longer be tolerated, and then backing that message with credible threats of enforcement and credible promises of assistance, i.e. 'pulling every lever' to influence offender behavior."[1]

We were already looking at a program along those lines when the report came out. Our foundation has worked with Catholic Relief Services in Latin America for many years and in a number of countries. CRS is a particularly strong organization in Latin America because of its religious roots. Catholicism is a respected institution in countries such as El Salvador, even among people who practice extreme violence on a daily basis. CRS can leverage this respect to try to work with people who will have nothing to do with the government or local law enforcement, which is widely seen as corrupt and sometimes co-opted by the gangs that hold so much power on the streets.

Several years ago, CRS came up with a plan to respond to horrific violence in El Salvador. One government project that CRS supports, Yo Cambio (I Can Change), works inside the federal prisons. The project provides counselors who talk with inmates about their past and try to encourage them to invest in their futures. It's fair to ask, Why would they work with inmates who may be looking at consecutive life sentences and have little hope for release? The answer is those inmates still are filling a powerful role within a gang and they direct gang murders and operations from within prisons. Counselors talk about the consequences of violence and how it is threatening their families' futures on the outside. The idea is to try to get them to change and move forward to working toward peace.

Another of CRS's projects involves working inside communities trying to steer the youth toward better futures. This was the project that most interested us, as diverting young people away from getting tightly enmeshed in MS-13 and other gangs seems like the only way to break the cycles so many young people find themselves in. Ideally, social programs would reach out to kids before they ever join gangs. It's theoretically cheaper and easier to steer kids into non-gang alternatives, and experts favor what are called primary, secondary, and tertiary programs. Primary programs work in communities to strengthen and build positive options; secondary programs work with families of at-risk kids to zero in on good options and coping skills in the presence of gang pressure; tertiary programs try to intervene with young gang members who have a chance of being convinced to reject violence.

But in looking to support CRS's effort and some other efforts to address young gang members, we realized there was a problem.

Distinctions without a difference

The Office of Foreign Assets Control (OFAC) is an agency of the U.S. Department of the Treasury. It enforces economic and trade sanctions based on U.S. foreign policy, specifically targeting terrorists, international narcotics traffickers, and other groups considered threats to the United States. The rationale for OFAC is sound: It regulates how U.S. funds are being spent overseas to make sure they are not funding terrorism or other behavior the U.S. has identified as problematic. Specifically, if the U.S. has passed sanctions on a specific group, then U.S. citizens and organizations are prohibited from giving those groups anything whatsoever of value—not money, not access to buildings to hold meetings, not medical services, and literally not a plate of cookies or a can of soda.

Here is the dilemma: The United States has issued sanctions

against MS-13, which it considers a transnational criminal organization operating in Honduras, Guatemala, El Salvador, Mexico, and the United States. MS-13 is the largest gang in Central America, but the United States does not have sanctions against all Central American gangs, and in fact we don't have sanctions against the second-largest gang in El Salvador, 18th Street, which I am told is equally (if not more) violent than MS-13.

CRS wants to work with both of these gangs to stop recruitment and provide positive alternatives to gangs, but because of OFAC regulations and sanctions, we can support CRS's work with the other gangs, but not MS-13. You can imagine why not working with one of the most significant gangs in a community could create problems.

We are trying to support exactly the focused deterrence that was the recommendation of our government's own report. And yet OFAC's rules make pursuing that approach impossible. We had our lawyers submit an application for guidance or a license to pursue these projects, which is what OFAC provides in these cases. We waited for over eleven months, and Congressional members registered their support of our petition. And the answer that came back from OFAC was, in essence: You are correct that the law states you can't work with MS-13, so you should certify that anyone you help is not a member of MS-13, and if not a member, that your help would not pass through and benefit anyone connected with MS-13.

CRS was in the process of developing a ten-year program to rehabilitate and reintegrate gang-involved youth, and our foundation also was considering additional infrastructure and programs for female juveniles who are incarcerated. It's hard for me to forget the words of a young woman we met in El Salvador in one of the few female juvenile jail facilities (which was filled to capacity). Anita* had joined a gang at a young age, and at seventeen, she had already been in jail for three years. She had a younger sister she hadn't seen since she went to jail, and she said, "I would tell her do things right and don't make the mistakes I did." It's the kind of weary, defeated comment you expect to hear from a middle-aged man in a prison movie, not a seventeen-year-old young woman who under different circumstances would be thinking about applying to college.

However, many inmates at this facility have backgrounds connecting them to MS-13, which would violate OFAC's instructions. Therefore, we cannot consider helping expand facilities designed to help these young women reform their lives, finish their education, and learn life skills, or fund programs to try to get messages like Anita's out to younger sisters and brothers most at risk for making exactly the same mistakes.

How do we reconcile OFAC's response with the U.S. government's expressed desire to address the violence in El Salvador that is driving so many Salvadorans to travel to and illegally enter the United States? This violence will bring more and more MS-13 members into U.S. communities. After waiting for two full years, the State Department's Bureau of International Narcotics and Law Enforcement Affairs (INL) and USAID were granted waivers by OFAC to implement anti-gang programs involving MS-13. Therefore, while parts of our government seem to understand that you cannot address violence in El Salvador without also addressing MS-13 directly, OFAC is providing different guidance to organizations like ours who want to work alongside them. When we come across this kind of self-defeating bureaucracy, I admit even I ask myself: If I could be home in the United States, what am I doing here?

We haven't given up; we're currently vetting a violence prevention initiative that will focus on a single, high-crime community and assess the perpetrators of crime, eventually developing a strategy to intervene in those critical primary, secondary, and tertiary levels. The approach is to treat violence as a public health crisis; you triage to stop its spread as you work toward a cure. Initially, and while the OFAC constraints are still in place, the program will focus on youth who are vulnerable to gangs but have not yet joined them. Among other elements, the program plans to help strengthen family units and increase the number of positive interactions between law enforcement and communities in order to reduce antagonism between them.

The bottom line remains the same. We all need to appreciate that our own safety and security depend on participating in the challenges affecting our neighbors in this hemisphere. Political rhetoric does not solve complicated problems; what brings progress is investing first in understanding what's going on, and then designing solutions that speak to the reality on the ground and are aligned with our government's activities. In the words of William R. Brownfield, the former assistant secretary of state for INL, "If we ignore these threats, these problems, and these crises in Central America today, we will address them on our own front porches tomorrow."

ORANGE SHOES IN ARIZONA

After I spoke with Oscar on the phone in June 2017, our foundation team touched base with him several more times. He was working in Mexico and said that he was saving money in hopes of making another attempt to cross into the United States and meet up with his friends in Maryland. He was always friendly, always upbeat.

And then in July, he stopped responding.

When we called his phone, it went straight to voice mail. We left messages, but he did not call back. He stopped posting on or communicating through Facebook. After a week or two of this silence, our Mexico City contact, who had previously connected with him on WhatsApp, sent me a screenshot from the account Oscar had been using. Instead of Oscar's photograph on his main account page, the page now showed the image of a tough gangster with tattoos all over his face and arms. "MS" was tattooed across his chin and across the back of his hands, which were held up flashing a gang sign.

I feared the worst. This was a young man who said he had fled Honduras after being threatened by MS-13. Had the gang killed him and left this as a message? Had he stopped resisting MS-13 and joined them?

We asked our NGO partners in Honduras who were in touch

with his family to try to find out. Within a couple of days, word came back: They said Oscar had again been apprehended trying to get into the United States in Arizona, this time many miles west of MOR. He was in good health, but he was again sitting in Florence, Arizona, awaiting deportation.

I was curious to learn what happened. We located Oscar in federal detention. We learned he was originally charged with a felony reentry, but had agreed to plead guilty to a misdemeanor charge. He had already served a thirty-day sentence for the misdemeanor and now was waiting for word of his deportation, which could be any day.

When we got this news I was on my way to Africa for meetings on several of our projects in Rwanda and the Democratic Republic of Congo, but within a few hours of us locating Oscar, one of our foundation team members flew to Arizona. We received permission to meet with Oscar the next morning. The next day, this is the report I received:

A guard led Oscar into a small room at the Florence Detention Center. We were grateful to meet inside with air conditioning, as it was 110 degrees outside. He was wearing standard-issue green prison scrubs and bright orange rubber Crocs. He looked to be in good health—and embarrassed.

Oscar says he was doing pretty well in Mexico, living near Mexico City. He said he was working for a paving company. He had a girlfriend. He didn't have any problems with cartels or gangs. He said he avoided them and things were "calm. I was fine. I had a place to live, clothes, food, work. I could buy shoes. I am ashamed to be back here again. I should have stayed in Mexico."

Instead, Oscar and a Honduran man named Esteban* became friends. They met up with some other Hondurans who passed through Mexico City on their way to the United States. When they talked, Oscar and Esteban decided they would also make another effort to go the United States. Esteban is forty-five, had lived in the United States in the past, and told Oscar he knew a good way to cross.

On what sounds like the spur of the moment, Oscar and Esteban made their way by train and bus to the U.S.–Mexican border. Although Oscar said on our previous call that he was working and trying to save money for the trip, he had not saved much money. They could not afford a *coyote*. He did not have a map, or a plan for what to do when they crossed. He said his phone was stolen on one of the trains, along with his shoes and some clothing. He said they planned on begging for food so did not bring much.

They made their way to what he described as a space in the border fence where someone had cut the pipes with a saw and they could squeeze through. It was clear Oscar had no idea where he was; he initially said he crossed near San Luis Río Colorado, Mexico, which would have been near Yuma, Arizona. However, the Border Patrol report said he and the other man were picked up near Why, Arizona, 150 miles east of Yuma, and BP believed he had crossed near Lukeville, a small town about thirty miles south of Why located within Organ Pipe National Monument.

Oscar said he and Esteban climbed through the fence and began walking across the desert. Oscar said he carried eight gallons of water. They thought it would be a six- or seven-day walk to Tucson (113 miles northeast), but they became lost. He claimed they walked for twelve days, and realized at times they were walking in circles. They did manage to refill their water jugs with rainwater and some runoff. "God provided for us and led us to water," Oscar said. But Esteban had a hernia, and by day twelve he was in severe pain and they were both starving.

They saw a town, including the bright lights of a casino. But by now Esteban was in terrible pain, and they had no money. They stood by the side of a paved road, and on July 22, they waved

309

down a Border Patrol vehicle and surrendered. Oscar was adamant that Esteban was not a *coyote* and this was not a three-punch ticket situation.

ICE initially charged Oscar with a reentry felony and processed him under Operation Streamline, so he was brought to court in a large group where everyone was in shackles and wearing the clothing they were apprehended in. Because they were being charged with a crime, each person had the right to a public defender, and Oscar said his public defender told him to plead guilty to misdemeanor illegal entry and serve thirty days. If Oscar tried to argue his felony case and lost, the lawyer said the judge would probably sentence him to six months or a year in prison. Said Oscar: "I didn't mean to disrespect the U.S. Since I was fourteen I would see movies and I'd see pretty buildings and people, and I'd say one day I'll be there.

"If I made it to Maryland I would find a job and I would work so hard. I wouldn't steal or be a criminal. I would find a job and produce something for your country and then I could help my family. I'm not going to cross again. I will try to find work."

Oscar served his first thirty days under the control of the U.S. Marshals Service in Florence, and then they handed him over to ICE, which uses the same facility—the Florence Correctional Center, which is operated by the private prison company CCA.

I asked what it was like. "In the prison there are delinquents, lots of tattoos, shaved heads, and they try to intimidate you. I just try to stay away from them. But it's ugly. They do not have to lock people up like this.

"I'm not a bad person. I made a bad choice."

I asked, What about the image of the gangster with the MS-13 tattoos on your profile image on WhatsApp?

Oscar replied, "Oh, I put that there. Sometimes I just use pictures I think are kind of cool and tough. That wasn't MS-13; that was just an image I thought was cool." He made a mean face like a gangster and grinned.

I asked, Do you realize the guy in the picture has "MS" tattoos all over himself, even his face? Did you get involved with MS in Mexico or after you crossed into the United States?

Oscar's smile went away. He said no. He claimed he never worried about MS-13 in Mexico because the cartels won't tolerate MS-13 doing anything in Mexico. He said, "The Mexican Mafia will kill Maras."

The interpreter asked: "Well, isn't it kind of dangerous if you're living in Mexico to be attaching yourself to an MS image?"

It was as if this had never occurred to him before. He looked down and he said, "Yes, you're right."

We all have wondered why Oscar had no coat or anything else with him when he arrived at MOR in winter. I asked about that. This time, he said he had a jacket, gloves, a scarf, a blanket, food, and some water in a backpack when he and the other four men started walking near the border. But he said when the armed guard of the smuggling group started chasing and shooting at him most of the items were in his pack. When he began running the pack slowed him down so he threw it off. His hat fell off, and his jacket was too hot as well, so he threw that away, too.

Our time was up, and we said goodbye.

Family business

We also asked our Mexico City contact to set up another visit with Oscar's family in Honduras. She talked at length with Oscar's brother Jaime. He told her he was going to school on the weekends and he talked about a small business he was developing for the family. He was going by bus to Tegucigalpa several times a week to purchase cheese and bananas and avocados, and

311

he and his aunts would sell the items at a storefront in the nearby small town.

Jaime talked a bit about his father and told our foundation team member that Oscar was a lot like him. He had trouble settling down and was often away from home, then he would suddenly reappear. The father had made other efforts to get to the United States, but was never successful. Jaime told our colleague he hoped Oscar would return to Honduras and go to work with him in the food stand, although he seemed to realize Oscar probably would not do that. He said the aunts and young cousins are excited about the food stand; they do not want to leave their village.

Not long after we visited with Oscar in Arizona, we learned ICE flew him back to San Pedro Sula, and then Oscar traveled by bus to visit his family—using money he made sweeping the detention center while incarcerated in Florence. But he didn't stay long. He reached out to us to say he had already made his way north again through Guatemala, and he was trying to find money for a boat to cross the river back into Mexico.

As these reports came to me, I was in Africa, where long flights and hours riding in vehicles gave me time to think about Oscar and what we had learned from following his activities. When we saw the MS-13 images on his profile, I thought there was at least a fifty-fifty chance that it was put there by the last people to see him alive. The more familiar you become with the stories of immigrants, gangs, cartels, and law enforcement in the Northern Triangle countries and Mexico, you realize violent harm and even death have become routine solutions to otherwise minor grievances or misunderstandings.

And if what Oscar told us in Florence about his last journey was accurate, I began to understand why his family was frustrated with him. Taking off with no map...no plan...no money...no food? Trying to cross the Arizona desert in the middle of summer?

I thought back to what that bishop in Texas said to me. That sometimes immigrants' faith is all they have. Oscar's frame of reference is so different from mine—and from that of most Americans. He is a twenty-year-old man who, just in the eight months I had known him, had described at least four separate life-threatening situations—watching his father get thrown from a train, being interrogated by cartel members in Mexico, encountering the armed drug mules near our MOR ranch and getting shot at, and now trying to cross the Arizona desert in the middle of summer. And yet Oscar thinks he's blessed. When he convinces himself that it is God's will that he go to the United States, despite having few resources, he does not see the obstacles and threats that crop up as a sign that he needs a new and better plan. He seems to process surviving them as proof he should keep trying.

Desperate people are always going to take on risks to reach a place of safety and a better life. What frustrates me is that our border vulnerabilities motivate Oscar to think that next time he's going to make it, and that could get him killed. I don't believe Oscar is a threat. I don't think he's violent. He is a naïve young guy who doesn't even realize the danger of putting an image of MS-13 on his phone. I think he believes somewhere in Maryland is a perfect job that will allow him to make enough money to buy all the shoes he wants and still send money back to his family and be a hero. And who knows, maybe that optimism keeps him out of gangs or working for the cartels.

It's often not easy to hold on to optimism in the developing world. For all the ambition and enthusiasm Jaime communicated to our colleague when she visited his village in Honduras, just a couple of months later, as we were finishing this book, we received word that he and his aunts had shut down the food business after their stand was robbed. As Gary Haugen said, the reality of development work in fragile communities is that bullies and criminals

313

are constantly watching and ready to pounce. Months of progress can evaporate in an instant.

In late November, we finally connected with Oscar again. He said he was in San Juan Del Río, Mexico, where he had found work in construction. In late December, Oscar posted a video on his Facebook page. He appears to be alone, riding on the top of a moving freight train. He is smiling and pointing the camera at beautiful scenery and a colorful sunrise. "Here on the Beast, going to Tepic, Nayarit right now. Relaxed," he says in Spanish.

Oscar and Jaime have been struggling to survive for their entire lives. They have made difficult and sometimes risky decisions in that struggle. But directly south of our border and throughout Central America, many others who are poor and struggling have sought survival among violent criminal organizations, including gangs and drug cartels. And make no mistake, these criminal organizations will do business with terrorists or other enemies of the United States if the price is right. They are a threat to us, and more times than we can even know, they cross back and forth over our border, smuggling drugs, people, cash, and weapons. We must intensify our defenses against those threats.

The humanitarian path is to focus on creating stability and opportunity in these countries of origin so young people like Oscar and Jaime can find a better life there. Meanwhile, we must protect stability and public safety in our own country by tightening up the border.

New role

I've explained that I began serving as a sworn auxiliary deputy volunteer in Macon County, Illinois, in 2012. Once I became involved with sheriffs and other frontline responders in Illinois and Arizona, I also interacted more closely with law enforcement organizations on the national level. I found that I wanted to learn more and try to contribute what I could to supporting public safety. By the fall of 2017, I had completed more than 3,400 hours of patrol and training and eighty-two weapons qualifications. Eventually, I became undersheriff in Illinois, and I worked alongside Macon County's outstanding elected sheriff Tom Schneider.

As I was completing this book, Sheriff Schneider decided to retire with fifteen months left in his term before the next election. Rather than choose among three excellent lieutenants who were running for sheriff, Sheriff Schneider asked me to serve out his term. I agreed to serve until the next election in November 2018, and I was sworn in as sheriff on September 15, 2017, and confirmed by the Macon County Board November 9, 2017.

I see our border from many angles: as a landowner, as a philanthropist, and now as the sheriff of a county in one of America's fifty border states. I cannot say this strongly enough: We must be committed and relentless in defending the rule of law in our country, and that defense must begin at the border.

ACKNOWLEDGMENTS

This book represents the insights and support of many people. First, I want to thank Senator Heidi Heitkamp of North Dakota, and Cindy McCain, chair of the Human Trafficking Advisory Council of the McCain Institute for International Leadership. Senator Heitkamp is a courageous leader who cares deeply about the security of the United States. Cindy McCain is a warrior in the global fight against human trafficking. Without their encouragement and support I would not have written this book.

I am grateful to my ranch neighbors in Arizona. They live every day with the consequences of inadequate border security, and they have been generous in helping me understand border issues. Thank you Scott and Toni Arena, Ed and Jean Ann Ashurst, Roger and Barbara Barnett, Bob and Ruth Cowan, Fred and Peggy Davis, Fred and Robyn Giacoletti, Gerry Gonzalez, Sadie and Sage Goodwin, Donny and Lynn Kimble, Wes and Brita Kimble, Bill and Michelle Kimble, Phil and Carrie Krentz, Frank and Sue Krentz, Ben Krentz, Jack and Marguerite Ladd, John and JoBeth Ladd, Bill and Mary McDonald, Louie and Susan Pope, and Gary Thrasher.

I especially thank Kelly, Kerry, and Mackenzie Kimbro and Warner Glenn for their support and encouragement and the lessons they have taught me.

Several years ago, I was standing near the U.S.–Mexico border with a friend who is a police officer from Illinois. Like me, he has seen the devastating impact of drugs and drug-related violence in his community. I pointed to the fence and said: "Border Patrol is the last line of defense." He corrected me and said, "No, Border Patrol is the first line of defense against drug smugglers. We're the last line of defense in Illinois and every other state."

With that insight in mind, I have a long list of friends in law enforcement all across the country I want to thank for their service and for their assistance in helping me shed a light on this nationwide problem. Thank you Sheriff Mark Dannels, Sheriff Bruce Kettelkamp, Sheriff Mike Lewis, Sheriff Benny Martinez, Sheriff Jim McDonnell, Sheriff Mike Miller, Sheriff Barry Virts, Sheriff Leon Wilmot, Chief of Police Charlie Beck, Chief of Police Jim Getz, Chief of Police Robert Maynard, States Attorney Jay Scott, Assistant States Attorney Michael Baggett, Chief Deputy Thad Smith, Retired Deputy Chief Cody Moore, Deputy Chief Robert Arcos, First Assistant Chief Michel Moore, Assistant Chief Jorge Villegas, Captain Civilian Commander Arif Alikhan, Captain Alfred Labrada, Captain Al Neal, Commander Tom Alinen, Commander John Black, Commander Jeffrey Bert, Commander Kenny Bradshaw, Commander Sam Farris, Commander Mark Genz, Commander Tad Williams, Deputy Commander Steve Ziegler, Lt. Larry Auton, Lt. Jamie Belcher, Lt. Tony Brown, Lt. Jon Butts, Lt. Kenny Foster, Lt. Sean Gijanto, Lt. Richard Morales, Lt. Jim Root, Lt. Jeff Scheibly, Lt. Kris Thompson, Lt. Curtis Wilkins, Lt. Scott Woods, Sgt. Ron Atkins, Sgt. Jason Brown, Sgt. John Filippelli, Sgt. Mike Finch, Sgt. Scott Flannery, Sgt. John Gjerde, Sgt. Mike Hawkins, Sgt. Jim Hermann, Sgt. Ty Hernandez, Sgt. Lou Ann Hollon, Sgt. Kevin Jamka, Sgt. Dan Keil, Sgt. Tod Linendoll, Sgt. Dale Pope, Sgt. Danny Romero, Sgt. Louie Tartaglia, Sgt. Tim Williams, DPS Special Agent Ben Dollar, Det. Ben Berry, Det. Juan Hoke, Det. Guy Hudson, Det. Eric Jamka, Det. Jake Kartchner, Det. Chad Larner, Det. Mike Magoffin, Det. John Monroe, Det. Tal Parker, Det. Jeremy Peuschold, Det. Jon Roseman, Det.

Matt Whetstone, Det. Randy Wilson, Det. Cody Woods, K-9 Det. Brando Reibschied, K-9 Officer Steve Jostes, Dep. Chris Adams, Dep. Shane Beck, Dep. Daniel Carr, Dep. Todd Choatie, Dep. Roger Clark, Dep. Robbin Cronin, Dep. Jesus Davidson, Dep. Ross Estavillo, Dep. Tom Fair, Dep. Jennifer Harris, Dep. Forest Hauser, Dep. Joseph Herbert, Dep. Bart Hickey, Dep. Brian Hickey, Dep. Tim Hoffman, Dep. Philip Hogan, Dep. Jorge Hoke, Dep. Matt Hunt, Det. Matt Jedlicka, Dep. Adam Kartchner, Dep. Adam Major, Dep. Joe Mannix, Dep. Ray McNeely, Dep. Sean Miller, Dep. Jessie Owens, Dep. Bradley Patient, Dep. German Paz, Dep. David Pittenger, Dep. Ursula Ritchie, Dep. Marshall Sharp, Dep. Clifford Shipley, Dep. Pat Smith, Dep. Adam Walter, Dep. Chad Wayne, Dep. Shane Wendell, Dep. Travis Wolfe, Dep. Bobby Zavala, SAR Coordinator David Noland, and the CCSO SAT Team. I also want to thank my friend Chuck Wexler, executive director of the Police Executive Research Forum, for his support and guidance on many issues covered in this book.

I am especially grateful to Tom Schneider, former sheriff of Macon County, who provided me the opportunity to, first, train and serve as a sworn auxiliary deputy, then serve as undersheriff, and to now serve as sheriff of Macon County.

I want to thank the leadership of Border Patrol and the rank and file who put their lives at risk every day to protect our country. Some are friends, and many agents helped me understand the challenges they face; however, because I quote many current and retired agents of both Border Patrol and ICE, I decided it was best not to name them individually. I could not have completed this book without their support and input.

Although I have protected their privacy, this book would have been incomplete without the generosity and courage of many people who shared very personal stories with me, from migrants in respite centers in Mexico and Texas, to rural farmers in Central

America, to those struggling with drug addiction and their family members in the Midwest. I will never forget their stories.

The following individuals provided important insights and support: President Ernesto Zedillo, David Aguilar, Admiral Thad Allen, Bruce Anderson, Ambassador Mari Carmen Aponte, Hugh Aprile, Kathleen Arnold, Gary Binning, Herminio Blanco, Rodrigo Bolaños, Eduardo Bours, Jessie Bovay, Neal Brackett, Paul Brinkley, Wesley Broquard, Lane Bunkers, Mike and Kathy Burkham, Gaye Burpee, Monica Campbell, Carol Capas, Cyntia Cardenas, Sue Cavanna, Dan Clegg, Hank Crumpton, General Kurt Crytzer, Marc D'Silva, Erica Dahl-Bredine, Lauren Dasse, Shannon Sedgwick Davis, Franco Domma, Sally Donnelly, Adam Finck, Senator Jeff Flake, Liam Forsythe, Huey Freeman, Jorge Salomon Garcia, Paula Goedert, Dave Groccia, General Carter Ham, Joe Hanss, Tom Hayes, Frank Hernandez, Paul Hicks, Mary Hodem, Kellie Hynes, Jeffrey Irvine, Deputy Chief of Mission Mark Johnson, Rick Jones, Scott Kafer, Julie Katsel, Mitch Kelldorf, Gil Kerlikowske, Erin Lane, Meghan Latcovich, Jeremy Lite, Sylvia Longmire, Larry Mackey, Ambassador Jean Manes, Lee Marple, General James Mattis, Golden McCarthy, Cindy Mora, Charlie Munger, Sonia Nazario, Erik Nicholson, Michael Palmer, Ashley Peterson, Dan Pickard, Sister Norma Pimentel, General Alberto Jose Mejia Ferrero, Maria Emma Mejia, Kevin Oaks, Pilar Frank O'Leary, Bruce Parks, Laren Poole, Jose Quiroga, Carrie Ray, Robin Reineke, Maria Roarick, Arturo Rodriguez, Sonny Rodriguez, Nelson Rood, Ashish Rughwani, Jeff Sanford, Jorge De Los Santos, Adam Schmidt, Rea Anne Servia, Michael Sheridan, Carlos Slim, Roberto Slim, Celina de Sola, Laura St. John, Cecilia Suarez, Schuyler Thorup, Glenn Tosten, Alberto Usobiaga, Conor Walsh, Peter Wataka, and Wendy Young.

Without the support and encouragement of my father, Warren E. Buffett, and my late mother, Susie Buffett, our foundation would not have the resources to focus on helping the world's most vulnerable and marginalized populations and on issues like citizen security, conflict mitigation, and the rule of law, without which little else can be accomplished. My brother, Peter, and sister, Susie, also have helped me in many ways.

Our foundation staff put in countless hours in support of this book. Mark Rigel spent many days and nights at significant risk collecting evidence of current border activity. Doug Oller provided invaluable assistance in many ways through his management and support of our ranches and farms. Charlie Jordan supported our ranch activities on the border, and the help of Tracy Coleman and "Hondo" was invaluable. Ann Kelly Bolten provided invaluable input, editing, and key recommendations. Sabra Brucker and Matraca Keller arranged and oversaw logistics to complete hundreds of interviews and dozens of trips. Jimmy McDonough, Manuela Nivia, Jessica Peck, and Cristina Camacho were diligent fact checkers, and Elaine Blackmore provided research support. A special thank-you to Jeannie O'Donnell, who supported my photography so that my experiences could be reflected in images, and Lauren Scribner, who worked on the photographic and graphic layouts in this book. Ana Vianei provided important research support in Mexico and Central America. Roslyn Ratliff, Ann Goode, Christine Fortney, Charlotte Ryan, and Ashley Pinney assisted me throughout the process. And a special thank you to Trisha Cook who filled in all the remaining critical gaps as she always does on everything I do.

My partner in writing this book, Joan Hamilton, put in hundreds of hours, including trips to prisons, mountain peaks, foreign countries, and desert washes; in Mexico we flew in helicopters above freight trains observing migrants headed north, and in El Salvador we sat with gang members who were convicted murderers. She helped me dissect some of the most complex problems facing our country, and I could not have completed this book without Joan. This book also benefited from the expert guidance of our agent, Jim Levine of Levine Greenberg Rostan Literary Agency. I appreciated the wise advice and editing of Paul Whitlatch, senior editor at Hachette Books, and the support of Hachette publisher Mauro DiPreta, publicity director Joanna Pinsker, director of marketing Michael Barrs, assistant editor Lauren Hummel, and production editor Melanie Gold.

NOTES

INTRODUCTION

1 Brownfield, W. Quotes in transcript of a Briefing on the International Narcotics Control Strategy Report, March 2, 2017. Retrieved November 26, 1017 from https://defenseoversight.wola.org/primarydocs/170302_inscr_launch.pdf.
2 National Drug Threat Assessment Summary (Rep.). (2015). Retrieved October 3, 2017, from U.S. Department of Justice and Drug Enforcement Administration website: https://www.dea.gov/docs/2015%20NDTA%20Report.pdf.
3 Grillo, I. (2011). Mexico's Narco Torpedoes. Retrieved October 3, 2017, from https://www.pri.org/stories/2011-12-21/mexico-s-narco-torpedoes.
4 LaSusa, M. (2016, October 4). 5 Clever Ways Mexico Cartels Move Drugs across US Border. Retrieved October 3, 2017, from http://www.insightcrime.org /news-analysis/5-clever-ways-mexico-cartels-move-drugs-over-us-border.
5 Zobeck, T. How Much Do Americans Really Spend on Drugs Each Year? Retrieved November 20, 1017, from https://obamawhitehouse.archives.gov/blog /2014/03/07/how-much-do-americans-really-spend-drugs-each-year.

PART I: COSTS AND CONSEQUENCES

1 National Institute on Drug Abuse. (2017, September 15). Overdose Death Rates. Retrieved October 13, 2017, from https://www.drugabuse.gov/related-topics/trends-statistics/overdose-death-rates.
2 Based on casualty statistics. Retrieved November 26, 2017, from http:// www.history.com/topics/9-11-attacks, and from https://www.thebalance.com /the-cost-of-war-3356924.
3 Kochanek, K. D. (2016, June 30). National Vital Statistics Report (Rep. No. 4). Retrieved October 19, 2017, from Centers for Disease Control website: https://www.cdc.gov/nchs/data/nvsr/nvsr65/nvsr65_04.pdf.
4 Lopez, G. (2017, June 6). In One Year, Drug Overdoses Killed More Americans than the Entire Vietnam War Did. *Vox*. Retrieved October 13, 2017, from https://www.vox.com/policy-and-politics/2017/6/6/15743986/opioid-epidemic -overdose-deaths-2016.
5 Katz, J. (2017, September 2). The First Count of Fentanyl Deaths in 2016: Up 540% in Three Years. *New York Times*. Retrieved October 13, 2017, from

https://www.nytimes.com/interactive/2017/09/02/upshot/fentanyl-drug-overdose-deaths.html.

6   From the CDC, retrieved December 21, 2017, from https://www.cdc.gov/nchs/data/databriefs/db294_table.pdf#1.

7   Centers for Disease Control and Prevention. (2015, July 7). New Research Reveals the Trends and Risk Factors behind America's Growing Heroin Epidemic. Retrieved October 13, 2017, from https://www.cdc.gov/media/releases/2015/p0707-heroin-epidemic.html.

8   ONDCP. (2016, December). Un-Adjusted Estimated Federal Drug Control Spending by Fiscal Year 2008–2016. Retrieved October 13, 2017, from http://www.drugwarfacts.org/chapter/economics#spending=&overlay=table/altfedspending.

9   FY 2017 Budget and Performance Summary (Rep.). (2016, December). Retrieved October 14, 2017, from Executive Office of the President of the United States website: https://obamawhitehouse.archives.gov/sites/default/files/ondcp/policy-and-research/fy2017_budget_summary-final.pdf.

10 Miron, J. and Waldock, K. The Budgetary Impact of Ending Drug Prohibition. Retrieved November 26, 2017, from https://object.cato.org/sites/cato.org/files/pubs/pdf/DrugProhibitionWP.pdf.

11 The Economic Impact of Illicit Drug Use on American Society (Rep.). (2011). Retrieved October 13, 2017, from United States Department of Justice and National Drug Intelligence Agency website: https://www.justice.gov/archive/ndic/pubs44/44731/44731p.pdf.

12 The Council of Economic Advisors. (2017, November). The Underrated Cost of the Opioid Crisis. Retrieved November 20, 2017, from https://www.whitehouse.gov/sites/whitehouse.gov/files/images/The%20Underestimated%20Cost%20of%20the%20Opioid%20Crisis.pdf.

13 Smith, S. (2014, March 11). Drug Abuse Costs Employers $81 Billion per Year. Retrieved October 13, 2017, from http://www.ehstoday.com/health/drug-abuse-costs-employers-81-billion-year.

CHAPTER 1. RED SHOES "WALK UP"

1   Reuters (2017, April 26). Honduras Murder Rate Falls Slightly in 2016: Report. Retrieved November 26, 2017, from https://www.reuters.com/article/us-honduras-violence/honduras-murder-rate-falls-slightly-in-2016-report-idUSKBN17S2YU.

2   Kopan, T. (2016, August 31). What Donald Trump Has Said about Mexico. CNN. Retrieved October 3, 2017, from http://www.cnn.com/2016/08/31/politics/donald-trump-mexico-statements/index.html.

3   Mohan, G., and Coronado, G. (2015, May 25). To Keep Crops from Rotting in the Field, Farmers Say They Need Trump to Let in More Temporary Workers. *Los Angeles Times*. Retrieved October 13, 2017, from http://www.latimes.com/projects/la-fi-farm-labor-guestworkers.

4   Linthicum, K. (2017, March 3). More and More People Are Being Murdered in Mexico—and Once More Drug Cartels Are to Blame. *Los Angeles Times*.

Retrieved October 3, 2017, from http://www.latimes.com/world/mexico-americas/la-fg-mexico-murders-20170301-story.html.

5 From the Criminal Justice Information Services website. Retrieved November 26, 2017, from https://ucr.fbi.gov/crime-in-the-u.s/2016/crime-in-the-u.s.-2016/topic-pages/violent-crime/murder.

6 Agren, D. (2017, June 21). Mexico's Monthly Murder Rate Reaches 20-Year High. *The Guardian.* Retrieved October 3, 2017, from https://www.theguardian.com/world/2017/jun/21/mexicos-monthly-rate-reaches-20-year-high.

7 Brazil's Igarape Institute, as quoted in *The Economist*, March 31, 2017; Retrieved October 13, 2017, from https://www.economist.com/blogs/graphicdetail/2017/03/daily-chart-23.

8 Hearing to Receive Testimony on U.S. Northern Command and U.S. Southern Command in Review of the Defense Authorization Request for Fiscal Year 2016 and the Future Years Defense Program, United States Senate Committee on Armed Services Cong., 47 (2015) (testimony of General John Kelly).

9 Drug Cartels and Heroin Addiction, Senate Foreign Relations Subcommittee on Western Hemisphere, Transnational Crime, Civilian Security, Democracy, Human Rights and Global Women's Issues Cong. (2016). Retrieved October 2, 2017, from https://www.c-span.org/video/?410188-1/hearing-examines-drug-cartels-heroin-addiction&start=3225.

10 CBS News. (2017, August 22). Mexican Troops Say They Seized 140 Pounds of Fentanyl at U.S. Border. Retrieved October 3, 2017, from https://www.cbsnews.com/news/mexican-soldiers-140-pounds-of-fentanyl-seized-at-u-s-border.

11 Miroff, N. (2017, November 13). Mexican Traffickers Making New York a Hub for Lucrative—and Deadly—Fentanyl. *Washington Post.* Retrieved November 19, 2017, from https://www.washingtonpost.com/world/national-security/at-the-new-york-division-of-fentanyl-inc-a-banner-year/2017/11/13/c3cce108-be83-11e7-af84-d3e2ee4b2af1_story.html?utm_term=.12a77eb701c6.

12 Markon, J. (2016, March 5). Can a 3-Year-Old Represent Herself in Immigration Court? This Judge Thinks So. *Washington Post.* Retrieved October 3, 2017, from https://www.washingtonpost.com/world/national-security/can-a-3-year-old-represent-herself-in-immigration-court-this-judge-thinks-so/2016/03/03/5be59a32-db25-11e5-925f-1d10062cc82d_story.html.

13 InSight Crime. (2015, December 9). Special Report: Gangs in Honduras. Retrieved October 3, 2017, from http://www.insightcrime.org/investigations/special-report-gangs-in-honduras.

CHAPTER 2. LIGHTS OFF, PISTOLS READY

1 The term "endangered" as used here refers to all five categories of conservation terminology for animal populations in jeopardy, including near threatened, vulnerable, threatened, critically endangered, and extinct in the wild.

2 Carroll, R. (2015, October 14). Altar, Mexico: How the "Migrant Oasis" for Would-Be Border Crossers Became a Trap. *The Guardian.* Retrieved October 13,

2017, from https://www.theguardian.com/world/2015/oct/14/altar-mexico-how
-the-migrant-oasis-for-would-be-border-crossers-became-a-trap.

3   McMillan, S. (2015, October and November). New Life in the Badlands. *Nature
Conservancy Magazine*. Retrieved October 13, 2017, from https://
www.nature.org/magazine/archives/new-life-in-the-badlands.xml.

4   Janofsky, M. (2000, June 17). Immigrants Flood Border in Arizona, Angering
Ranchers. *New York Times*. Retrieved October 13, 2017, from http://
www.nytimes.com/2000/06/18/us/immigrants-flood-border-in-arizona-angering
-ranchers.html.

5   Johnston, G. (2017, May 30). 2017 Cattle Outlook: Prices Haven't Hit the Bottom. *Agriculture.com*. Retrieved October 13, 2017, from http://www
.agriculture.com/markets/analysis/livestock/2017-cattle-outlook-prices-havent
-hit-the-bottom.

6   Villarreal, A. (2014, December). Explaining the Decline in Mexico-U.S. Migra-
tion: The Effect of the Great Recession. *US National Library of Medicine*.
Retrieved October 3, 2017, from https://www.ncbi.nlm.nih.gov/pmc/articles
/PMC4252712.

CHAPTER 3. STEPPING ON THE BALLOON

1   Filzen, A. (2013, February 22). Clash on the Border of the Tohono O'odham
Nation. Retrieved October 13, 2017, from https://pulitzercenter.org/education
/clash-border-tohomo-oodham-nation.

2   Migration Policy Institute. (2016, October 18). Largest U.S. Immigrant Groups over
Time, 1960–Present. Retrieved October 13, 2017, from http://www.migrationpolicy
.org/programs/data-hub/charts/largest-immigrant-groups-over-time.

3   U.S. Department of Justice, Office of the Inspector General, Operation Gatekeeper. Retrieved October 13, 2017, from https://oig.justice.gov/special/9807
/gkp01.htm.

4   U.S. Customs and Border Patrol. (1994, August 8). Border Patrol Strategic Plan
(Rep.). Retrieved October 13, 2017, from https://assets.documentcloud.org
/documents/355856/border-patrol-strategic-plan-1994-and-beyond.pdf.

5   Government Accountability Office. (2017, November). Border Patrol: Issues
Related to Agent Deployment Strategy and Immigrant Checkpoints. Retrieved
November 26, 2017, from http://www.gao.gov/assets/690/688201.pdf.

6   U.S. Border Patrol. Southwest Border Sectors, Total Illegal Alien Apprehensions by
Fiscal Year. https://www.cbp.gov/sites/default/files/assets/documents/2016-Oct/BP
%20Southwest%20Border%20Sector%20Apps%20FY1960%20-%20FY2016.pdf.

7   United States Department of Homeland Security, Office of Immigration Statistics. (2017, September). Efforts by DHS to Estimate Southwest Border Security
between Ports of Entry. Retrieved October 13, 2017, from https://www.dhs.gov
/sites/default/files/publications/17_0914_estimates-of-border-security.pdf.

8   Becker, A. (2013, April 4). New Drone Radar Reveals Border Patrol "Gotaways" in
High Numbers. Center for Investigative Reporting. *Reveal*. Retrieved October 3,

2017, from https://www.revealnews.org/article/new-drone-radar-reveals-border
-patrol-gotaways-in-high-numbers.

9   Ibid.

10 Ibid.

11 Rempell, C. (2009, May 18). Why Are Mexican Smugglers' Fees Still Rising?
New York Times. Retrieved October 13, 2017, from https://economix.blogs
.nytimes.com/2009/05/18/the-rise-in-mexican-smugglers-fees.

12 United States Department of Homeland Security, U.S. Customs and Border Protection, Southwest Border Deaths by Fiscal Year. Retrieved January 3, 2018, from
https://www.cbp.gov/sites/default/files/assets/documents/2017-Dec/BP%20South
west%20Border%20Sector%20Deaths%20FY1998%20-%20FY2017.pdf.

13 Gonzalez, D. (n.d.). Border Crossers, and the Desert that Claims Them. USA Today
Network. Retrieved October 13, 2017, from https://www.usatoday.com/border-wall
/story/immigration-mexico-border-deaths-organ-pipe-cactus/608910001/.

14 Drug Enforcement Administration. 2016 National Drug Threat Assessment
Summary (Rep). November 2016. Accessed November 15, 2017, from
https://www.dea.gov/resource-center/2016%20NDTA%20Summary.pdf.

CHAPTER 4. AN EXPENSIVE JUGGLING ACT

1   Nowrasteh, A. (2015, July 14). Immigration and Crime—What the Research
Says. Cato Institute. Retrieved October 13, 2017, from https://www.cato.org
/blog/immigration-crime-what-research-says.

2   Ghandnoosh, N., and Rovner, J. (2017, March 16). Immigration and Public
Safety. The Sentencing Project. Retrieved October 13, 2017, from
http://www.sentencingproject.org/publications/immigration-public-safety.

3   DeForest, L. (n.d.). Chiricahua National Monument Has Wild, Colorful History.
AZCentral.com. Retrieved November 26, 2017, from http://archive.azcentral
.com/travel/arizona/features/articles/archive/hearthistory.html.

4   Wittig, A. S. (2017, March 22). Jury Finds Gaxiola Guilty in Chiricahua Assault. *Willcox Range News.* Retrieved October 13, 2017, from http://www.willcoxrangenews
.com/news/article_cc18ded8-0e5d-11e7-bc34-bf3c0964da27.html.

5   Morrison Institute for Public Policy. (2010, September 28). Annual Cost Per Inmate. Retrieved October 13, 2017, from http://arizonaindicators.org/criminal-
justice/corrections/annual-cost-per-inmate.

6   Quick Facts; Illegal Reentry Offenses. Retrieved October 13, 2017, from U.S.
Sentencing Commission https://www.ussc.gov/sites/default/files/pdf/research
-and-publications/quick-facts/Quick_Facts_Illegal_Reentry_FY15.pdf.

CHAPTER 5. SANCTUARIES AND "SLAM DUNKS"

1 U.S. Customs and Border Patrol, CBP Public Affairs. (2017, April 18). Border Patrol Agents Arrest 2 Men Convicted for Sex Crimes against Children [Press release]. Retrieved October 13, 2017, from https://www.cbp.gov/newsroom /local-media-release/border-patrol-agents-arrest-2-men-convicted-sex-crimes- against-children.

2 Eichler, A. (2017, March). Previously Deported Illegal Alien Murders Woman, Kidnaps Daughter. *CNS News*. Retrieved October 13, 2017, from https://www.cnsnews .com/news/article/andrew-eicher/previously-deported-illegal-alien-murders-woman -kidnaps-daughter.

3 Gerber, M., and Quea, J. (2017, March 7). Man Who Had Been Deported to Mexico Five Times Charged in Deadly L.A. Car Crash. *Los Angeles Times*. Retrieved October 13, 2017, from http://www.latimes.com/local/lanow/la-me-ln -alvarado-crash-immigration-20170307-story.html.

4 Dickerson, C. (2017, September 13). A Sheriff's Bind: Cross the White House, or the Courts. *New York Times*. Retrieved October 13, 2017, from https://www.nytimes .com/2017/09/13/us/sheriffs-immigration-enforcement-jails.html.

5 The defendant was originally identified as Juan Francisco Lopez-Sanchez and mentioned in news accounts using that name. However, it turned out that was an alias and he was charged as José Inéz Garcia Zárate.

6 Yan, Holly, and Dan Simon. Undocumented Immigrant Acquitted in Kate Steinle Death. CNN. http://www.cnn.com/2017/11/30/us/kate-steinle-murder -trial-verdict/index.html.

7 Romney, L., Chang, C., and Rubin, J. (2015, July 6). Fatal Shooting of S.F. Woman Reveals Disconnect between ICE, Local Police; 5-Time Deportee Charged. *Los Angeles Times*. Retrieved October 13, 2017, from http://www.latimes.com/local/crime/la-me-sf-shooting-20150707-story.html.

8 Luhby, T. (2016, September 1). Trump Condemns Sanctuary Cities, but What Are They? CNN. Retrieved October 4, 2017, from http://www.cnn.com/2016 /09/01/politics/sanctuary-cities-donald-trump/index.html.

9 Wexler, C. (2017, March 6). Police Chiefs across the Country Support Sanctuary Cities Because They Keep Crime Down. *Los Angeles Times*. Retrieved October 13, 2017, from http://www.latimes.com/opinion/op-ed /la-oe-wexler-sanctuary-cities-immigration-crime-20170306-story.html.

10 Santos, F. (2016, November 9). Sheriff Joe Arpaio Loses Bid for 7th Term in Arizona. *New York Times*. Retrieved October 13, 2017, from https://www .nytimes.com/2016/11/09/us/joe-arpaio-arizona-sheriff.html.

11 Hirschfeld Davis, J., and Haberman, M. (2017, August 25). Trump Pardons Joe Arpaio, Who Became Face of Crackdown on Illegal Immigration. *New York Times*. Retrieved October 13, 2017, from https://www.nytimes.com/2017/08/25 /us/politics/joe-arpaio-trump-pardon-sheriff-arizona.html.

12 Krogstad, J. M., Passel, J. S., and Cohn, D. (2017, April 27). 5 Facts

about Illegal Immigration in the U.S. Pew Research Center. Retrieved October 4, 2017, from http://www.pewresearch.org/fact-tank/2017/04/27/5-facts-about-illegal-immigration-in-the-u-s.

13 Mejia, B., Carcamo, C., and Knoll, C. (2017, February 9). L.A., Orange Counties Are Home to 1 Million Immigrants Who Are in the Country Illegally, Analysis Shows. *Los Angeles Times*. Retrieved October 13, 2017, from http://www.latimes.com/local/lanow/la-me-illegal-immigration-los-angeles-20170208-story.html.

14 Zamora, L. Sanctuary Cities and Immigration Detainers: A Primer. (2017, April 25). Bipartisan Policy Center. Retrieved October 13, 2017, from https://bipartisanpolicy.org/blog/sanctuary-cities-and-immigration-detainers-a-primer.

15 Ho, V. New S.F. Sheriff to Reverse Ban on Communicating with Immigration. SF-Gate. Retrieved October 13, 2017, from http://www.sfgate.com/bayarea/article/New-S-F-sheriff-to-reverse-ban-on-communicating-6754468.php.

16 Immigration. *Miranda-Olivares v. Clackamas County*, No. 3:12-cv-02317-ST, slip op. (D. Or. April 11, 2014) (Stewart, Magistrate Judge). crImmigration. Retrieved October 13, 2017, from http://crimmigration.com/2014/04/17/oregon-federal-court-detainer-led-to-fourth-amendment-violation.

17 United States, Government Publishing Office. (2012). United States Code. Retrieved October 13, 2017, from https://www.gpo.gov/fdsys/granule/USCODE-2011-title8/USCODE-2011-title8-chap12-subchapII-partVIII-sec1325.

18 Jarrett, L. (2017, February 24). Are Undocumented Immigrants Committing a Crime? Not Necessarily. CNN. Retrieved October 13, 2017, from http://www.cnn.com/2017/02/24/politics/undocumented-immigrants-not-necessarily-criminal/index.html.

19 Gramlich, J., and Bialik, K. (2017, April 10). Immigration Offenses Make Up a Growing Share of Federal Arrests. Pew Research Center. Retrieved October 13, 2017, from http://www.pewresearch.org/fact-tank/2017/04/10/immigration-offenses-make-up-a-growing-share-of-federal-arrests. During this same period, arrests for drug crimes, supervision violations, property crimes, and weapons offenses all dropped.

20 Motivans, Mark (March 2017). Federal Justice Statistics, 2013–2015. Retrieved October 13, 2017, from https://www.bjs.gov/content/pub/pdf/fjs1314.pdf.

21 Light, M. T., Lopez, M. H., and Gonzalez-Barrera, A. (2014, March 18). The Rise of Federal Immigration Crimes. Pew Research Center. Retrieved October 4, 2017, from http://www.pewhispanic.org/2014/03/18/the-rise-of-federal-immigration-crimes.

22 Ibid.

23 Ibid.

24 Immigration. *Miranda-Olivares v. Clackamas County*, No. 3:12-cv-02317-ST, slip op. (D. Or. April 11, 2014) (Stewart, Magistrate Judge). crImmigration. Retrieved October 6, 2017, from http://crimmigration.com/2014/04/17/oregon-federal-court-detainer-led-to-fourth-amendment-violation.

25 Gonzales, R. (2017, March 20). DHS Publishes List of Jurisdictions That Rejected Immigrant Detainer Requests. NPR. Retrieved October 14, 2017, from http://www.npr.org/sections/thetwo-way/2017/03/20/520851267/dhs-publishes-list-of-jurisdictions-that-rejected-immigrant-detainer-requests.

CHAPTER 6. DRUG CARTELS AND DECATURS

1   Inspection Service Authority. Retrieved January 26, 2018, from https://www.ecfr.gov/cgi-bin/retrieveECFR?gp=1&SID=6b9726d27974b907c0f76b92f3a4fdfc&h=L&n=pt39.1.233&r=PART&ty=HTML#se39.1.233_111.
2   STOP Act of 2016, S. 3292, 114th Cong. (2016).
3   Melendez, S. (2016, September 12). How America Gets Its Deadliest New Drug. *Fast Company*. Retrieved October 14, 2017, from https://www.fastcompany.com/3063518/carfentanil-synthetic-opioids-heroin.
4   Shesgreen, D. (2017, September 22). An Inside Look at the Hunt for Fentanyl, the Deadly Opioid Driving the Overdose Crisis. *USA Today*. Retrieved October 14, 2017, from https://www.usatoday.com/story/news/nation/2017/09/17/opioid-crisis-how-customs-officers-find-fentanyl-mail/662838001.
5   WHO TV report. Marijuana Bust: Cartels' Large Grow Operation. Retrieved October 14, 2017, from http://whotv.com/2013/11/18/marijuana-bust-cartels-large-grow-operation.
6   Welsh-Huggins, A. (2017, May 4). "Gray Death" Causes Worry. *Associated Press*. Retrieved October 14, 2017, from https://www.usnews.com/news/best-states/ohio/articles/2017-05-04/gray-death-dangerous-opioid-combo-is-latest-mixing-trend.
7   News Channel 5. (2017, April 4). Nearly $13 Million in Fentanyl Seized in Drug Bust. Retrieved October 14, 2017, from http://www.newschannel5.com/news/nearly-13-million-in-fentanyl-seized-in-drug-bust.
8   Hughes, A. (2017, May 02). Suspected Drug Dealer Arrested in Decatur County. Retrieved October 14, 2017, from http://www.wbbjtv.com/2017/05/02/suspected-drug-dealer-arrested-decatur-county.
9   Grass, J. (2014, June 19). Alleged Cartel Hit Man Pleads Guilty to Murdering Decatur Man. Retrieved October 14, 2017, from http://www.al.com/news/huntsville/index.ssf/2014/06/alleged_cartel_hit_man_pleads.html.
10 Fischer, J. (2016, March 11). MAP: Indiana Drug Overdoses by County. *The Indy Channel*. Retrieved January 26, 2018 from https://www.theindychannel.com/about/map-indiana-drug-overdoses-by-county.

CHAPTER 7. WHAT ABOUT DEMAND?

1   Law enforcement leaders quoted in this chapter spoke at the PERF conference and their comments also appear in the September 2017 report of the Police Executive Research Forum: *The Unprecedented Opioid Epidemic: As Overdoses Become a Leading Cause of Death, Police, Sheriffs, and Health Agencies Must Step Up Their Response*. This report is available online at http://www.policeforum.org/assets/opioids2017.pdf.
2   Thompson, D. (2017, May 8). Legalized Pot Sends More Teens to ER in Colorado, Study Finds. CBS News. Retrieved October 14, 2017, from https://www.cbsnews.com/news/pot-legalized-colorado-teens-hospital-er.

3 Mitchell, K. (2017, July 12). Crime Rate in Colorado Increases Much Faster Than Rest of the Country. *Denver Post*. Retrieved October 14, 2017, from http ://www.denverpost.com/2017/07/11/colorado-sees-big-increase-crime-10-percent -higher-murder-rate.

4 Fiedler, M., et al. (2015). Colorado's Legalization of Marijuana and the Impact on Public Safety: A Practical Guide for Law Enforcement (Rep.). Retrieved October 14, 2017, from Police Foundation and the Colorado Association of Chiefs of Police website: https://www.policefoundation.org/publication/colorados-legalization-of-marijuana-and -the-impact-on-public-safety-a-practical-guide-for-law-enforcement2.

5 Associated Press. Pot-Sniffing Dog Not Enough to Search, Colorado Court Rules. *U.S. News & World Report*. Retrieved November 25, 2017, from https:// www.usnews.com/news/best-states/colorado/articles/2017-07-15/pot-smell-not -enough-to-search-car-colorado-court-rules.

6 Paul, J. (2016, September 28). More Illicit Pot Being Grown in Colorado Homes, Shipped out of State. *Denver Post*. Retrieved October 14, 2017, from http://www.denverpost.com/2016/04/15/more-illicit-pot-being-grown-in-colorado -homes-shipped-out-of-state.

7 Pilkington, E. (2012, November 28). Painkiller Addiction: The Plague That Is Sweeping the US. *The Guardian*. Retrieved October 14, 2017, from https:// www.theguardian.com/society/2012/nov/28/painkiller-addiction-plague-united -states.

8 Eyre, Eric. (2016, December 17). Drug Firms Poured 780M Painkillers into WV Amid Rise of Overdoses. *Charleston Gazette-Mail*. Retrieved January 13, 2018, from https://www.wvgazettemail.com/news/cops_and_courts/drug-firms -poured-m-painkillers-into-wv-amid-rise-of/article_99026dad-8ed5-5075-90fa -adb906a36214.html.

9 Whalen, J. (2017, May 31). Ohio Sues Five Drugmakers, Saying They Fueled Opioid Crisis. *Wall Street Journal*. Retrieved October 14, 2017, from https://www.wsj.com/articles/ohio-sues-five-drug-firms-saying-they-fueled-opioid -crisis-1496248317.

10 City of Everett. (2017, September 25). City of Everett's Lawsuit against Purdue Pharma, Everett, WA, official website. Retrieved October 14, 2017, from https://everettwa.gov/1681/Purdue-Lawsuit.

11 Le, P. (2017, March 14). City Alleges Drugmaker Let OxyContin Flood Black Market. *Associated Press*. Retrieved October 14, 2017, from https://apnews.com /967208c49e3d4e7ea6a9453076ae3ec7/city-says-drugmaker-knowingly-let-pills -flood-black-market.

12 Quinones, S. (2015). *Dreamland: The True Tale of America's Opiate Epidemic*. New York: Bloomsbury Press.

13 Deutsche Welle (2016, December 2). Mexican Cartels Shift to Heroin for US Market. Retrieved January 26, 2018, from https://www.youtube.com/watch ?time_continue=3&v=Ec9PMHCFpjI.

14 National Institute on Drug Abuse. (2017, August). What Are Marijuana's Long-Term Effects on the Brain? Retrieved October 14, 2017, from https://www .drugabuse.gov/publications/marijuana/what-are-marijuanas-long-term-effects -brain.

15 Kennedy, M. (2014, December 19). Cigarette Smoking Costs Weigh Heavily on the Healthcare System. Reuters. Retrieved October 14, 2017, from https://www .reuters.com/article/us-healthcare-costs-smoking/cigarette-smoking-costs-weigh -heavily-on-the-healthcare-system-idUSKBN0JX2BE20141219.

16 Langston, S. (2017, August 18). District Attorney: Marijuana Laced with Fentanyl Is in Tennessee. Retrieved October 14, 2017, from http://wkrn.com/2017 /08/18/district-attorney-marijuana-laced-with-fentanyl-is-in-tennessee.

17 Schwartz, N. D. (2017, July 24). Economy Needs Workers, but Drug Tests Take a Toll. *New York Times*. Retrieved October 4, 2017, from https://www.nytimes .com/2017/07/24/business/economy/drug-test-labor-hiring.html.

CHAPTER 8. TOO MUCH, TOO FAST

1 Taylor, S. (2008, February 8). U.S. to Raise Texas Levees in Lieu of Border Wall. *Reuters*. Retrieved October 14, 2017, from https://www.reuters.com/article /us-usa-borderwall-levees/u-s-to-raise-texas-levees-in-lieu-of-border-wall-idUS N0851616320080208.

2 Office of Immigration Statistics (2017, September). *Efforts by DHS to Estimate Southwest Border Security between Ports of Entry*. Retrieved October 13, 2017, from https://www.dhs.gov/sites/default/files/publications/17_0914_estimates-of-border -security.pdf.

3 This calculation includes the border between Alaska and Canada, which is 1,538 miles; the U.S.–Mexico border is 1,933 miles, and the International boundary with Canada is 3,987, according to the U.S. Geological Survey.

4 Longmire, S. (2014). *Border Insecurity: Why Big Money, Fences, and Drones Aren't Making Us Safer*. New York: St. Martin's Press.

5 Coburn, Sen. Tom. (2015, January). A Review of the Department of Homeland Security's Missions and Performance, https://www.documentcloud.org /documents/2298505-senator-coburn-dhs-report-final.html.

6 Moran, G. (2017, March 13). Last Border Hiring Binge Had Some Bad Outcomes. *San Diego Union-Tribune*. Retrieved October 14, 2017, from http:// www.sandiegouniontribune.com/news/immigration/sd-me-border-enforcement -20170302-story.html.

7 Ortega, B. (2014, September 11). Report: CBP Wasted Millions on Ajo Housing for Agents. *AZ Central*. Retrieved October 14, 2017, from http://www .azcentral.com/story/news/arizona/politics/2014/09/11/report-cbp-wasted-millions -ajo-housing-agents/15471201.

8 Davidson, J. (2014, July 6). Border Patrol Agents under Fire for Excessive Force. *Washington Post*. Retrieved October 14, 2017, from https://www .washingtonpost.com/politics/federal_government/border-patrol-agents-under -fire-for-excessive-force/2014/07/06/2e507bd2-02d7-11e4-8572-4b1b969b6322 _story.html?utm_term=.593870eef53b.

9 Ortega, B. (2014, September 14). Border Killings: 46 People Killed, No Agents Disciplined. *AZ Central*. Retrieved October 14, 2017, from http://www

.azcentral.com/story/news/arizona/investigations/2014/09/14/border-deaths-agents
-transparency-secrecy/15616933.

10   Sullivan, J., Thebault, R., Tate, J., and Jenkins, J. (2017, July 1). Number of Fatal
Shootings by Police Is Nearly Identical to Last Year. *Washington Post*. Retrieved October 5, 2017, from https://www.washingtonpost.com/investigations/number-of-fatal
-shootings-by-police-is-nearly-identical-to-last-year/2017/07/01/98726cc6-5b5f-11e
7-9fc6-c7ef4bc58d13_story.html.

11   As reported by cnsnews.com. Retrieved October 14, 2017, from https://www
.cnsnews.com/news/article/susan-jones/chief-border-patrol-agents-among-most
-assaulted-7542-2006. Number of fatalities according to the U.S. CBP's "In
Memoriam" web page. Retrieved November 20, 2017, from https://
www.cbp.gov/about/in-memoriam/memoriam-those-who-died-line-duty.

12   U.S. Customs and Border Protection Use of Force Review: Cases and Policies
(2013, February). *Police Executive Research Forum*. Retrieved October 14, 2017,
from https://www.cbp.gov/sites/default/files/documents/PERFReport.pdf.

13   Wootson, C. R. (2017, February 2). A Border Agent Didn't Behead a Man for a Cartel, Jurors Ruled. But They Still Found Him Corrupt. *Washington Post*. Retrieved
October 14, 2017, from https://www.washingtonpost.com/news/post-nation/wp
/2017/02/02/a-border-agent-didnt-behead-a-man-for-a-cartel-jurors-ruled-they-still
-found-him-corrupt.

14   Prendergast, C. (2017, October 4). Douglas Border Agent Accused of Lying, Disguising $70K in Deposits. *Arizona Daily Star*. Retrieved October 14, 2017, from
http://tucson.com/news/local/douglas-border-agent-accused-of-lying-disguising-k
-in-deposits/article_b64fc5ab-2c21-5936-912e-d8e570c0edda.html.

15   Longmire, S. (2014). *Border Insecurity: Why Big Money, Fences, and Drones Aren't
Making Us Safer*. New York: St. Martin's Press.

16   Associated Press. (2017, January 13). Two out of Three Border Patrol Job Applicants Fail Polygraph Test, Making Hiring Difficult. *Los Angeles Times*. Retrieved
October 13, 2017. http://www.latimes.com/local/lanow/la-me-border-patrol
-lies-20170113-story.html. The story also notes that the average failure rate for
eight other law enforcement agencies consulted was 28 percent.

17   Tomsheck, J. (2017, May 16). Why Is Congress Proposing to Increase Customs and Border Protection Corruption? *The Hill*. Retrieved October 14, 2017,
from   http://thehill.com/blogs/congress-blog/homeland-security/333698-why
-is-congress-proposing-to-increase-customs-and.

18   Sheriff Martinez's comments here are based on interviews and also an article in
The Blaze. Retrieved October 14, 2017, from http://www.theblaze.com/news
/2015/03/24/a-sheriffs-shocking-testimony-texas-children-are-being-recruited-by
-criminals-to-smuggle-people-drugs-into-the-u-s.

19   Operation Stonegarden. Retrieved October 13, 2017, from http://www
.homelandsecuritygrants.info/GrantDetails.aspx?gid=21875.

20   Nanez, D. (2017, September). A Border Tribe, and the Wall That Will Divide It.
AZ Central. https://www.usatoday.com/border-wall/story/tohono-oodham-nation
-arizona-tribe/582487001/.

21   Miller, Todd. (2014). *Border Patrol Nation: Dispatches from the Front Lines of
Homeland Security*. San Francisco: City Lights Books, p. 145.

22   ICE Shadow Wolves. (2014, June 3). Retrieved October 14, 2017, from https://www.ice.gov/factsheets/shadow-wolves.

23   Markon, J., and Partlow, J. (2015, December 16). Unaccompanied Children Crossing Southern Border in Greater Numbers Again, Raising Fears of New Migrant Crisis. *Washington Post*. Retrieved October 16, 2017, from https ://www.washingtonpost.com/news/federal-eye/wp/2015/12/16/unaccompanied -children-crossing-southern-border-in-greater-numbers-again-raising-fears-of -new-migrant-crisis.

24   NBPC website http://www.bpunion.org/newsroom/press-releases/1858-chief -morgan-does-not-have-the-will-to-secure-the-border.

25   National Border Patrol Council. (n.d.). Media FAQ. Retrieved October 14, 2017, from http://www.bpunion.org/newsroom/media-faq#7-corruption.

26   Stearns, B. (2017, August 4). DHS May Not Have Capacity to Hire 15,000 Officers Trump Promised. Cronkite News. Retrieved October 14, 2017, from https://cronkitenews.azpbs.org/2017/08/04/dhs-may-not-have-capacity-to-hire -15000-officers-trump-promised.

27   National Border Patrol Council. (n.d.). Retrieved October 13, 2017, from http://www .bpunion.org/newsroom/press-releases/1786-statement-integrity-advisory-panel.

28   As quoted in *Congressional Record: Proceedings and Debates of the 107th Congress*, 2002.

29   The intent of DACA, to address the complicated issues of youth brought illegally to the United States when they were children, is something I support. However, as this chief's comments indicate, the practical implications of the administration's executive order were far more complicated, and a U.S. Appeals Court said the administration exceed its statutory authority in bypassing Congress. In 2017, the Trump administration announced it was ending the program and gave Congress six months to propose a legislative solution. For more details see U.S. Citizenship and Immigration Services. (n.d.). Consideration of Deferred Action for Childhood Arrivals (DACA). Retrieved October 16, 2017, from https://www.uscis.gov/archive/consideration-deferred-action -childhood-arrivals-daca.

30   U.S. Department of Justice. (2015, March). FY 2014 Statistics Yearbook (Rep.). Retrieved October 14, 2017, from https://www.justice.gov/eoir/pages /attachments/2015/03/16/fy14syb.pdf.

31   Department of Homeland Security. (2016, June 20). Affirmative Asylum Application Statistics and Decisions Annual Report (Rep.). Retrieved October 14, 2017, from https://www.dhs.gov/sites/default/files/publications/U.S.%20Citizenship%20and%20 Immigration%20Services%20-%20Affirmative%20Asylum%20Application%20 Statistics%20and%20Decisions%20Annual%20Report%20-%20FY%202016.pdf.

32   International Justice Resource Center. (2017, July 03). Asylum and the Rights of Refugees. Retrieved October 14, 2017, from http://www.ijrcenter.org/refugee- law. See also: Obtaining Asylum in the United States, U.S. Citizenship and Immigration Services. Retrieved December 26, 2017, from https://www.uscis.gov /humanitarian/refugees-asylum/asylum/obtaining-asylum-united-states.

33   Comments made by Shawn Moran on the Fox Business Network's *Risk & Reward* show broadcast October 7, 2016.

34 Steller, T. (2017, May 16). Steller: Border Patrol Union Embraces Hard-Line Politics. *Arizona Daily Star*. Retrieved October 14, 2017, from http://tucson .com/news/local/columnists/steller/steller-border-patrol-union-embraces-hard -line-politics/article_1a406237-8433-5870-83f6-5cffc0c91b75.html.

35 Archibold, R. C. (2010, April 04). Ranchers Alarmed by Killing Near Border. *New York Times*. Retrieved October 14, 2017, from http://www.nytimes.com /2010/04/05/us/05arizona.html.

36 Wallace, J. D. (2005, May 18). Illegal Immigration Costly for Southeastern Arizona Ranchers. KOLD News 13. Retrieved November 15, 2017, from http://www.tucsonnewsnow.com/Global/story.asp?S=3364733.

37 Duara, N. (2017, June 23). Death on the Border: Arizona Used Rancher's Killing to Justify Harsh Immigration Laws, but the Truth of the Case Is Unclear. *Los Angeles Times*. Retrieved October 14, 2017, from http://www.latimes.com/nation /la-na-arizona-krentz-20170623-story.html.

38 Morse, A. (2011, July 28). Arizona's Immigration Enforcement Laws. Retrieved October 14, 2017, from http://www.ncsl.org/research/immigration/analysis-of -arizonas-immigration-law.aspx.

39 DiLeonardo, R. (2012, June 25). Supreme Court Partially Strikes Down Arizona Immigration Law but Upholds Controversial Section. Jurist. Retrieved October 14, 2017, from http://www.jurist.org/paperchase/2012/06/supreme-court-partially -strikes-down-arizona-immigration-law-but-upholds-controversial-section.php.

40 Bandler, A. (2016, March 8). Border Ranchers: Where the Hell Is Border Security? *Daily Wire*. Retrieved October 14, 2017, from http://www.dailywire.com /news/3951/border-ranchers-where-hell-border-security-aaron-bandler.

41 Lopez, C. A. (2017, June 16). Two Arrested in Attack on Off-Duty Border Patrol Agent." *Las Cruces Sun-News*. Retrieved October 14, 2017, from http://www.lcsun-news.com/story/news/crime/2017/06/16/two-charged-border -agent-assault/403991001.

42 Based on my personal conversations with border area law enforcement, and also on Falzarano, F. (2017, June 26). Sinaloa Cartel Cell Conducting Surveillance on U.S. Law Enforcement in Plot to Uncover and Murder Confidential Informants in Arizona. *JammedUp*. Retrieved October 14, 2017, from http://news.jammedup .com/2017/06/26/exclusive-mexican-cartel-spying-on-u-s-cops-in-plot-to-identify -murder-informants-in-arizona.

CHAPTER 9. BARRIERS

1 Jacobo, J., and Marshall, S. (2017, January 26). Nearly 700 Miles of Fencing at the US-Mexico Border Already Exist. ABC News. Retrieved October 5, 2017, from http://abcnews.go.com/US/700-miles-fencing-us-mexico-border-exist/story?id=4 5045054.

2 Robbins, T. (2006, April 6). San Diego Fence Provides Lessons in Border Control. NPR. Retrieved October 5, 2017, from http://www.npr.org/templates/story /story.php?storyId=5323928.

3   Civic Impulse (2017). H.R. 6061—109th Congress: Secure Fence Act of 2006. Retrieved from https://www.govtrack.us/congress/bills/109/hr6061.

4   Burnett, J. (2014, August 18). In South Texas, Few on the Fence over Divisive Border Wall Issue. NPR. Retrieved October 16, 2017, from http://www.npr.org/2014/08/18 /340628014/in-south-texas-few-on-the-fence-over-divisive-border-wall-issue.

5   Blakeslee, S. (2006, October 9). Gone for Decades, Jaguars Steal Back to the Southwest. *New York Times*. Retrieved October 14, 2017, from http:// www.nytimes.com/2006/10/10/science/10jaguar.html.

6   Secret, 905-Foot-Long Drug Tunnel Found along U.S.–Mexico Border in Arizona (2015, February 27). Fox News. Retrieved October 14, 2017, from http://www.foxnews.com/world/2015/02/27/secret-05-foot-long-drug-tunnel-found -along-us-mexico-border-in-arizona.html.

7   Greaber, J. (2017, April 28). Two Tunnels Discovered by Border Patrol. KGUN9. Retrieved October 14, 2017, from http://www.kgun9.com/news/local -news/tunnels-discovered-by-border-patrol.

8   Testimony of Mr. Leon N. Wilmot, Yuma County Sheriff, Arizona, before the House Committee on Homeland Security Hearing "Ending the Crisis: America's Borders and the Path to Security" on February 7, 2017.

9   Yuma County Chamber of Commerce. Agriculture. Retrieved October 5, 2017, from http://www.yumachamber.org/agriculture.html.

10 Partlow, J. (2014, February 10). Under Operation Streamline, Fast-Track Proceedings for Illegal Immigrants. *Washington Post*. Retrieved October 14, 2017, from   https://www.washingtonpost.com/world/the_americas/under-operation -streamline-fast-track-proceedings-for-illegal-immigrants/2014/02/10/87529d24 -919d-11e3-97d3-f7da321f6f33_story.html.

CHAPTER 10. RED SHOES IN HONDURAS

1   Colibri Center. (n.d.). About Us. Retrieved October 16, 2017, from http://www.colibricenter.org/about-us.

2   Beatrice, J. S., and Soler, A. (2016). Skeletal Indicators of Stress: A Component of the Biocultural Profile of Undocumented Migrants in Southern Arizona. *Journal of Forensic Sciences*, 61(5), 1164–1172. Retrieved October 16, 2017, from https://www.ncbi.nlm.nih.gov/pubmed/27321251.

3   Food and Agricultural Organization of the United Nations. (n.d.). Food and Nutrition Security in Latin America and the Caribbean. Retrieved October 16, 2017, from http://www.fao.org/americas/perspectivas/seguridad-alimentaria/en.

4   Nazario, Sonia (2007). *Enrique's Journey*. New York: Random House Trade Paperbacks.

5   Food and Agriculture Organization of the United Nations. (2002). The Spectrum of Malnutrition. Retrieved October 16, 2017, from http://www.fao.org /worldfoodsummit/english/fsheets/malnutrition.pdf.

CHAPTER 11. STOLEN HARVESTS

1 Inter-American Development Bank, Consultative Group for the Reconstruction and Transformation of Central America. Central America after Hurricane Mitch: The Challenge of Turning a Disaster into an Opportunity. https://web.archive.org/web/20051026083640/http://www.iadb.org/regions/re2/consultative_group/backgrounder4.htm.

2 Central Intelligence Agency, The World Factbook: El Salvador. https://www.cia.gov/library/publications/the-world-factbook/geos/es.html.

3 Allison, M. (2012, March 1). El Salvador's Brutal Civil War: What We Still Don't Know. *Al Jazeera.* Retrieved October 16, 2017, from http://www.aljazeera.com/indepth/opinion/2012/02/2012228123122975116.html.

4 Martínez, Ó., et al. (2016, November 20). Killers on a Shoestring: Inside the Gangs of El Salvador. *New York Times.* Retrieved September 15, 2017, from https://www.nytimes.com/2016/11/21/world/americas/el-salvador-drugs-gang-ms-13.html.

5 Lopez, R., Connell, R., and Kraul, C. (2005, October 30). Gang Uses Deportation to Its Advantage to Flourish in U.S. *Los Angeles Times.* http://www.latimes.com/local/la-me-gang30oct30-story.html.

6 Overseas Security Advisory Council. (2017, February 22). El Salvador 2017 Crime and Safety Report. Retrieved September 15, 2017, from https://www.osac.gov/pages/ContentReportDetails.aspx?cid=21308.

7 Lopez, G. (2013). Hispanics of Salvadoran Origin in the United States. Pew Research Center. Retrieved October 16, 2017, from http://www.pewhispanic.org/2015/09/15/hispanics-of-salvadoran-origin-in-the-united-states-2013. More information at CIA World Factbook, retrieved October 16, 2017, from https://www.cia.gov/library/publications/the-world-factbook/geos/es.html.

CHAPTER 12. TWO-LEGGED PREDATORS

1 U.S. Department of Homeland Security. Obtaining Asylum in the United States. https://www.uscis.gov/humanitarian/refugees-asylum/asylum/obtaining-asylum-united-states.

2 Proujansky, A., and Currier, C. (2017, March 12). Refugees Fleeing Violence in Central America Hope for Asylum in Mexico. *The Intercept.* Retrieved September 18, 2017, from https://theintercept.com/2017/03/12/refugees-fleeing-violence-in-central-america-hope-for-asylum-in-mexico.

3 Sherman, C. (2016, April 13). Gangs Declare War on Police as El Salvador Violence Rages. Associated Press. Retrieved September 19, 2017, from https://apnews.com/2b359687e4124126ad9cbe74884739c4/gangs-declare-war-police-el-salvador-violence-rages.

CHAPTER 13. PRISON OR THE CEMETERY

1   Tjaden, S. (2016, June 8). Court Rules El Salvador Prison Crowding Unconstitutional. InSight Crime. Retrieved October 17, 2017, from http://www.insightcrime.org/news-briefs/court-rules-el-salvador-prison-crowding-unconstitutional.

CHAPTER 14. SILENCING THE CANARY

1   Linthicum, K. (2017, March 3). More and More People Are Being Murdered in Mexico—and Once More Drug Cartels Are to Blame. *Los Angeles Times*. Retrieved October 17, 2017, from http://www.latimes.com/world/mexico-americas/la-fg-mexico-murders-20170301-story.html.
2   Agren, D. (2017, June 21). Mexico's Monthly Murder Rate Reaches 20-Year High. *The Guardian*. Retrieved October 17, 2017, from https://www.theguardian.com/world/2017/jun/21/mexicos-monthly-rate-reaches-20-year-high.
3   Agren, D. (2017, May 5). Mexico after El Chapo: New Generation Fights for Control of the Cartel. *The Guardian*. Retrieved October 17, 2017, from https://www.theguardian.com/world/2017/may/05/el-chapo-sinaloa-drug-cartel-mexico.
4   Berenson, T. (2016, January 8). Timeline of El Chapo's Major Escapes and Captures. *Time*. Retrieved October 17, 2017, from http://time.com/4173454/el-chapo-capture-escape-timeline.
5   Morici, L. H. (2014, August 1). Managing Risks in Mexico. *Harvard Business Review*. Retrieved October 2, 2017, from https://hbr.org/1993/07/managing-risks-in-mexico.
6   O'Neil, Shannon K. (2013). Mexico Makes It: A Transformed Society, Economy, and Government. *Foreign Affairs* 92(2): 52–63. Retrieved September 20, 2017, from http://www.jstor.org/stable/23527456.
7   De la Garza, P. (1997, February 21). Drug Czar's Arrest Puts Mexico on Thin Ice with U.S. *Chicago Tribune*. Retrieved September 20, 2017, from http://articles.chicagotribune.com/1997-02-21/news/9702210097_1_drug-cartels-supply-largest-drug-consuming-nation-gen-jesus-gutierrez-rebollo.
8   Hernandez, F. D. (2015, June 7). What Is the Order of the Aztec Eagle?!, Mexico News Network. Retrieved October 17, 2017, from http://www.mexiconewsnetwork.com/art-culture/order-aztec-eagle/.
9   Mexican Government. (2000, November 21). Orden Mexicana del Aguila Azteca a Promotores del TLCAN [Press release]. Retrieved October 17, 2017, from http://zedillo.presidencia.gob.mx/pages/vocero/boletines/com2540.html.
10 Conservation Agriculture Going Strong in Sonora. (2009, April 27). Retrieved October 17, 2017, from http://www.cimmyt.org/conservation-agriculture-going-strong-in-sonora/.
11 Norman Borlaug Biography, Nobel Prize. (n.d.). Retrieved October 17, 2017, from https://www.nobelprize.org/nobel_prizes/peace/laureates/1970/borlaug-bio.html.

12 Department of State, Bureau of Consular Affairs. (2017, November 22). International Travel, Mexico. Retrieved January 26, 2018, from https://travel.state.gov/content/travel/en/international-travel/International-Travel-Country-Information-Pages/Mexico.html.

13 The World's Most Dangerous Cities. (2017, March 31). *The Economist*. Retrieved October 17, 2017, from https://www.economist.com/blogs/graphicdetail/2017/03/daily-chart-23.

14 Bender, J. (2016, April 25). The Most Violent Cities in the World: Latin America Dominates List with 41 Countries in Top 50. *The Independent*. Retrieved October 17, 2017, from http://www.independent.co.uk/news/world/the-most-violent-cities-in-the-world-latin-america-dominates-list-with-41-countries-in-top-50-a6995186.html.

15 Office of the United States Trade Representative. (n.d.). Mexico. Retrieved October 17, 2017, from https://ustr.gov/countries-regions/americas/mexico.

16 Linthicum, K. (2017, July 22). Mexico's Bloody Drug War Is Killing More People Than Ever. *Los Angeles Times*. Retrieved October 17, 2017, from http://www.latimes.com/world/mexico-americas/la-fg-mexico-murders-20170721-story.html.

17 Angel, A. (2017, May 1). Mexico Narco Messages Reflect Weakness of State Institutions: Study. Retrieved October 17, 2017, from http://www.insightcrime.org/news-analysis/narco-messages-reflect-weakness-state-institutions-study.

18 Longmire, S. (2011). *Cartel: The Coming Invasion of Mexico's Drug Wars*. New York: St. Martin's Press.

19 Archibold, R., Cave, D., and Malkin, E. (2011, October 15). Mexico's President Works to Lock in Drug War Tactics. *New York Times*. Retrieved October 17, 2017, from http://www.nytimes.com/2011/10/16/world/americas/calderon-defends-militarized-response-to-mexicos-drug-war.html.

20 Lee, B., and Renwick, D. (2017, May 25). Mexico's Drug War. *Council on Foreign Relations*. Retrieved October 17, 2017, from https://www.cfr.org/backgrounder/mexicos-drug-war.

21 The Library of Congress has compiled a web site with many resources addressing the complexities of the nineteenth-century "Mexican War." Retrieved at http://www.loc.gov/rr/program/bib/mexicanwar/.

22 Whelan, R. (2017, July 5). 11,155 Dead: Mexico's Violent Drug War Is Roaring Back. *Wall Street Journal*. Retrieved October 17, 2017, from https://www.wsj.com/articles/11-155-dead-mexicos-violent-drug-war-is-roaring-back-1499270119.

23 Malkin, E. (2017, April 19). Corruption at a Level of Audacity "Never Seen in Mexico." *New York Times*. Retrieved October 17, 2017, from https://www.nytimes.com/2017/04/19/world/americas/in-mexico-mounting-misdeeds-but-governors-escape-justice.html.

24 Mejia, D. (2017, July). Plan Colombia: An Analysis of Effectiveness and Costs. *Foreign Policy at Brookings*. Retrieved October 17, 2017, from https://www.brookings.edu/wp-content/uploads/2016/07/Mejia-Colombia-final-2.pdf.

25 Lee, B., and Renwick, D. (May 25, 2017). Mexico's Drug War. Council on Foreign Relations. Retrieved October 17, 2017, from https://www.cfr.org/backgrounder/mexicos-drug-war.

26 Ibid.
27 Frassica, M. (2014, November 30). Mexico's "Narco State" Gets a Cultural Boost from New, More Gory Pop Ballads. Public Radio International. Retrieved October 17, 2017, from https://www.pri.org/stories/2014-11-30/mexicos-narco -state-gets-cultural-boost-new-more-gory-pop-ballads.
28 Villarreal, A. (2014). Explaining the Decline in Mexico-U.S. Migration: The Effect of the Great Recession. *Demography*, 51(6), 2203–2228. Retrieved October 17, 2017, http://doi.org/10.1007/s13524-014-0351-4.
29 Fertility Rate, Total (Births per Woman). (n.d.). *The World Bank*. Retrieved September 20, 2017, from https://data.worldbank.org/indicator/SP.DYN.TFRT .IN?locations=MX.

CHAPTER 15. RED SHOES ON THE ROAD AGAIN

1 Widespread Abuse against Migrants Is Mexican Human Rights Crisis (2010, April 28). *Amnesty International*. Retrieved October 2017 from https:// www.amnesty.org/en/press-releases/2010/04/widespread-abuse-against-migrants -mexican-e28098human-rights-crisise28099/.
2 Trevizo, P. (2013, May 20). Ministering in Brutal Altar, Mexico. *Arizona Daily Star*. Retrieved October 2, 2017, from http://tucson.com/news/local/border/ministering -in-brutal-altar-mexico/article_aacee843-0c7a-5b0a-bbce-3afbfe8c8ba4.html.
3 Moore, G. (2011, September 19). Unravelling Mysteries of Mexico's San Fernando Massacre. InSight Crime. Retrieved October 17, 2017, from http://www .insightcrime.org/investigations/unravelling-mysteries-of-mexicos-san-fernando -massacre.

PART III: WHAT NEEDS TO CHANGE

1 Alvarez, L. (2017, June 20). Haven for Recovering Addicts Now Profits from Their Relapses. *New York Times*. Retrieved October 17, 2017, from https://www.nytimes.com/2017/06/20/us/delray-beach-addiction.html.
2 Wootson, C. R. (2017, July 8). Why This Ohio Sheriff Refuses to Let His Deputies Carry Narcan to Reverse Overdoses. *Washington Post*. Retrieved October 17, 2017, from https://www.washingtonpost.com/news/to-your-health /wp/2017/07/08/an-ohio-countys-deputies-could-reverse-heroin-overdoses-the -sheriff-wont-let-them.

CHAPTER 16. REBOOT COMMAND OF THE BORDER

1   Jervis, R. (2014, June 17). Immigrant Children Continue to Surge into South Texas. *USA Today*. Retrieved October 17, 2017, from https://www.usatoday.com /story/news/nation/2014/06/17/children-surge-immigration-texas/10643609.

2   Associated Press (2014, June 29). Border Patrol Has Lots of Agents—in Wrong Places. *USA Today*. Retrieved October 18, 2017, from https://www.usatoday .com/story/news/nation/2014/06/29/border-patrol-has-lots-of-agents-in-wrong -places/11705315/.

3   Government Accountability Office. (2017, November). *Border Patrol: Issues Related to Agent Deployment Strategy and Immigrant Checkpoints.* Retrieved November 26, 2017, from http://www.gao.gov/assets/690/688201.pdf.

4   Rittgers, D. (2011, September 11). Abolish the Department of Homeland Security (Rep. No. 683). Retrieved October 5, 2017, from Cato Institute website: https://object.cato.org/sites/cato.org/files/pubs/pdf/PA683.pdf.

5   Kean, T. H., et al. (2004). The 9/11 Commission Report (Rep.). Retrieved October 17, 2017, from National Commission on Terrorist Attacks upon the United States website: http://govinfo.library.unt.edu/911/report/911Report.pdf.

6   Kean, T. H., and Hamilton, L. H. (2014, July). Today's Rising Terrorist Threat and the Danger to the United States: Reflections on the Tenth Anniversary of the 9/11 Commission Report (Rep.). Retrieved October 18, 2017, from Bipartisan Policy Center website: http://bipartisanpolicy.org/wp-content/uploads/sites /default/files/%20BPC%209-11%20Commission.pdf.

7   Eichenwald, K. (2012, September 10). The Deafness before the Storm. *New York Times*. Retrieved October 18, 2017, from http://www.nytimes.com/2012/09 /11/opinion/the-bush-white-house-was-deaf-to-9-11-warnings.html.

8   Government Accountability Office. (2001, August). INS' Southwest Border Strategy: Resource and Impact Issues Remain After Seven Years (Rep.). Retrieved October 5, 2017, from http://www.gao.gov/new.items/d01842.pdf.

9   Department of Homeland Security. (2015, September 15). Who Joined DHS. Retrieved October 17, 2017, from https://www.dhs.gov/who-joined-dhs.

10 President George W. Bush. (2002, June). The Department of Homeland Security (Rep.). Retrieved October 5, 2017, from https://www.dhs.gov/sites/default /files/publications/book_0.pdf.

11 Perl, R. (2004). Terrorism: Reducing Vulnerabilities and Improving Responses (Rep.). Retrieved October 5, 2017, from National Academies Press website, https://www.nap.edu/read/10968/chapter/24.

12 Homeland Security Advisory Council. (2015, June 29). Interim Report of the CBP Integrity Advisory Panel (Rep.). Retrieved October 18, 2017, from U.S. Department of Homeland Security website, https://www.dhs.gov/sites/default /files/publications/DHS-HSAC-CBP-IAP-Interim-Report.pdf.

13 Border Security: Frontline Perspectives on Progress and Remaining Challenges, Senate Committee on Homeland Security and Governmental Affairs

Cong. (2013). (Testimony of U.S. Immigration and Customs Enforcement Homeland Security Investigations Executive Associate Director James Dinkin.)

14 Coast Guard History. (n.d.). Retrieved October 18, 2017, from http://www.military.com/coast-guard-birthday/coast-guard-history.html.

15 Today, Plum Island has four hundred employees who "provide a host of high-impact, indispensable preparedness and response capabilities, including vaccine R&D, diagnostics, training, and bioforensics among others." Department of Homeland Security. (n.d.). Science and Technology. Retrieved October 17, 2017, from https://www.dhs.gov/science-and-technology/plum-island-animal-disease -center.

16 Markon, J. (2014, September 25). Department of Homeland Security Has 120 Reasons to Want Streamlined Oversight. *Washington Post.* Retrieved October 18, 2017, from https://www.washingtonpost.com/news/federal-eye/wp/2014/09 /25/outsized-congressional-oversight-weighing-down-department-of-homeland -security.

17 Annenberg Foundation Trust at Sunnylands and Aspen Institute Justice and Society Program. (2013, September). Task Force Report on Streamlining and Consolidating Congressional Oversight of the U.S. Department of Homeland Security (Rep.). Retrieved October 18, 2017, from the Aspen Institute Justice & Society Program website, https://assets.aspeninstitute.org /content/uploads/files/content/upload/DHS%20whitepaper%20final_0.pdf.

18 Longmire, S. (2014). *Border Insecurity: Why Big Money, Fences, and Drones Aren't Making Us Safer.* New York: St. Martin's Press.

19 Higgins, U.S. Representative Clay. (2017, July 20). House Passes Landmark DHS Authorization Act, News release. Retrieved October 18, 2017, from https://clayhiggins.house.gov/media/press-releases/house-passes-landmark-dhs -authorization-act.

20 Ibid.

21 Kelly, C., and Gillman, T. (2017, July 6). Trump's Plan for Border Patrol, ICE Hiring Surges Face Timing, Security Obstacles. *Dallas News.* Retrieved October 5, 2017, from https://www.dallasnews.com/news/politics/2017/07/06/trumps-plan -border-patrol-ice-hiring-surges-face-timing-security-obstacles.

22 Dinan, S. (2017, July 31). Homeland Security Inspector General Says Trump Administration Can't Hire 5,000 New Border Agents. *Washington Post.* Retrieved October 18, 2017, from http://www.washingtontimes.com/news/2017/jul/31 /john-roth-says-trump-administration-cant-hire-5000/.

23 Johnson, J. C. (2017, January 5). Record of Progress and Vision for the Future (Rep.). Retrieved October 18, 2017, from U.S. Department of Homeland Security website, https://www.dhs.gov/sites/default/files/publications/17_0105_exit -memo.pdf.

24 Healy, G. (2005, October 7). What of "Posse Comitatus"? Cato Institute. Retrieved October 18, 2017, from https://www.cato.org/publications/commentary /what-posse-comitatus.

25 From the National Travel and Tourism Office. Retrieved November 26, 2017, from http://tinet.ita.doc.gov.

26 Bureau of Transportation Statistics. (2016). Border Crossing/Entry Data (Rep.). Washington, District of Columbia. Retrieved October 18, 2017, from https://www.bts.gov/content/border-crossingentry-data.
27 U.S. Southern Command. (n.d.). About Us. Retrieved October 18, 2017, from http://www.southcom.mil/About/.
28 Coast Guard Seizes $350 million Worth of Cocaine in the Caribbean (2014). CBS News. Retrieved October 18, 2017, from https://www.cbsnews.com/news/coast-guard-seizes-350-million-dollars-of-cocaine-in-the-caribbean/.
29 Posture Statement of Admiral Kurt W. Tidd Commander, United States Southern Command, 115th Cong. (2017). (Testimony of Admiral Kurt W. Tidd.) Retrieved October 18, 2017, from https://www.armed-services.senate.gov/imo/media/doc/Tidd_04-06-17.pdf.

CHAPTER 17. RESPECT AND WORK WITH MEXICO

1 Migration Policy Institute. (2017, February 8). U.S. Immigration Trends. Retrieved October 18, 2017, from http://www.migrationpolicy.org/programs/data-hub/us-immigration-trends#source.
2 Krogstad, J. M., Passel, J. S., and Cohn, D. (2017, April 27). 5 Facts about Illegal Immigration in the U.S. Pew Research. Retrieved October 18, 2017, from http://www.pewresearch.org/fact-tank/2017/04/27/5-facts-about-illegal-immigration-in-the-u-s.
3 Yee, V., Davis, K., and Patel, J. (2017, March 6). Here's the Reality about Illegal Immigrants in the United States. *New York Times*. Retrieved October 18, 2017, from https://www.nytimes.com/interactive/2017/03/06/us/politics/undocumented-illegal-immigrants.html.
4 Gonzalez-Barrera, A., and Krogstad, J. M. (2017, March 2). What We Know about Illegal Immigration from Mexico. Pew Research. Retrieved October 18, 2017, from http://www.pewresearch.org/fact-tank/2017/03/02/what-we-know-about-illegal-immigration-from-mexico/.
5 Krogstad, J. M., and Passel, J. S. (2014, December 30). U.S. Border Apprehensions of Mexicans Fall to Historic Lows. Retrieved October 18, 2017, from http://www.pewresearch.org/fact-tank/2014/12/30/u-s-border-apprehensions-of-mexicans-fall-to-historic-lows/.
6 Villarreal, A. (2014, December). Explaining the Decline in Mexico–U.S. Migration: The Effect of the Great Recession. *Demography*. Retrieved October 18, 2017, from https://www.ncbi.nlm.nih.gov/pmc/articles/PMC4252712/.
7 Lesser, G., and Batalova, J. (2017, August 3). Central American Immigrants in the United States. Retrieved October 18, 2017, from http://www.migrationpolicy.org/article/central-american-immigrants-united-states.
8 Beaubien, J. (2011, July 7). Drug Cartels Prey on Migrants Crossing Mexico. NPR. Retrieved October 18, 2017, from http://www.npr.org/2011/07/07/137626383/drug-cartels-prey-on-migrants-crossing-mexico.
9 Congressional Research Service. (2017, June 29). U.S.–Mexican Security Coop-

eration: The Merida Initiative and Beyond. Retrieved October 18, 2017, from https://fas.org/sgp/crs/row/R41349.pdf.

10 Statement of Admiral William E. Gortney, United States Navy Commander, United States Northern Command and Northern American Aerospace Defense Command, Senate Armed Services Committee Cong. (2016). (Testimony of Admiral William E. Gortney.)

11 Martin, P., and Jackson-Smith, D. (2013, April). An Overview of Farm Labor in the United States. https://wrdc.usu.edu/files-ou/publications/pub__1454925.pdf.

12 NBC 4. (2017, July 24). Shortage of Farm Workers Leaving Entire Fields to Rot. Retrieved October 18, 2017, from http://nbc4i.com/2017/07/24/shortage-of -farm-workers-leaving-entire-fields-in-california-other-states-to-rot.

13 Morris, C. (2017, August 8). California Crops Rot as Immigration Crackdown Creates Farmworker Shortage. *Fortune*. Retrieved September 21, 2017, from http://fortune.com/2017/08/08/immigration-worker-shortage-rotting-crops/.

14 Tillman, L. (2017, February 5). In Mexico, Trump Triggers a Surge in Patriotism, Anti-American Sentiment. *Los Angeles Times*. Retrieved November 19, 2017, from http://www.latimes.com/world/mexico-americas/la-fg-mexico-patriotism-trump -2017-story.html.

15 O'Connor, S. (2016, July 18). *Meth Precursor Chemicals from China: Implications for the United States* (Rep.). Retrieved October 18, 2017, from U.S.-China Economic and Security Review Commission website, https://www.uscc.gov/sites/default /files/Research/Staff%20Report_PrecursorChemicalReport%20071816_0.pdf.

CHAPTER 18. CREATE A PERSISTENT PRESENCE

1 Longmire, S. (2014). *Border Insecurity: Why Big Money, Fences, and Drones Aren't Making Us Safer*. New York: St. Martin's Press.

2 Beebe, D. Watch This Surveillance Master Dissect a Murder from the Sky. Bloomberg News. Retrieved October 19, 2017, from https://www.bloomberg.com /news/articles/2016-08-23/watch-this-surveillance-master-dissect-a-murder-from -the-sky.

CHAPTER 19. REDUCE DEMAND FOR DRUGS AND ILLEGAL LABOR

1 Bradley, J., Powers, R., and French, M. (2011). *Flags of Our Fathers: Heroes of Iwo Jima*. New York: Ember.

2 Bradley, J. (2016). *The China Mirage: The Hidden History of American Disaster in Asia*. New York: Back Bay Books, Little, Brown and Company.

3 Meyer, Karl. (1997, June 28). The Opium War's Secret History. *New York Times*. Retrieved January 13, 2018, from http://www.nytimes.com/1997/06/28/opinion /the-opium-war-s-secret-history.html.

4 McCoy, A. W. (n.d.). Opium. Retrieved September 22, 2017, from

https://www.opioids.com/opium/history. See also *Medication-Assisted Treatment for Opioid Addiction in Opioid Treatment Programs*, Chapter 2. Treatment Improvement Protocol (TIP) Series, no. 43. Center for Substance Abuse Treatment. Rockville, MD: Substance Abuse and Mental Health Services Administration (US); 2005.

5   Higham, S., et al. (2016, December 22). Drug Industry Hired Dozens of Officials from the DEA as the Agency Tried to Curb Opioid Abuse. *Washington Post*. Retrieved November 24, 2017, from https://www.washingtonpost.com/investigations /key-officials-switch-sides-from-dea-to-pharmaceutical-industry/2016/12/22/55d2 e938-c07b-11e6-b527-949c5893595e_story.html?utm_term=.89b84d4f98bf.

6   Deprez, E, and Barrett, B. (2017, October 5). The Lawyer Who Beat Big Tobacco Takes on the Opioid Industry. Bloomberg News. Retrieved November 24, 2017, from https://www.bloomberg.com/news/features/2017-10-05/the -lawyer-who-beat-big-tobacco-takes-on-the-opioid-industry.

7   Interview with Michael Moore by Chris Bury, PBS NewsHour. (2017, October 7). https://www.pbs.org/newshour/show/ohio-sues-big-pharma-increase-opioid -related-deaths.

8   Berlanga, M. (2016, September 27). Want to Make Ethical Purchases? Stop Buying Illegal Drugs. *New York Times*. Retrieved October 19, 2017, from https://www.nytimes.com/2016/09/27/opinion/want-to-make-ethical-purchases -stop-buying-illegal-drugs.html.

9   Passel, J., Cohn, D., and Gonzalez-Barrera, A. (September 2013). Population Decline of Unauthorized Immigrants Stalls, May Have Reversed. Pew Research. Retrieved October 19, 2017, from http://www.pewhispanic.org/2013/09 /23/population-decline-of-unauthorized-immigrants-stalls-may-have-reversed.

CHAPTER 20. SUPPORT PEACE AND SECURITY IN OUR HEMISPHERE

1   Abt, T. (2016, February). What Works in Reducing Community Violence: A Meta-Review and Field Study for the Northern Triangle. Retrieved October 19, 2017, from https://www.usaid.gov/sites/default/files/USAID-2016-What -Works-in-Reducing-Community-Violence-Final-Report.pdf.

INDEX

ABOUT THE HOWARD G. BUFFETT FOUNDATION

The Howard G. Buffett Foundation was established in 1999 with gifts from my parents, Warren and Susie Buffett. Our initial philanthropic investments were in conservation and projects designed to support endangered and threatened species such as the mountain gorilla and the cheetah.

Within a few years, I realized that endangered animal species will never survive if the people around them suffer from extreme poverty and violence. And so our focus evolved. I used my experience as a farmer to help communities in the developing world improve food security. As I traveled widely I learned that conflict undermines most development, and we could not afford to disregard it.

Through the years my parents' gifts to my brother and sister and my foundations increased substantially. In 2004, my father pledged an additional $1.1 billion worth of Berkshire-Hathaway stock to each foundation. On his birthday in 2012, he doubled that commitment.

As of the end of 2017, our foundation has distributed over $1 billion, with $870 million dedicated to projects supporting food security and conflict mitigation in Africa and Latin America.

We feel we have a unique opportunity as a private family foundation: We can afford to take significant risks because we do not have to raise funds from other sources or show success to please donors. We see our mission as trying to catalyze change and progress in regions where some of the most vulnerable people on Earth live and in situations where others cannot or will not work. And when we fail, we feel it is important to communicate what went wrong in order to contribute to the larger body of knowledge and prevent others from wasting resources.

In recent years I have broadened our foundation's areas of emphasis again. We are still investing heavily in projects designed to help some of the world's most vulnerable people, such as developing projects in the Democratic Republic of Congo and creating a practical agriculture education institute in Rwanda designed to be a model for all of Africa.

However, violence and erosion of the rule of law in Central America's Northern Triangle countries of El Salvador, Honduras, and Guatemala as well as in Mexico have reached unprecedented levels. As these nations have become overrun with corruption and gang- and cartel-related violence, their people are fleeing north to safety. Their problems have become our problem. The influx of refugees who have been entering the United States illegally is a humanitarian crisis, but the criminal smuggling of drugs and other crimes undermines our strength and future as a nation. I believe it is the biggest threat we face on our soil.

I have always been inspired by my father's testimony before the U.S. Senate shortly after he became chairman of Salomon Brothers following a financial scandal in 1991. "Mr. Chairman," he said, "I would like to start by apologizing. The nation has a right to expect its rules and laws to be obeyed." Inconsistent strategies to secure the U.S. border, including policies that seemed to contradict the law, have not only made us less safe and helped escalate our nation's problems with illegal narcotics, they have exacerbated the humanitarian crisis for people seeking safety in our country. Ignoring the rule of law in our country to address the erosion of the rule of law in another does not make sense. Today, one of our foundation's primary missions is to advocate for public safety so we can again be a model of peace and strength in our hemisphere.